Social Work Education and Practice Engagement

Social Work Education and Practice Engagement

Edited by

Sanjai Bhatt
Suresh Pathare

SHIPRA

Rs. 1150; US$ 57.50

ISBN: 978-81-7541-757-1

First Published in India in 2015

Social Work Education and Practice Engagement

Published by:
SHIPRA PUBLICATIONS
LG 18-19, Pankaj Central Market, I.P. Ext.
Patparganj, Delhi-110092
Tel: 91-11-2223 5152, 2223 6152
E-mail: info@shiprapublication.com
www.shiprapublication.com

Preface

Social Work as a human service profession has moved through various phases of change and has evolved through various ideological phases. Beginning with the philosophy of charity, which was preached and practised across various cultures and religions, social work has been wedded with the idea of reaching out to others through planned welfare measures, followed by development for all and all for development. At present, the dominant ideology of the discipline focuses on empowerment and liberation of people. With the changing social order and social demands, this dynamic discipline has undergone a mammoth transformation in its scope, fields/areas, and approaches, and in line with the same, it embarked on working with the welfare model of development and social change. With the opening up of the economy and the advent of globalisation, the needs of society and the social systems have drastically changed, and so have the priorities of the profession. The same is also reflected in the two global definitions of social work, which have evolved in less than one and half decade.

In July 2001, both the IASSW and the IFSW reached an agreement on adopting an international definition of 'social work' which states that "the social work profession promotes social change, problem-solving in human relationships and the empowerment and liberation of people to enhance well-being". Utilising the theories of human behaviour and social systems, social work intervenes at the points where people interact with their environments. The principles of human rights and social justice are fundamental to social work (IASSW, 2001). The latest global definition of social work is much broader as it emphasises that "Social work is a practice-based profession and an academic discipline that promotes social change and development, social cohesion, and the empowerment and liberation of people. The principles of social justice, human rights, collective responsibility and respect for diversities are central to social work. Underpinned by theories of social work, social sciences, humanities and indigenous knowledge, social work engages people and structures to address life challenges and enhance wellbeing (IASSW, 2014). The official commentary on this definition also substantiates that structural barriers contribute to the perpetuation of inequalities, discrimination, exploitation and oppression. The development of critical consciousness through reflecting on structural sources of oppression and/or privilege, on the basis of criteria such as race, class, language, religion, gender, disability, culture and sexual orientation, and developing action strategies towards addressing structural and personal barriers are central to emancipatory practice, where the goals are: empowerment and liberation of people. In solidarity with those who are disadvantaged, the profession strives to alleviate poverty, liberate the vulnerable and oppressed, and promote social inclusion and social cohesion.

A closer scrutiny of the two definitions reveals that in the new definition of social work, the inclusion of the word 'social cohesion' in place of 'problem-solving in human relationships' may not be appropriate in reflecting the genuine nature of social work profession fully, but it surely does this on one parameter and that is, in terms of its emphasis on *collective responsibility and respect for diversities.* This reflects that the social work profession has evolved much beyond its traditional boundaries. Indeed it has transcended into multivariate issues with a rights-based frame of intervention. The discipline has witnessed a wide scale expansion of scope in-different areas ranging from the traditional domains of women, family and children to newer domains like environment, disaster management, occupational social work and corporate social responsibility.

In India, the past two decades have witnessed a changing relationship between the government, market and civil society institutions. The new paradigms under the cover of public-private partnership and corporate social responsibility are gaining ground. The welfare, service delivery and development models have also undergone drastic transformation. There is visible impact of science and technology on the quality of life of people in both positive and negative manners. To comply with constitutional commitments and international obligations, we have moved to a rights-based approach, entitlements, and empowerment. The country has also seen a couple of debates and public movements for addressing the hitherto unnoticed issues towards issues demanding change. This includes the most debated Jan Lokpal Bill to prevent and halt corruption from the core of Indian bureaucracy, right to information, movements based on health issues, Gay and Lesbian Rights, movement for securing safe work place for women, food security, climate change, environmental degradation, millennium development goals, decent work, social security for workers, child abuse and child labour, land rights, and activism for the rights of tribals and other vulnerable and displaced groups in mining belts and SEZs and so on. The social work "consciousness" has spread to various media, be it the print media, social networking sites like facebook and twitter or the method of promoting socially conscious views through "blogs". Interestingly, the social work profession has been a witness to several legislations and has been a contributory to the formulation and amendments of major legislations in this country. Through an active and consistent discourse, it has been instrumental in convincing the government for being a signatory to many international commitments like the Convention of Child Rights and Millennium Development Goals.

Empowerment being a multi-dimensional, social process of increasing the capacity of individuals or groups to make choices and to transform those choices into desired actions and outcomes, it leads to the emancipation and liberation of people. This process creates for the marginalized communities the power to use these choices in his or her own life, community and society, and the capacity to act on issues that they define as important. Thus, it is the empowerment and right-based approaches which presently dominate the social work paradigm.

II

Against this backdrop, we have consciously driven to create platforms to meaningfully engagements with the critical social realities and one such platform is the Indian Social Work Congress. This platform not only envisages the facilitation of threadbare discussions and deliberations on issues related to social work education and practice in India, but also works towards ensuring the framing of a collective response of the social work profession to the taxing contemporary realities. Within the aegis of the First Indian Social Work Congress, 2013, the issues, challenges and gaps in social work education and practice in the country were discussed, so that the bridges to close the gaps could be built.

The purpose of the Congress was to bring the fraternity of professional social workers together to discuss and deliberate upon the issues related to the social work education, practice and research in India. The Congress aimed at strengthening the social work profession to ensure social justice and human rights for all; record the response of the profession with regard to various social concerns; and redraw the boundaries that should position the profession of social work in the contemporary times.

The present volume is a diverse set and subsumes within itself an array of themes, all of which have significant potential to inform and impact social work education and practice. These are arranged in two parts: part *one* relates to select papers having an appraisal of various aspects of social work education in India, and part *two* contains papers reflecting the nature, trends, challenges and engagement of social work practice. Prof H. Y. Siddiqui in his paper on 'Social Work in India' takes a bird's eye view towards the trend of social work education in India. He raises the question on the professional status of social work in the country and also offers way ahead in order to provide a clear direction to the fraternity. Prof Vidya Rao's paper titled 'From Social Service Administration to Anti-Oppressive Social Work: A Critique of 'Professional Social Work', reflects the journey of professional social work as a discipline in India with several paradigm shifts. Interestingly, there is almost no evidence of this paradigm shift in formal scholarly professional social work literature of the past twenty-thirty years. The paper attempts to delineate the historical shifts in social work perspectives drawing evidence and arguments from the Indian context. Prof Suresh Pathare in his paper titled 'Social Work Education in India: Transition from Westernization to Indigenization', seeks to document the contribution of the individuals and organizations from outside and within the country that influenced the shaping of social work education. Further, it identifies the conditions that facilitated the starting of the initial schools of social work. It also seeks to explore the extent of Western influence in general, and American influence in particular, on social work education. Lastly, it investigates the process of indigenization of social work education and identifies the challenges and issues for future direction. In his paper on 'Social Work Education through Distance Learning in India: A Reality', Gracious Thomas presents a picture of open and distance learning systems. He compares the correspondence and distance education modes. He also highlights the salient features of social work education through the latter mode. Lastly, he traces the background of the establishment and functioning of the School of Social Work at IGNOU. In his paper on 'Bridging Gaps in Professional Social Work Education in India', Teddy Andrews J. looks at the strengths and gaps in social work training and also attempts to suggest strategies to bridge the gaps. His paper focuses on discussion on the nature of social work based on selected literature, author's experience and MSW trainees' feedback through focus group discussions at Manipal University. In his paper on 'Development of Social Work as a Profession in India: Challenges Faced by the Social Work Fraternity', Kaivalya T. Desai traces the historical development of social work in India. He highlights the different roles of professional bodies existing in India. He also explores the notable challenges faced by social work fraternity in India. Namita Jainer's paper titled 'Social Work Education: Educating for Social Change', discusses the role and significance of social work education in contributing to the agenda of social change. It further gives insights about the ways to meet this agenda. In order to bring out this connection, the paper makes a commentary on the book titled 'Education and Knowledge: The Structured Misrepresentation of Reality' authored by Kevin Harris. In the paper titled 'Field Work Practicum in Social Work Education', Atul Pratap Singh formulates SMART Objectives and makes an attempt to provide at least some basic ingredients along with supportive annexure for generic nature of field work practice learning which can be easily translated into practice. He also answers several important questions, such as—How to begin the field work? How to complete it? How to supervise the students? What should be the criteria to evaluate the students?

The second part of the book deals with the nature, trends, challenges and social work practice engagement. It contains largely new emerging areas of social work practice in India as well as a few traditional fields of social work engagement. Abraham Francis while examining strengths-based practice in social work seeks to explore, understand and discuss strengths-based perspectives in social work with a special emphasis on practice in the mental health field. There has been a shift away from the mere focus on deficits to a strengths-based in the delivery of services to clients. The strengths-based approach is a specific method of working with a person while earlier social work practices were based more on disease, deficits, problems, and pathologies; it was further assumed that clients have become clients because they have deficits. The author observes that much of the social work literature on practice with families and individuals continues to use treatment, dysfunction, and therapy metaphors and tends to ignore strengths perspectives as the focus continues to be on deficits rather than strengths. Jaimon Varghese's paper titled 'Spiritually Sensitive Social Work: An Emerging Model of Practice', highlights various dimensions of spiritually sensitive social work. It presents the findings of a field study on the attitude of professional social work trainees on spiritually sensitive social work. It also advocates that undoubtedly spiritually sensitive social work is an emerging model of social work practice and very much in tune with the Indian ethos. J. H. Christopher's paper titled 'Signature Pedagogy in Social Work and Psychological Well-Being of Social Work Trainees: An Evidenced-Based Evaluatory Process', lays out the findings of an empirical study carried out in five of the ten departments of Social Work, affiliated to Bangalore University. The paper highlights major problems and challenges of implementation of field work. It also offers some fruitful suggestions in order to strengthen the field work. The joint paper of Suneel Vatsyayan, Ajay Vats and V. Vindhya titled 'NADA Protocol for Protection, Treatment and Recovery: A Social Worker's Perspective', focuses on issues related to addiction treatment, NADA Protocol, its spread globally and how NADA protocol can meet the needs and challenges in the field of addiction treatment and protection and recovery in India. Faseela Jaleel, B.P. Nirmala and Jagadisha Thirthalli presented their experiences at day care centre in their paper titled 'Recovery Oriented Services (ROSES) for Persons with Psychiatric Disability. The paper is based on vocational rehabilitation efforts made by psychiatric rehabilitation unit of NIMHANS in providing recovery oriented services to fine cases with similar clinical diagnosis (Schizophrenia to its subtypes with any comorbidity). Tarun Bikash Sukai's paper titled 'Globalization and NGO Response to HIV/AIDS: Concerns for Social Work Practice', provides some insights on NGOs engaged in HIV/AIDS prevention and care in West Bengal. The paper also analyses the impact of globalization on the NGOs engaged in combating AIDS in general with the help of secondary data and perceptions of NGO-functionaries in West Bengal about the future trends in particular.

Ms. Subhashree Sanyal's paper titled 'Foreign Aid, Voluntary Sector and Social Work Practice in India', provides a view of foreign aid and its impact and importance on the third sector. The paper also suggests that despite the adoption of the stringent measures by the state to regulate the inflow of foreign funds, the effectiveness of aid for non-profit, is under questions from different quarters. Broadly, the paper focuses on how important the foreign aid is to the voluntary sector and largely social work practice in India today. Dr Jitendra Kumar Misra in his paper titled 'Management and Service Delivery of Civil Society Organisations: A Study' explores the dimensions of management and service delivery practices of Civil Society Organizations (CSOs) and develop a self assessment tool for CSOs. Findings show an average performance of the level of management and service delivery of CSOs in Delhi as CSOs operate under a relatively moderate developed framework of infrastructure and resources, with and required organizational, programme management and service delivery practices. The study provides guidance to adhere to the norms of internal governance; operations; accountability, transparency, disclosure of information, development of report, personnel policies and accounting procedures, programme planning, implementation, monitoring and evaluation practices. On the basis of the findings, a self assessment tool for CSOs has also been been developed. Iqball Majeed Bhat has made an excellent attempt to explore the issues of Identity and Marginalization of Gujjar and Bakkarwal Communities of Jammu and Kashmir. He explains that Gujjars constitute eight per cent of the total population of the state and are one of the most economically backward and socially isolated tribal groups, who are caught between the two identities of Muslim and Gujjars. For them, even the attainment of the Schedule Tribe status could not bring too much change in the overall socio-economic backwardness of the group. The politics of exclusion has influenced the cultural milieu of this group in the form of changing livelihood patterns. The author has proposed that social work intervention in the form of creation of Gujjar welfare councils or boards may prove beneficial for the empowerment and welfare of this community. Zothankimiralte and Kalpana Sarathy presented a paper on the Sexual Behaviour of Urban Gay Men in Mizoram. They found that gay men and lesbian women find little acceptance in this society because the Bible does not allow its practice. Although Mizos are heavily influenced by modernization and westernization, the general population has negative attitudes and perceptions toward homosexuality, which result in stigmatization and discrimination of people who practise it. They argued that if discrimination, stereotyping and stigmatization of gay population along with inappropriateness of discussions about sex heighten in society, then it is likely that these groups will continue to hide their sexuality, which in turn will make them more vulnerable to sexual risk behaviour. Shivani Chauhan Barooah in her paper titled 'Decent Work for Home-based Workers in India: Implications for Social Work' explains the notion of decent work which emphasizes four main elements: work and employment; social protection; rights at work; and social dialogue. She argues that the extent and magnitude of the informal economy has increased tremendously over the past few decades with a sudden spurt of newer and different types of economic activities. Due to the rise of complex global chains of production over the past half-century, home-based work has grown in leaps and bounds. The paper brings home an element of the multi-directionality of social work practice, as home-based work is found to be an area which requires social work intervention.

We would like to put on record our sincere appreciation of all the eminent scholars and delegates of the First Social Work Congress, whose meaningful contribution, both by way of presentations on the diverse dimensions of contemporary social problems and the scope of social work practice, as also in terms of their active participation in the discussions and deliberations within the sessions enriched the collective consciousness of the social work fraternity. We owe our sincere gratitude to NAPSWI for allowing us to bring out this volume. The editing work took quality time of our family members, and we gratefully appreciate the cooperation of our family members especially our spouses—Ms Madhu Bhatt and Ms Vaisahli Pathare. We also acknowledge the last minute help by Dr. Neera Agnimitra, Dr. Atul Pratap and Dr. Digvijoy Phukan. We are thankful to Mr. D. Kumar and Mr. Nalin Sharma of Shipra Publications, New Delhi for showing interest in the publication of the volume.

October 31, 2014

Sanjai Bhatt
Suresh Pathare

Contents

SECTION II
SOCIAL WORK PRACTICE ENGAGEMENT

Section I

Social Work Education

1
Social Work in India

H. Y. Siddiqui

In the early 20th century, the main role assigned to social workers was providing assistance to the needy (*see* Cheyne, 1926, Witmer, 1942), which forever tilted the natural thrust of social work to deal with poverty, and deprivation of all kind. Later the definitions started calling it a professional service to satisfy 'individual needs along with removing barriers' (Clarke, 1947; Friedlander, 1955), based on scientific knowledge. The concept of providing help in social functioning came later. The review of the literature during the period and the current makes it inevitable to concur with what Morales and Sheafor said. However, even before Sheafor reached that conclusion, Khinduka had faced the same difficulty and in 1965, observed in his edited volume 'Social work in India', that the principle difficulty in defining social work is that of finding a suitable differentia, one that is brief, inclusive and conceptually flawless (p. 11). Simply calling it a helping profession or activity does not serve the purpose, as almost all professions, help people to solve their problems, such as nurses, doctors, lawyers and so on. Further, helping in the Indian subcontinent in particular and elsewhere too is seen as a social and religious obligation, and hence poses difficulty in its acceptance as a professional domain, as almost all politicians and many others, take pride in claiming themselves as social workers. Any professional expected to help the needy without specifying a need area, given the task of poverty alleviation, or removing barriers in the path of success of the individuals, is asking for trouble, a sentiment Gore expressed along with many others in 1980s. The definition has to be inclusive yet brief, which conceptually define each activity or role carried out by social workers. To be precise, what is the thread that binds you from helping an individual to bringing about social change. Further, professional expertise consisting of a body of knowledge, both about the problem area and possible solutions, discovered through a scientific process, is a necessary requirement as well.

It shows that an academic and descriptive approach was used to define social work rather than professional. A variety of social work academics individually, and collectively as professional bodies of social workers, struggled to define the nature and scope of 'professional' social work, the most recent being an attempt by IFSW and IASSW (2013). The difficulty is the variety of tasks being currently pursued by social workers and a lack of consensus about the core expertise needed to accomplish these tasks. I dealt with the subject way back (Siddiqui, 1987) when I was trying to work out a course curriculum for social work students. The dilemma I faced was, do I design it for students dealing with problems of adjustment/service delivery/ need fulfilment/welfare, chose the term you like, or bringing about social change. I had then argued that a social worker would need a different theoretical knowledge base for accomplishing these tasks. Further, the time available for doing that and the academic background of students, coupled with faculty expertise, made it very difficult. It is not mandatory for students to have studied social work or even social sciences at the bachelor level to pursue a course in social work. However, I must admit that I had no clarity about the basic expertise then. Social work was all about values and philosophy, methods and fields, where you can practise those methods theoretically. The body of knowledge and skills that a social worker needs, and which is common to all social workers, no matter what they are doing, to qualify for professional practice, remains unidentified even now. Just to pick up the debate in UK in 2009, Sheldon and Macdonald wrote:

> " Social work's disciplinary territory is the poor, troubled, abused or discriminated against, neglected, frail and elderly, mentally ill, learning disabled, addicted, delinquent, or otherwise socially marginalized... This is a dauntingly broad remit.... The sheer range of social and personal problems for which we acquired some responsibility has lead to the development of a discipline which has always been forced to borrow...from adjacent fields."

The problem is they are only worried about borrowing from adjacent fields, which I think is referring to psychology, sociology and psychiatry and maybe other social science disciplines, but they are not worried about the vast range of tasks or how well these disciplines provide the practical wisdom. As Specht (1986) noted a profession with a weak knowledge base is vulnerable to 'de-professionalisation', and the practitioners will be vulnerable to identify with anything more popular such as change agent or development workers or consultant.

It is quite tempting to quote a few definitions to stress the point, but instead let us refer to the main themes running through these, to describe the confusion prevailing in defining social work. Let us begin by referring to the definition adopted by IAFSW and IASSW in 2002. It refers to social work as providing help to sort out problems of human relations, bring about social change, ensure human rights and social rights, etc. Of course, the scientific knowledge, professional nature of interventions, and emphasizing the skills needed, are routine as well. It is a common theme running through many definitions. The definition given by NASW is referring to what social workers do, which is basically providing services to their clients. It goes on to elaborate these by noting that they (social workers) help people increase their capacities for problem solving and coping, obtain needed resources, facilitate interaction between people and their environment, make organizations responsible to people and influence social policies etc. The definition describes the tasks as is obvious, but not how these are linked by a central conceptual framework, thus making it part of social work. The problem these definitions create in the mind of a practitioner or a student is what exactly their job as a professional? Further, if they are not able to provide a solution to the problem, but help the person to reach the professional person, since left on their own they will not be able to access that, will it dilute their professional status? Are they supposed to be proficient in all the tasks or only in some, which they prefer? Is there a shared understanding or theory of carrying out all the tasks, if all these are social work tasks and require an expertise?

For example, what is common between an expertise to increase individual capacities for problem solving and coping on the one hand and to influence the structural change in a society on the other. In other words, what is the common thread running across these tasks. Let us take the example of Law as a profession. The common expertise with lawyers, which make them a professional is their knowledge of law. So whereever they work the main expertise is law whether in civil matters or criminal or corporate matters or whether they help an individual, a group or an organization. Further, the task of reform of existing laws or enactment of new laws, to reform the justice system in the country, is a collective responsibility, as part of ethical and social considerations rather than considered as a professional task. Although it can be argued that the two has some linkages.

Mary Richmond, one of the founders of social work profession, in 1917 raised similar issues:

> "*With other practitioners—with physicians and lawyers, for example—there was always a basis of knowledge held in common. If a neurologist had occasion to confer with a surgeon, each could assume in the other a mastery of the elements of a whole group of basic sciences and of the formulated and transmitted experience of his own guild besides. But what common knowledge could social workers assume in like case? (Richmond, 1917: 5)*

Sheldon and Macdonald (2009) are not questioning the ability to acquire the range of expertise, maybe because they thought different social workers will acquire different expertise through different courses, but that is not the trend reflected by a review of social work education, which remained confined to BSW and MSW courses with marginal variation in the content. Specific courses such as Family Therapy, Child Welfare, Woman Welfare, Drug addiction or development practice, etc., for at least one year duration dealing with these issues in depth are not very easily found, in schools of social work. Further, Mary Richmond's query what is common knowledge among all these workers is still not answered with any degree of clarity.

The most recent attempt to arrive at a definition is the draft of a global definition put on the website of International Federation of Social Workers recently, and they expect you to participate in deciding the future of social work (*see* Appendix I). I produce the definition below for us to take our own stand.

The Global Definition of Social Work Profession

"Social work facilitates social development and social cohesion. Core to social work is supporting people to influence their social environments to achieve sustainable wellbeing. The profession is underpinned by theories of social work, social sciences, and indigenous knowledge. Principles of human rights, collective responsibility and social justice are fundamental to practice."

The definition uses the word core at least to centralize all social work efforts towards supporting persons to influence their social environments. The argument in this paper is about identifying an objective, which is vague and not defined or discussed by any discipline or theory, hence the expertise remains vague thus it makes the professional knowledge base weak. It thus makes it difficult, for the society to accept social workers as a professional.

The clarity of professional task a social worker is expected to perform based on his knowledge and skills, at all levels is the first requisite for defining social work. Friedlander (1955), Khinduka (1965) and many others used two clear terms: social adjustment and/or social functioning and human relationships. Let us describe in detail these terms and how these explain human problems or issues, with which social work, as a profession, has to deal with.

Boehm (1958) first proposed social functioning as a central focus of social work practice. Bartlett (1970) defined it as normative behaviour in social situations, and added that it has an overarching concern in all social work fields and methods including service delivery roles. Blackely and Dziadosz (2009) in a recent article have endorsed this view by giving example from a mental health setting. The term, however, is not found in the dictionary of sociology edited by Abercrombie, Nicholas, Stephen Hill and Bryan S Turner (1994). According to functionalists, it refers to the roles society evolves to guide members of a society. G H Mead (1934) was the first to use the concept in a very creative way to suggest how children learn about the society and develop their own social being (the self) by role-taking i.e., imaginatively taking the role of others such as fathers, mothers, etc. The purpose of doing so is to help the members understand the manner in which they will interact with each other, to fulfil their multifarious needs in society. An online medical dictionary refers to the term as ability of the individual to interact in the normal or usual way in society.

Skidmore, Thackeray, and Farley, (1988) noted that social functioning includes the activities that are essential to satisfying relationships in the variety of social experiences, of daily living. They draw a triangle to describe the social functioning, (*see* Figure 1.1).

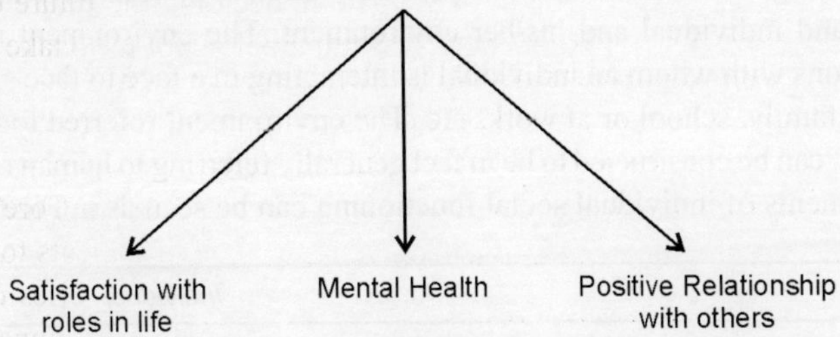

Fig. 1.1

The base of the triangle is self worth, the right side of the triangle is positive relationship with others, and the left side of the triangle reads satisfaction with roles in life, and the end outcome is noted in the centre as mental health. They then go on to emphasize enhancement of social functioning as the key area of social work, which differentiates it from other professions. Sociology simply provides a description of social roles and social change, but no practice wisdom to fill the generation gap, or explain the gap within a generation.

Human responses to social roles constitute the other end of the problem of social functioning, and hence we cross the disciplinary boundary to entre the domain of psychology. The problem is immensely complex, as social science discovered, that each individual is a unique entity, hence it is difficult both to generalize and/or theorize, human needs and perception and response to the environment.

The beginnings of social work in the United States usually dealing with poverty and deviance in Columbia University, in New York, saw the problem originating in the development of human beings. The Columbia School as it came to be known, thus invented the first method of social work, now known as working with individuals, but then termed as case work by Mary Richmond. She searched for the causes of poverty and social exclusion in the interaction between an individual and his/her environment, but she argued that care has to be taken to focus on the person within her/his situation, which she termed as social diagnosis. Yet soon after, the Chicago University in Chicago, again dealing with poverty and deprivation, came up with a different notion of human maladjustment, focusing on the environment of the individual, thus giving rise to settlement house movement and retaining children in school and training of youth to help them find work and better values. In a way the focus is again on interaction between individuals and their environment, the service is helping them to get better results, which are expected to provide individual's need fulfilment and better social functioning.

The expertise needed for a professional in dealing with these problems, is knowledge of social sciences, primarily sociology and psychology, to understand individual and his/her environment. The environment refers to the persons with whom an individual is interacting in a face to face situation, such as family, school or at work, etc. The environment referred to by early scholars, can be constructed to be in fact generally referring to human relations. The elements of individual social functioning can be seen as in Figure 1.2.

	Individual
Self-Concept	Relationships with self and others
Self Confidence	Need fulfilment
	Relationships with self and others
For Example	
Parents	Peer Group
Siblings	Teachers
Spouse	Boss, Colleagues, Sub Ordinates
Children	
Family	Group Relations
Neighbourhood	Community Relations
Gender,	
Religious Groups	
Caste	
Linguistic Groups	
	Social Relations
With in a nation	
	International Relations
Between Nations	

Fig. 1.2

Now it is obvious that the range of human relations cover a wide range, beginning from the relationship a person has with self, to human relations within a nation or even between nations. The purpose of doing this exercise is to highlight the scope of practice on one hand and the need for developing relevant theoretical material, to guide the practice. Given the recent developments in social sciences, we can find enough literature dealing with human relations at all these levels. Scholars have developed a number of perspectives to explain self-concept, group relations in general including family, peer groups, gangs, communities and so on, to provide some understanding of human relations, but to what extent such knowledge can guide practice of social work, has been a subject of debate in social sciences since long (*see* Pathak, 1989, Gellner, 1986, Davies, 1981).

Applicability has never fascinated sociologists the way it has economists, Van Nieuwenhuize (1982) noted, and went on to explain that sociologists hardly ever bother to develop a theory into a planning model, hence the link between sociological theory and community development or between sociology and social work remains weak (Pathak, 1989). Pathak quoted Martin Davies to emphasize that the contribution of sociology to social work has been primarily a negative one. He even went on to add that various change or control strategies are normally of only limited value and may be counter productive (*ibid*, p.5). And finally sociology may yct succeed in proving that social work is irrelevant and misguided in its assumed role (*ibid*).

What Timms (1970: 2) noted is equally significant,"*social workers do not usually enjoy a reputation for sustained critical thought about what they do. They are seen characteristically in feminine terms, high-souled, low-heeled women somewhat anxious to intervene in the lives of others.*" We must also take into account the cultural differences that shape human relations, in different countries and in different places and time periods to make it impossible for sociologists or social scientists to come up with knowledge which can really guide practice. Further, to attain a greater consistency in outputs of an intervention it is necessary to focus on specific relationships rather than covering all. In the US, the tendency has been to focus on intimate personal relations of an individual, which are more given to theorising and also where the professional is dealing with a more concrete reality. We will however suggest covering group and community relations as well, since in developing countries these are equally relevant, as these cultures are collectivist in their orientation. Some authors have suggested different approaches in handling human relations based on the cultural influence (*see*, McGoldrich and Hardy, 2008).

Social work, hence, can be defined as a profession providing help to person/s in dealing with the problems arising out of their 'Social Functioning', or 'Interaction with their Social Environment', I see the core expertise needed by social workers to help people in their social functioning as their expertise and skills in human relationships. Social work, therefore, can simply be defined as a profession to facilitate human relations to promote social development. I am using the term social development, both as defined by psychologists and as defined by sociologists. The psychologists are referring to the capacity of individual to handle all relations around him or her, while the sociologists are using a macro perspective of relations in the society, though there is no unanimity. The social workers will have to choose the level they will specialize in practice. It should be noted that a social worker will find it difficult, if not impossible, to deal with issues of human relations effectively at all levels. The expertise of social workers, thus, can be used by individuals, groups including families, communities and organizations to deal with their problems arising out of human relations. Social workers can and do take up the role of bringing about changes in societies to ensure better human rights compliance scenario, including social rights as a socially conscious member of society.

The theoretical framework social workers can use to analyze all the professional tasks, *see* the Figure 1.3:

	Problem	*Source/Cause/s*
1.	Behaviour Problems in Children:	Relationship with self and relationships in family
2.	Learning Problems in Children:	Relationship with self and relationships in school/family
3.	Alcoholism:	Relationship with self and relationships with friends/family/work
4.	Unemployment/Poverty:	Relations with self/others
5.	Domestic Violence	Relations with self/partner/spouse/children
6.	Group Problems	Relationships in a group
7.	Community Problems	Relationships in community
8.	Organizational Problems	Relationships in an organization
9.	Social Problems	Relationships in society

Fig. 1.3

The social work profession thus would claim human relationships as their main area of knowledge and skills. A social worker thus would know very specifically what is expected of her/him, and how to deal with the professional nature of his obligation. We already know that we use our relationship with our clients/s as our core skill to interact with them.

Dealing with relationships at the macro level is a very complex task beyond the scope of an individual or even a whole organization, but it is possible to include it as a practice area, so long as we are clear about the theoretical expertise needed. We are including it as a practice area to take care of the often cited argument that social justice can only be ensured by raising social awareness and promoting social action. Since a number of social work definitions feel uncomfortable, in diluting the social justice and human rights concerns, and perhaps rightly so, we should retain these as our core values. However, studying development and human relationships, example tribal-rural-urban continuum, should be an important agenda for our research efforts.

Radical left wing movements emerged in 60's and reached their peak in 70's, and then became non-functional, since they were not able to demonstrate any specific successes. A training programme for professional training of social workers will find it difficult to do justice with radical ideas, which are political in nature. I have earlier dealt with these (*see* Siddiqui, 1984, 2005). It also did not help the student to find any opportunity for professional practice as Sheldon & McDonald (2009: 30) commented, and I quote:

> "Salaried revolutionaries saw their own employers as the main targets of change and they naturally stopped employing them."

Discussing poverty in a society and its impact on human relationships is a very valid area of social work research. Thus increasing livelihood opportunities, working conditions or conditions of work, through better human relationships can be attempted, as has already been demonstrated in community practice. The reasons for decline of radical social work are more complex, as emergence of a capitalist world indicates, despite continuing poverty and a very wide gap between rich and poor both within and between nations. It requires a much wider discussion to consider the issue in depth and look at arguments from different perspectives. The recent changes in China and their experiments with new forms of democratic state are some other developments in the area.

Social Work Education

Social work education in India is now more than 75 years old. It has covered a lot of ground from making a modest beginning in 1936. The total number of schools, according to a latest update by TISS, is growing rapidly, and is estimated to be around 300. The growth of schools of social work has increased many fold in the last two decades. However, exact figures about these schools or details about these, such as courses offered and intake of students, number of faculty, etc. are not available as there is no mechanism to collect this data on a regular basis. The existing schools/departments present a wide variety of structures, resources including faculty strength and expertise to impart social work education in India. There are independent Faculties of Social Work, Departments within the Faculty of Social Sciences in a university, Departments within a college affiliated to a university or constituent college of a University, Department/s in a Distance Education University, and Departments within a private university/college.

Needless to say that their location is indicative of resources they have access to and the monitoring mechanism, both academic and administrative, to supervise their functioning. It also determines the courses they can offer, for example, departments at college level generally offer undergraduate programmes or at best Masters level programmes, but are not entitled to offer research programmes such as M.Phil and Ph.D Courses. The post graduate courses predominate and the need for under graduate education in social work is now gradually being recognized. Recently TISS has started a five year integrated programme in places outside its main campus in Mumbai.

Review of Social Work Education in India

A thorough review of social work education in India is long overdue. The University Grants Commission has appointed a committee for the purpose long ago but unfortunately it could not complete its job, although the committee deliberated for some time and visited some schools. The last exercise of delivering some useful information on the subject was the Second UGC Committee report (1978), which at the time listed only 34 social work education institutions in the country. Seminars on the theme of review of social work education have been organized frequently and some have published the proceedings (*see* Nair, 1981; Jacob, 1994; Singh and Srivastava, 2005). The issues raised all these seminars reflect a familiar pattern. A more recent effort by TISS was done to review all the problems faced by social work departments/ schools, with a view to set up a network to support and strengthen social work education in the country. Five meetings were held in different zones of the country, the regional reports were discussed in a meeting at TISS. The report of these deliberations (Nadkarni and Desai, 2012) is available on the net. I have taken a few facts from the report to highlight the issues, which conform to the pattern with a few changes.

South Zone: Prof. Ramana presented the trends in social work education in South India, highlighting the following points:

- Growth of social work institutions mostly at the post graduate level,
- The quality of education in these institutions is sub-standard both academically and administratively with skewed teacher-student ratios.
- The programmes are self-financed and have expensive fee structures.
- The fieldwork training component in these institutions is weak.
- Distance education in social work is getting promoted, with poor quality of contact classes.
- The supervised fieldwork component is absent in the distance education mode.
- The personnel management and industrial relations specialisation is not suited to social work.
- Licensing in social work is needed and hence the need to establish a National Council for Social Work Profession.
- Need to indigenise social work education.
- The generic programmes in social work to be changed to specialisations with focus on rural issues.

North Zone: Professor Zubair Meenai presented the report and highlighted the following points:

- The schools are generally located in the university System and have low autonomy.

- Some schools are offering Diplomas besides PG and Other programmes.
- Mushrooming of private schools in UP and Rajasthan.
- The new schools do not have adequate faculty members and inadequate infrastructure such as space, library, administrative staff, etc.
- Innovative methods of education are found in some schools such as skill labs, for improving the quality of education.
- Wide variation in curriculum contents and new schools has poorly designed curriculums.
- Rural exposure of students is low.
- No faculty development programmes.
- More research needed to provide a sound theoretical base.

East Zone: Dr Nabor Soreng presented the report and highlighted the following points:

- Curriculum is generally outdated;
- Field work facilities are not adequate;
- Assessment of social work students being undertaken by non social work faculty;
- Faculty strength is insufficient as reflected by high student-teacher ratio;
- Insufficient research efforts and lack of sharing of research findings.

West Zone: Professor Geeta Balakrishnan presented the report and highlighted the following point:

There are more than 300 schools in India out of which 67 are in Maharashtra, and 60 in Gujarat, thus 40 per cent of schools are in Western region.

Gujarat

- Mushrooming of self finance institutions with high fees;
- Faculty is generally sub-standard;
- Student teacher ratio very high even in state run institutes reflecting low faculty strength;
- Overcrowding of students in field work agencies as there are not enough field work agencies;
- Distance education becoming popular and nearly 800 students enrolled in the state;
- The students with distance education qualifications get very low salaries.

Maharashtra

- Despite the large number of schools in Maharashtra, the quality is sub-standard.

- Lack of adequate field work agencies;
- Students have to pay to get field work exposure;
- Low salary for teachers;
- Students are admitted without following any selection criteria;
- Absence of indigenous literature;
- Motivation of students to find jobs;
- Field work orientation currently is to carry out programmes, not sufficient attention paid to process learning;
- Field Action projects lacking;
- Literature in local language needed as English competencies are weak;
- Specialization courses, core courses and practice courses need to be identified.

North East: No. of Participants not given: Fr. Jerry Thomas presented the report and highlighted the following points:

- No recognition of professional nature of social work by other professionals;
- Problems of curriculum;
- Core base of social work education and regional issues needs to be blended;
- Lack of adequate field work agencies;
- Quality of faculty poor;
- No research experience with faculty;
- Non social work teachers;
- General discussion which followed identified following issues;
- Distance Education;
- Ideology of Social work debate inconclusive;
- Mushrooming of market driven social work education to be stopped;
- Change from market driven to Ideology driven education suggested.

What conclusions can we draw from the rather grim scenario presented by the regional reports? At least one trend is obvious: social work has been recognized by employers and the job market is expanding, pushing the growth of social work institutions, from 34 schools around three decades ago to three hundred plus schools in the country now. Almost all well known universities are adding social work departments. This is a clear indication of social work programmes being positively evaluated both by students and the administration of higher education officials. The darker side is the commercialisation of social work education but then that has happened to other more established professions in the country such as medicine, engineering and law, particularly with strong professional bodies in place, still unable to prevent it. So let us take it as a professional hazard of being located in world's largest, thriving but still poor democracy.

The trend of having institutions of social work in India, which can be classified as very professional to moderate to very weak is not unique to social work alone. Similar trend is found with many other professional institutions, including medicine and engineering. As Bawa noted, worldwide there is a deliberate planned shift toward massification of higher education as a strategy of development. Between 1960 and 2004 the number of participants in some form of higher education grew from about 13 million to about 132 million (Bawa, 2009). Such mass scale expansion is bound to dilute the quality.

There are three issues which are common in all the reports: (i) dissatisfaction with the curriculum, (ii) faulty strength and its quality, and (iii) field work. The conclusion one can draw from these observation is obvious. There is a lack of clarity about what is to be taught, expertise to deliver this, and particularly to develop the skills of practice, which largely depends on, apart from other things, well designed field work experiences. This affects the overall professional competence of social workers coming out of these institutions. Distance education as someone jokingly remarked distances students from education particularly in places, where even the on campus mode is not able to do justice with the learners (*See* Siddiqui, 2011). The curriculum and its delivery, in many schools, are generally academic, theoretical and devoid of practice orientation. It does not provide knowledge of any practice tools to learners, which are hallmarks of professional practice. Field work is the only saving grace, which is generally getting diluted in many schools.

On the positive side, attempts at preparing guidelines for curriculum development have been made and a report has been published by UGC (2001). As Professor Meenai mentioned, some institutions are focusing attention on skill development, but it remains an unstructured non documented exercise generally. Another positive feature of social work education appears to be that social work education of whatever quality is still influencing the students in a positive way, which has resulted in their greater acceptance by the job market in the service delivery sector, which led to the commercialization of social work education. Further, if they are accepting jobs at a low salary and still taking interest in the job, reflects a positive approach as well. If they are not able to do it very professionally is a shortcoming of social work education in particular and the system of higher education in general.

These are rather serious issues, which require a subtle but a firm approach if we are serious about rectifying the situation. However, we can attempt a holistic approach to identify future challenges, once we finish taking a look at all aspects of social work in India.

Social Work Research

Let us look at the state of social work research in India. Research is crucial for professionalization of social work and for that matter all practising professions. All professions are looking for more innovative ways to provide services to their clients. They are, therefore, continuously identifying areas where particularly epistemological understanding is inadequate, therefore limiting the capacities of the practitioners to provide effective solutions. The disciplines providing theoretical inputs are therefore trying to come up with the epistemological issues but how a particular theory relates to a social phenomenon in a particular context is experienced by a practitioner alone. Therefore, a successful professional is always recording the details of what knowledge s/he applied in a context, with what result. This as we all know is what is known as outcome research. Greenwood (1957) therefore made it amply clear the function of social work research when he said, "Social work is not a science, whose aim is to derive knowledge; it is a technology whose aim is to apply knowledge."

Ramchandran (1968) in order to define the term social work research observed that, "social work is a practice profession. Social work research then has the function to search for answers to questions raised regarding alternate interventions or treatments in social work practice, and for answers to problem or difficulties faced by social work practitioners in the practice of their profession." A committee of social science research while reviewing the studies done by social workers commented, "much of the research in social work cannot meet the standards of rigorous professional work," (Govt. of India, 1968). The committee giving an example noted, even where a number of studies have been conducted on the same problem, these are invariably incomparable because the methodological tools differ, the basic concepts vary and the very presentation of findings is divergent. (Govt. of India, *ibid*). In 1972, Ranade felt that "social work research is far from impressive from either qualitative or quantitative angle. In 2008 Lal Das commented, "there has been little growth and practically no development in the field of social work research in India."

+Turning to global scenario of social work research some commonality is visible, as Rosen *et al.* (1999) in their article, "Social Work Research and the Quest for Effective Practice," wrote that the tension between basic and applied research remain unresolved within the profession. Basic studies (descriptive, explanatory, theory testing) vastly outnumbered well controlled outcome studies (Thyer, 2000). Joel Fischer (1973) found only 11 studies that used experimental or quasi-experimental designs, in a review of research on effectiveness of case workers that spanned approximately four decades. Zimbalist (1977) remarked that Social Survey method has failed to provide any useful answers to make welfare practice more effective. Austin (1998) reported that only 15 per cent of all published studies till mid nineties can be called well controlled outcome research. The research scenario in India is no exception. We do not have a separate journal publishing only social work practice research in India. A cursory look at research efforts in some major schools will provide the same conclusion that well controlled outcome studies account for a very low percentage. Most of the research is generally carried out by students for their degrees like MA, M.Phil or Ph.D. Their resources are limited and methodological understanding far from satisfactory. Most of the studies use descriptive or diagnostic designs and are generally quantitative in nature. Most of these are never published, and so no documentation takes place and hence sharing is low. For paucity of a better term we can call it forced research. The outcome and use of such research is rather limited.

The research projects undertaken both by academic institutions or NGOs are not very different either in methodology or sharing. The tradition of social work practitioners documenting their practice accounts, with any degree of methodological sophistication, is almost non-existent in India.

Attempts of reviewing the state of social work research goes on at different periods either independently or as part of review of social work education and practice. The most recent being the TISS effort to review social work education (2012) mentioned earlier. It noted paucity of research interest and competence among the faculty of so called newly emerging institutions. The most recent independent review of social work research in India is done by Lal Das and Bhaskaran, (2008). It is more of a useful guide line to do social work practice research, using quasi-experimental designs and emphasizing the need for using qualitative methods as well, rather than a review of social work research in India, yet Lal Das did comment on the lack of growth in social work research in India.

Ramchandran (1975) is trying to identify the reasons for poor state of social work research in India, listed eight problems quoting ICSSR. Reviewing the current scenario in a historical perspective, two things are clear. Research is a fulltime job and requires sufficient material resources and competent persons to do it well. Ramchandran, therefore, suggested the only possible way to improve social work research, by advocating for an independent body to carry it out. He went on to specify the whole process to carry it out (see Ramchandran, 1991). I need not add anything further at this juncture since it can be discussed and debated by a competent group of experts. I had long back suggested to ICSSR to undertake a process of developing tools to facilitate studies of different types. I think Lal Das and Bhaskaran (2008) has taken a step in the right direction.

Social Work Practice

A review of social work practice in India is long overdue. There are only three studies of social work manpower that have been published so far. The earliest was by Ramchandran (1977), limited in scope to the state of Maharashtra. Pathak (1983) did a general survey of social welfare manpower, and Nair (1983) did a study of social welfare manpower, in the state of Tamil Nadu. These studies provide information about where the social workers are working, their role and responsibilities, the remuneration they are getting and how satisfied they are with what they are doing. Any attempt at judging the quality of the services rendered or the strategies used and the success etc. was not part of the scope of the studies. No serious research effort has been undertaken to document the specific roles social workers are carrying out at any level, in any setting or field either in a state or nationally. The information about number of social workers and their practice settings is not available even about a single city.

A more recent in-house effort was done by TISS in (2008) and it is titled, Contextualizing Social Work Practice in India: Some Explorations. It has been published as a special volume of Indian Journal of Social Work. The editor Narayan (2008) in her editorial observed, "Professional social work is focused on the facilitation of empowerment and change. Social work has been constantly evolving and attempting to redefine its mandate as per the changing needs of society." She obviously is referring to changes the academic institutions made in their curriculum, since she has no data about practice to support her observation. The volume is an attempt to provide more theoretical inputs to practitioners in different areas rather than a review of practice currently on in the field. It is obvious, that the idea to research what is the nature of social work practice in the country, the strategies used or successes achieved, the difficulties encountered, the frustrations, burn outs or self doubts encountered, is not very popular among the academic world in India. However, it is very essential to revise our curriculum and add more opportunities for learners to improve the practice competence. An effort of this nature was undertaken by Ramchandran at the time of global Centenary of TISS, where he interacted with the alumnae of the institute to record their practice experiences. He produced a report entitled the 'Great Divide', which somehow has not been published. The great divide obviously referred to what we are discussing today as an unresolved issue developmental or remedial practice.

There are two ways one can reflect on social work practice in India: What methods are currently being used in the practice or what fields or areas social workers are engaged in. Even a cursory look at jobs being advertised, discussions during placement interviews, reveals that working with communities both rural and urban, generally for service delivery roles predominates. Case work and counselling is being used in a variety of settings, for example medical, psychiatric, school social work, correctional services, alcoholism, drug addiction and HIV/AIDs, marriage and family counselling including domestic violence, handling trauma victims and so on, but the details are missing. Group work is being used in working with women, children and youth but no records are available about its process, nature and effectiveness.

Advocacy practice is found but does not appear to be a very popular area of practice. Similarly method of social action for achieving any goals has generally not been very wide spread by social workers. The instances of private practice by individual social workers are non-existent or negligible. But the trend of social workers forming their own organization is gradually taking shape. But all this is just speculative and impressionistic account of social work practice. One can make an educated guess that the social work practice covers a fairly wide ground in India. A list of tasks being performed globally by social workers is available on the internet for us to compare notes.

Professional Status of Social Work in India

In the 1950's, the profession of social work was in search of an identity, recognition and a status, the position has not materially changed even now. It is still knocking at the door for acceptance as a profession and an identity different from that of a social science discipline (Bose, quoted in Pathak, 2012).

Professional status to any activity is granted first by its clients in a society, when they start recognizing the importance of the same and later by the state, when it recognizes the provider of the service and lays down a criterion to be fulfilled by the professionals. The state thus creates a body or rather give state sanction to a body of professionals to safeguard its own interest, that of the clients and in the final analysis that of society. The allotment of professional status, therefore, is a political process, intermediated by bureaucracy as well. In order for the political will to act in a democracy, it needs sufficient support from both the professionals and the bureaucracy, to prove to the political will, that it is in the larger interest of the society to do so and that it will not create any major problems including financial obligation for the state. In the history of the social work profession in India, the moment came and went, since the professionals among themselves could not decide, who should corner the glory, for making it happen, while the bureaucracy and politician were ready to do so. So the profession remained where it is today, although the practice has expanded phenomenally. Whether the moment will recur in the future I have no means of knowing, but if you take into account the current happenings in other professional bodies, it is not likely to happen. The possibility of the clients granting a professional status to the services provided by social workers can happen if the competence of social workers significantly improves in near future, and their clients see beyond any doubt that the intervention by the social workers brought significant gains for them, individually or collectively not once, but time and again. It can, however, only happen if the service offered by social worker is needed by the person in his/her day to day life, and the client, therefore, seeks it on his/her own. So far the workers have been trying to convince the clients that they are trying to help them but they have not been very sure or convinced about it.

So the struggle to become a profession will go on in India, and we can all hope that someday it will happen. A significant point to keep in mind is that generally social workers are employed by organizations to help common persons who do not feel the need for service being offered, or they are helping persons to access services such as medicine, employment, market, banks or education etc.

The Way Ahead

The future of social work at the level it is functioning seems to be secure for the time being, as the service delivery role it is performing will go on. Despite the tall claims of ensuring social justice and safeguarding human rights by social work educators, the worker on the ground, will go on working and earning a moderate living and making a dent here and there. They will be quite happy doing just that. Yet, for the sake of academic clarity we should recall what Gore said long back, a profession needs special skills in a problem area and clients with problems in that area to survive. It is high time that social work decided to choose an area, which is understood by all concerned to specialize in. Do keep in mind some key concepts like social change, macro-micro levels and structures, inter linkages between them, empowerment and so on have neither been adequately and clearly conceptualized nor discussed in operational terms, and existing literature has failed to provide guidelines of practice. (Pathak, 2012, 216).

- Identify your concrete expertise area,
- Develop assessment measures to be able to explain it to the client/s about the nature of the problem,
- Develop specific strategies to solve the problem in a given time frame, if possible,
- Develop indicators and measurement to depict change.
- Document feedback from clients, to support your claim of having helped them in a concrete manner.
- Professionalise social work education to produce professionals who will possess the requisite practice skills.
- Develop further programmes to develop professional skills beyond the Masters level around any number of feasible practice areas.

- M.Phil and Ph.Ds should be awarded for producing practical knowledge.
- Develop greater interaction between teaching and practice.
- Set up an independent body to carry out regular studies of social work interventions to refine these.
- Develop professional bodies to safeguard the professional interests.

Appendix

The Future of Social Work is Being Discussed…

Add your voice to the international debate on how social work should be described in the coming years. Does the current definition of social work reflect your reality and understanding of social work? Does the current definition reflect the daily realities for social workers in Afghanistan, America, Armenia, Angola, Argentina, Australia, Algeria, Albania, American Samoa, Aruba, Azerbaijan, and Austria. It makes you think?

The new Draft Global Definition of Social Work below is a result of extensive consultation carried out independently but in a coordinated fashion by IFSW and IASSW. To reach this point each organization ran regional workshops, and many countries, organizations and individuals also submitted their contributions into the process. These submissions were brought together by nominated representatives of both organizations and have resulted in this Draft Global Definition of Social Work that will enable further comments, reactions and feedback.

In the process of developing this draft each organization tried to respect the following, and sometimes competing considerations:

- To include the wide range of perspectives that have been voiced in the submission process;
- To keep the definition short;
- To ensure that the words and meaning are easily translatable;
- To make the wording relevant to governments and their policy development departments;
- To ensure that it is understandable to people who are not social workers;
- To maintain the depth and complexity of the profession.

The next steps involve both the IASSW and IFSW board's consideration of the draft. These processes may result in changes and it is anticipated that there will be further consultation and feedback. A final draft will be voted upon by members of both organisations.

2

From Social Service Administration to Anti-Oppressive Social Work

A Critique of 'Professional Social Work'

Vidya Rao

The journey from Social Service Administration in 1936 to social work with specialization in Medical and Psychiatric Social Work (1948), Criminology and Correctional Administration (1950s), Family and Child Welfare (1950s), Urban and Rural Community Development (1960s), and Social Welfare Administration (1972), Rural Social Work (1980s) marks the first phase of the shift in which scope of social work expanded into specific fields of practice. This phase lasted till about the mid 1990s. The next shift to rights based approach can be said to have begun in the mid 1990s. Especially when 'rights based approach' was adopted at the international forums, and when the idea percolated to professional social work in India, that social work is political in nature and content was acknowledged first by radical sections among the professional social workers. It was also acknowledged that the causes of the 'problems' faced by individuals belonging to the excluded sections were structural in nature. Anti-oppressive social work phase commenced from 2005 in which Dalit and Tribal Social Work, Disability Studies and Action, Women Centered Social Work, Social Work to reduce Impoverishment and Vulnerability, Socio-legal Rehabilitation Practice, Youth and Change, Gerontology Social Work, Social work for Peace and Human Security emerged as new areas of study and practice. The structural social work – the current phase that commenced from 2009, represents deeper social work theoretical knowledge required to resist neoliberal anti-people forces.

In the West, especially in the US, a new well developed discipline known as "Non-profit Management" evolved by the Schools of Social Work in collaboration with Business Management Schools in various universities in the 1990s. By the beginning of the first decade of the 21st century, due to concern about threat of terrorism, many national governments, including India were required to strictly regulate NPOs/NGOs. A slew of laws were enacted to regulate the voluntary non-government sector as a whole. This necessitated much more transparency and accountability on the part of NPOs/NGOs than was the case in the 1980s and the 1990s. A CEO of a voluntary organization is required to know the intricacies of these regulations and have sophisticated skills to balance autonomy with accountability. These measures helped in the development of in-depth knowledge about management of NGOs. Ironically during the same period when anti-oppressive social work emerged, management oriented professional social work also emerged in an endeavour to retain autonomy of non-government voluntary organizations as an arena of professional social work education and practice. This was different from the erstwhile Social Welfare Administration which included Public Welfare Administration and few aspects of legal framework of NGO sector.

Due to the Foucauldian influence in the early 2000s, a process of 'driving a person mad' within family and society as a structural exercise of social power to exclude certain inconvenient members recognized mental illness as a social construct. This recognition, contrary to the medical model of yester years, required professional social work to adopt a more humane, inclusive approach based on theoretical knowledge about social structural processes of power, dominance and exclusion and specialized skills for building capacities of the mentally ill to become ordinary members of society like others. This perspective gave rise to what is known as 'structural social work'.

These paradigm shifts and other developments influenced professional social work education and practice; but the influence of these paradigm shifts was not evenly spread. This is an attempt to trace the intellectual trajectory traversed by professional social work as a discipline in a premier social work education institution in India.

Social Work as a Discipline

Social work is primarily a helping activity. Helping process involves a set of values regarding the dignity and worth of every human being, principles regarding an individual's or a society's right to self-determination, methods and techniques to enable an individual, a group or a section of society to learn from experience, change and function. And, 'professionalism in social work education and practice, is about theoretically sound, value-based ethical processes of systematic, objective, rational, appropriate intervention strategies to deliver welfare services to alleviate hardship experienced by individuals, families, communities and societies. Delivery of welfare services has to be specific to the person, family, community, the problem and the context. Professional social work is an attempt to facilitate attitudinal and behavioural changes in the 'person' in need of welfare services, in the system delivering welfare services and in the society as a whole not only to alleviate a person's and/or the family's difficulty but also to ensure protection of human rights, equality, social justice and promotion of human security.

Owing to the fact that professional social workers conduct their activities in relation to others, every intervention is based on a political world view irrespective of the fact whether they are conscious of it or not. The purpose of professional social work, therefore, is to: (i) enhance the problem solving and coping capacities of individuals, (ii) link people with systems that provide them with resources, services and opportunities, (iii) promote effective and human operation of the systems, and (iv) to contribute to the social policies and development (Pincus and Minahan, 1973: 9).

Conventionally, professional social workers face difficult choices in the process of helping individuals in difficulty; they do their utmost to work out fair compromises among valid and competing claims and pressures to achieve their vision and mission rather than attempt changing the system. In the process of helping, professional social work encounters systemic barriers such as mass poverty, unemployment, population explosion, illiteracy, malnutrition, ill health, low productivity, partisan state and other social and economic barriers. Gore argues for a distinct shift from an emphasis on individual adjustment to social structural modification if professional social work is to engage in helping effectively. Professional social workers must participate in the policy formulation, planning and administrative processes of implementation at grass-roots, state and national levels (Gore: 1973: 47-49).

Essentially then, the thrust of professional social work involves understanding, changing the position of the oppressed and the oppressive structures at the societal level while simultaneously counter acting the negative effects of social change at the micro individual level. Viewed this way, professional social work is primarily concerned with conventional micro-level helping processes, while simultaneously being engaged at societal-level social change. From this, three distinct foci emerge namely, (i) core of direct service delivery to the marginalized disadvantaged vulnerable groups, (ii) planning, administration and implementation of welfare programmes and (iii) social action and social advocacy (Gore as cited in Nair: 1981: 13).

In this, several political realities stand out. It was expected of professional social work to move from performing the conventional system maintenance function to the task of changing the social structures in favour of the vulnerable, the victimized, the excluded and the marginalized (Desai as cited in Nair: 1981: 211-212). Because professional social work deals with prevention of insecurity and vulnerability, protection of people's rights, satisfaction of human need and alleviation of insecurity, the scope of social work extends over wide range of fields of knowledge. And, professional social work knowledge base perforce has to be eclectic and inter-disciplinary in nature. The body of social work theoretical knowledge has grown out of continuous interaction between social work practice and behavioural and social sciences theories. Professional social work as a discipline in India has developed over a period of seventy five years.

By paradigm shift one refers to professional discourse that includes the profession's written texts and/or the language spoken between specialists in the same profession (intra-professional discourse), between those in different professions (inter-professional discourse), and between professionals and clients. It also includes different forms of non-verbal communication. It is a form of social practice operating according to conventions and generally accepted rules, even if those are not explicitly stated or formalized or consciously complied with. The more formal the discourse (e.g. written documents such as codes of ethics, mission statements, public professional reports), the more it tends to reflect the profession's declared ethos and ethical codes. The more informal the discourse (e.g. oral discourse, intra-profession conversations, staff meetings, corridor talk), the less self-conscious it is.

Professional discourse reflects and structures reality by defining thc role and status of the profession in society, its values and norms, and the normative relationships between professionals themselves and between them and recipients of their services. Professional social workers tend to adopt the professional jargon used in the institutions in which they studied or work, and this jargon influences the type of interaction they create with their clients. Thus, analysis of professional discourse is an important instrument for understanding the profession, its practice and the links between everyday practice, larger issues of social structure, meanings and shifts in the perspectives. Examining professional discourse in the context of public discourse regarding social problems is especially relevant for social work. Social work per se, and more so professional social work in India has always been a contested activity, characterized by a history of uncertainty regarding its identity, mandate, methods and its status as a profession. However, unlike education, law and medicine, professional social work discourse in India has been the subject of surprisingly limited empirical research.

Nevertheless, the profession's exclusive domains have expanded over time. Most social workers enjoy a relatively high degree of professional autonomy. They are employed in a wide variety of social settings, mainly in the private, non-government, non-profit voluntary sectors but also in state services. Professional social workers engage in protection of populations at risk, extend material assistance, take up advocacy, organization and development of community, integration of labour market, counseling of individuals and families, and capacity building etc.

Job descriptions are formal documents prepared by employers in order to define the nature of their employees' work, the tasks they are expected to perform and their place in the organizational hierarchy. A job description constitutes a quasi-contract that indicates what is expected of the employee, and usually reflects the values and priorities of the organization and/or the profession. It may not always be in formally written format. At the same time it might be influenced by abstract professional commitments and values of the interests of politicians, elite, other professions, civil society or administrators. Social work job descriptions in the voluntary sector, where most professional social workers in India are employed, are usually written by social workers themselves. Social work job descriptions in the public sector, where few social workers are employed, are usually not written by social workers. Social work job descriptions constitute an important source of the professional discourse.

The ways in which poverty, poverty alleviation, need, problem, marginalization, helping, intervention etc. are represented in social work professional discourse reflect and construct the profession's attitude towards people and conditions and causes of poverty, marginalization, deprivation, victimhood, etc. It has the potential to reveal declared and tacit attitudes regarding these conditions and causes, social workers' role in this regard and appropriateness of the intervention strategies. Analysis of different levels of the social work discourse reveals distinctive attitudes toward the phenomenon of social need and the solutions.

Social work profession in India is an interesting case for the study of paradigm shifts that have taken place through the discourse due to the professional standing of social work, the structuring of social care and protection, the role played by professional social workers in representing the interests and the rights of the marginalized. Since its beginnings in the early decades of twentieth century, professional social work has undergone a constant process of professionalization.

Critique of Professional Social Work Discipline

When professional social work education was accepted by a small section of intellectuals as necessary for systematic and effective intervention in 1936, it was presumed that only professionally educated social workers would be able to do value-based, ethical, systematic, objective social work. Public opinion held that a strong commitment to a cause and passion for humanitarian work was sufficient for anyone to engage in social work. At that time, the need for professional social work education was not widely recognized nor was the idea of social work as a profession, especially when many social reformers were engaged in abolition of superstitious practices, running orphanages, promoting women's education and in the freedom movement without professional social work education. Without a tradition of imparting formal professional education for doing social work, accepting professional social work education as necessary marked the first shift from charity to systematic social service administration.

When professional social work education was accepted as necessary, the curriculum was developed in English by English knowing urban elite with exposure to western ideas of equality, freedom, social justice, citizenship, etc. The curriculum content of professional social work education prevalent in the US was adopted for preparing professional social work human-power in India. Because there was no consciousness about professionalism in social work in India, indigenous knowledge about society and social processes that was not documented in English, was scattered, was not easily available and hence did not get included.

Extant American curriculum content of professional social work education was based on Judeo-Christian liberal values and psychoanalytic theories prevalent at the time. Judeo-Christian values gave importance to 'individual' as an autonomous entity with freedom of choice in life and living. And, medical model followed by American professional social work that viewed individual with problems as deviance, personal inadequacy and as illness that had to be diagnosed and treated using theories of psychoanalysis and psychology.

"Administration" was understood as institutionalization of widely accepted principles, organizational norms and procedures that would deliver social and welfare services objectively and would solve the persons' problems systematically. Before independence, state's role was limited to providing legislative framework that would legitimize delivery of specific social and welfare services by voluntary agencies. It was left to the native elites to take the initiative to deliver social and welfare services to the needy persons personally or through the agency of a voluntary initiative. Credibility and acceptability of the processes and contents of social and welfare services delivered by the voluntary agencies depended on the perception of the ruling elites about the needs of the unfortunate recipients. The quality of service delivered was never questioned.

During the initial expansion phase, although it claimed to be a change agent, professional social work unwittingly was promoting status quo. Preoccupation of the discipline with the methods and the agency setting till the mid 1980s inhibited the development of eclectic theoretical knowledge base and social work's more important role – that of change agent. Professional social work consciously or unconsciously felt inadequate to deal with the larger social structural issues such as caste system, mass poverty, etc.

Though there was a perceived misfit between Indian cultural values and the received ideas about individual, culture, society, social problems, equality, freedom and justice, professional social work in India adopted the received values and ideas. This orientation towards the individual in difficulty as a deviant overlooked the power relations in a hierarchical society and its consequences for an individual. Society and the way society was organized were completely absolved of any responsibility for causing hardships for individuals.

There was some amount of unarticulated "us" and "they" feeling on the part professional social workers and the recipients of professional social work services. At the time, 'us' was taken to refer to all the natives and 'they' referred to the colonial rulers. Perceiving the professional social workers and the recipients of their services as belonging to this or the other "community" or as belonging to this or the other 'class' or as 'son of the soil' or an 'outsider' was considered divisive and unpatriotic because a country aspiring for independence from colonial rule and as a newly independent country had to focus on national unity and inculcation of patriotic feelings and not unleash fissiparous forces.

In the early years after independence, the Indian state had to attempt introduction of democracy, nation building and economic development – three formidable tasks simultaneously; as part of this effort, the state was keen that voluntary organizations extend welfare services to the disadvantaged because a newly independent developing nation could ill afford to spend much of its scarce resources on welfare although the poverty, mass illiteracy, morbidity and mortality levels were challenging. Nationalist fervour blinded professional social workers working both within government and outside to differential perceptions of need, poverty, welfare state, etc. to an extent.

This blindness to differential perceptions about the needs of different sections of Indian population might have been appropriate in the first few decades after independence as the nation was engaged in the task of nation-building and economic development. The language used in the professional social work literature of the time is generic and does not have evidence of professional social workers' awareness about their own class, caste gender or ethnic differences nor the differences in identities of their clientele. Professional social workers' focus was on 'helping' fellow country persons in difficulty. They considered themselves to be 'change agents' in the sense that they had gotten rid of the colonial mantle by participating in freedom movement and were engaged in nation-building and development by being engaged in helping activities.

Professional social workers' claims raised the expectations of the ruling classes from professional social work to unprecedented levels. Professional social work was expected to identify the problems, draw up plans, mobilize resources, implement them, provide feedback, change the policies, counter–act the ill–effects of change and so on without large financial implications to the state. Professional social worker's own expectations about their own role in planned development proved to be a tall order.

The emphasis was on 'unity in diversity'. As such, hierarchies, identities and other 'structural' aspects were quickly "managed" by homogenizing competing demands in the name of national integrity and equality of opportunity by the ruling elite; and professional social work educators and practitioners also subscribed to this way of homogenizing the differences. This resulted in overlooking the needs of individuals located in the periphery of the caste, gender and other power relations or geographical locations. Looking back, unquestioning subscription to 'unity in diversity' mantra amounted to holding a smoke screen to hide the unequal power relations. Though it was the need of the hour, naiveté on the part of professional social workers not only ran the risk of neglecting the needs of the excluded but also proved to be the origin of "elitism" among the professional social work in India. And, however well intentioned it was, unspoken element of condescension—professional social worker as the giver (superior) and the person with a 'problem' as the receiver of 'help' (inferior) in the professional social work 'helping process' — that had crept in reinforced existing hierarchies, especially because professional social workers in those early decades came from English educated upper strata of urban society with vested interests in rural areas.

Having been a British colony, Indian professional social workers had not got rid of colonial mindset and looked to the 'west' for theories and theoretical frameworks and applied them in practice until the mid 1980s. As such, the early professional social workers used psychology and psychoanalysis theories prevalent in the west to understand the "person" and her/his "problem" in Indian context. Even Karma theory in the Bhagavat Gita was interpreted from these perspectives. In this conservative perspective, the person with problem was seen as a deviant requiring "correctional" treatment by professionally trained social workers. The causes of the 'problem' experienced by an individual and its solutions were located within the individual herself/himself according this perspective; and the individual with a problem was goaded to accept "treatment" from professional social workers to become "normal" member of the society again. This approach used the authority of 'agency' of professional social worker and her employing organization as tools for helping. The language of the social work literature of the time indicates social worker as a change agent—change being limited to changing the person per se. The overall approach was remedial and residual. Humanitarianism was the main ideology undergirding social welfare services delivered by social work professionals working in voluntary agencies.

While professional social work discipline stirred a great deal of hope and expectation in the first two decades after independence, *social psychological* perspective adopted by professional social workers subscribed to the necessity of welfare state to deliver welfare services. In keeping with the 'national consensus' and Fabian Socialist ideology prevalent among the ruling elite at the time, professional social work also unwittingly took statist position because it had no clear understanding of the implications of universal adult suffrage, secularism, democracy, party politics, electoral politics and politics of development. Initially, political leaders themselves were ambivalent about how democratization of Indian polity, universal adult franchise and decentralized democratic decision-making system would pan out in a hierarchical society. Gradually, the elite upper caste and class utilized the democratic political processes to keep themselves entrenched in positions of power. Naiveté of professional social workers prompted them to keep a distance from politics regardless of the fact whether professional social workers were working within or outside the government. Professional social workers did their best to portray welfare services delivery system, of which they were part, as being apolitical. It did not occur to professional social workers that individual's problems could be caused by hierarchical social structure, that the state itself was peopled by vested interests and the state could not be expected to give effect to equality and social justice principles enshrined in the Indian Constitution. Despite Gandhi's and Ambedkar's efforts to annihilate caste system, to professional social workers, caste system was something that could not be changed in the immediate future. Despite virulent anti-brahmin movement taking place in Tamil Nadu in the 1960s, openly debating caste system, equality and social justice was preposterous for professional social workers at the time.

Keeping the responsibility for nation-building, national integration and planned change in mind, professional social workers believed that they were identifying individuals in genuine need regardless of their caste or creed. Professional social workers gave an impression as if they were promoting equality, social justice and rights on behalf of the vulnerable and the marginalized by creating 'caring' self-rule, by being part of the 'policy formulation processes' and by persuading government to establish social welfare service delivery systems at national, state and district levels to benefit the vulnerable and the marginalized without being conscious of the gaps and contradictions in their thinking, articulation and actions.

Professional social work had proliferated into new arenas of practice beginning from the 1940s and the 1950s into such fields as medical and psychiatric social work, family and child welfare, labour welfare, criminology and correctional administration; rural and urban community development and social welfare administration were added subsequently. These arenas of professional social work were seen as their contribution to the integration of social dimension to the state-sponsored economic development policies and plans. Several social legislations were enacted and social welfare divisions were created within the national and state governments in the 1950s and the early 1960s. The role of government expanded phenomenally. However, entry into government employment was through civil service only even for professional social workers. Professional social work educational centers could not scale up quickly to meet the human-power requirements of a nascent welfare state. As a result, educated persons without professional social work education were recruited to deliver public welfare services in the early 1970s.

The shift from social service administration located outside government to social welfare administration situated within government sponsored social welfare system marked the second shift. And some professional social work graduates from the elite professional social work educational institutions entrenched themselves in the newly created positions at national and state levels to 'administer' social welfare programmes of the government—an obligation of a so-called 'welfare state'. At this stage, four modes of professional social work response in India could be delineated: (1) concentration on what activities one was doing, (2) production of reports but remaining indifferent about its utilization by the state, (3) lobbying vigorously to get policy recommendations accepted by the state, and (4) critical evaluation of policies as complementary to effective governance.

By the 1970s, most of the professional social workers identified with the evolving public welfare system and were seen as being part of it by the general public. During this period, community organization (CO), community development (CD) social welfare administration (SWA), medical and psychiatric social work, family and child welfare and correctional administration disciplines of professional social work practice had much currency. Though CO, CD and SWA methods were built into professional social work education curriculum and practice as necessary, case work and group work methods were portrayed as *the USP* of professional social work. Professional social work as a discipline began to be distinguished from other social sciences and humanities because professional social work was 'practical' application of social science 'theories'. And social science theories without applicability had no value. Judeo-Christian values and psychology/psycho-analysis theories had crept into all branches of professional social work practice even when they were working in the public social welfare system in the country. Despite being aware that a 'person' was not seen as autonomous entity in Indian culture, but was a member of different collectives – family, clan, caste and community, the focus of professional social work intervention in practice continued to be the 'person' in need per se. As professional social work had had its origin in trade union movement and welfare of industrial workers in urban areas, the urban bias also got built into professional social work during the initial years. Professional social work focused on 'organizing' the urban poor to help themselves while government provided water, sanitation and other obligatory civic and social services. The need for structural change continued to be seen as being outside the scope of professional social work. Professional social work in rural and tribal areas was almost absent.

Out of Sync with Changing Socio-Political Reality

In the early 1960s, most professional social workers, both practitioners and educators were not known to take public stand on such contentious issues as identity politics (caste, ethnic, communal), persistence of traditional unclean occupations, caste and gender based discrimination, unjust traditional practices such as child marriage, untouchability, blatant human rights violations, and public policy of preferential treatment etc. in deference to national integration and political stability concerns that the nation faced after Nehru.

Movements, social and political, past and present, were contributing to the maturation and deepening of India's democracy. From Vaikom where there was a move to enable Dalit entry to temples to anti-zamindari movements that had helped India break the back of feudalism, have created conditions for middle-class to emerge. Periyar and Ambedkar led movements for backward castes in southern and western states of India in the initial decades after independence, political agitations and Mondal movement for the OBCs in north India many years later not only had deepened democracy by exploring the meaning of equality and opportunity for social, political and economic ascendance of the sections hitherto denied opportunities to improve their social status. These movements drew more people into the discourse by giving them a vote and a voice, and thereby opening up access to power.

Professional social work's response to these movements in the southern states and in Bihar was one of ambivalence. And their awareness about ethnic insurgency in the north eastern border-states was nil because those states had not become part of 'India' in their mind. Professional social work's engagement with relief work to war victims, refugees, widows, orphans and mobilization of cash donations for government relief funds etc. was their response to wars with Pakistan, China and liberation of Bangladesh; these engagements helped in gaining legitimacy.

In the mid 1960s, India witnessed widespread political instability in the wake of power struggle after Nehru. Dominance of one national political party came under attack from emerging regional political parties. Professional social work's response to severe drought situation was luke warm. For the first time 'poverty' was put on the political agenda. Their response to JP movement was one of fence-sitting. Professional social work found legitimacy in supporting state's efforts to attain food sufficiency, increased industrial growth, maintain political stability and raise resources for planned development during the 1960s.

Reflection on the events and developments in professional social work literature of the 1970s speaks about the involvement of professional social work in social policy formulation. Their response to abrogation of democracy during Emergency in 1975 was at best timid. All this gave professional social work politically inappropriate elitist status quoist character. The status quoist ideological stance and their reticence on the emerging caste, ethnic and class aspirations were viewed as naiveté, statist and strategic by the excluded sections, political class, activists and intellectuals.

The mid 1970s was a turning point in the Indian democracy; this period marked the starting point of the exploration of the ideas of citizenship and enfolded identity into a brand of inclusive nationhood through a series of stirring agitations, including agitation against communalism, casteism and identity politics. Realization that the freedom movement was not just about the overthrow of colonial rule and that what Ambedkar had predicted—'brown sahibs' had replaced the 'white sahibs' gave an impetus to civil society activism in the country. This was the period when activists who were not professional social workers had succeeded in getting a law guaranteeing employment-Employment Guarantee Act—to those who demand employment in rural areas enacted and implemented in the state of Maharashtra. Silence of professional social work to these developments is eloquent.

By early 1980s, professional social work's belief that welfare state can be transforming was belied. Public control of the means of production and distribution as part of policy of mixed economy was not only stifling private initiatives, but the ruling class had become self-serving and corrupt. By this time, ruling elite could not brook political dissention and used state's authority to quell protest using coercive power vested in it to oppress its own people and abrogate democratic norms of governance. Professional social work found itself unable to take a decisive stand on the issue of the nature of relationship that state should maintain with its citizen. Naiveté of professional social work not only disappointed the disadvantaged groups, but also stood discredited in the eyes of left-of-center intellectuals and political class. In addition, opinion on the issue divided professional social workers in the middle. Inclusion of social advocacy, equal access to education, policies of positive discrimination and Constitutional provisions for the development of backward classes and human rights violations etc. in the curriculum in some of the elite professional social work educational institutions in the 1980s was the first sign that professional social work had become aware of the necessity to address disparities and other structural issues, and intervene to reduce inequality at societal level rather than be pre-occupied with case work and community development. These gestures were no more than after-thought and amounted to piece-meal lip service because even by the late 1980s professional social work had not accepted that social work is political and that professional social work as a stakeholder was expected to participate in the politics of development. For instance, violence against women was treated more from criminality angle. That police and criminal justice system were deeply entrenched in patriarchy was not acknowledged and piece-meal attempts at gender sensitization of police and judiciary were conducted. Though appointment of social workers in police stations and family courts were pioneering initiatives, these initiatives did not recognize the caste, class and gender intersection in the manifestation of violence against women. As such to the general public, the excluded groups, to the political leaders and to social activists, professional social work appeared ineffective, inadequate, unprepared, hypocritical and irrelevant.

Professional social work came to be seen as being part of the hegemonic regime of the urban upper echelons of the political class perpetrating status quo. This was partly due to the fact that some of the visible professional social workers were engaged in expanding the scope of social policy, the jurisdiction and responsibilities of the Indian state without clear ideological and theoretical knowledge or clarity necessary for understanding and analyzing the centrifugal and centripetal forces unleashed by state sponsored planned development and representative democracy. Even at this stage, professional social workers presumed that state was benevolent; and universal adult franchise and the democratic processes were capable of responding to aspirations of diverse people and to the competing demands for social justice from the excluded. Having created state social welfare agencies, professional social workers were able to create space for themselves within government. Upon entering government, by making use of democratic processes, professional social workers were able to entrench themselves and their own people in powerful positions, neglecting the needs of their clientele. And those professional social workers who were outside government became 'rent seekers' as consultants and contractors.

Beginning from the mid 1980s, the idea of professional social work had acquired a different meaning altogether. Professional social workers were seen as 'rent seekers' in contrast to selfless Gandhian constructive social work and Ambedkarite radical social work, whose goals were equality and social justice that required deliberate efforts to secure the rights of the excluded. Professional social workers were seen as disengaged with these socio-political discourses. Professional social work principle of individualization resulted in atomization, stigmatization and fragmentation. By not retooling, professional social work had unwittingly become party to the stigmatization, dehumanization and marginalization processes of domination. Unable to re-orient itself, professional social work briefly found itself directionless.

Professional social work's engagement with the state policy processes depended on the nature of prevalent social-economic and political thinking of the time, changes in the social relations between state, civil society and economic institutions and between different sections of society. Social work professionalism was questioned for lack of theoretical social sciences knowledge and conceptual clarity by social scientists, especially sociologists, economists and political scientists. These developments brought home the fact that it was not sufficient to assume that their "work" will speak louder than their public posture, it was not sufficient to be delivering welfare services using case work, group work and community organization social work methods or by being part of 'policy formulation processes' without theoretical knowledge, conceptual clarity and analytical skills.

Despite the short comings, some of the professional social work activists started questioning the development model pursued by the state, the so called 'democratic' processes of policy formulation and the relationship between state and its people (civil society) in the country. While they called for participatory democratic decision making, they drew people's attention to peoples' sovereignty in a social democratic set up. This had a ripple effect and it not only galvanized the excluded sections to organize and assert their citizenship rights guaranteed in the Constitution, but also resulted in sensitizing the politicians and bureaucrats about the inter-connectedness of people, rights, natural resources, governance and the state.

Grudgingly professional social work started acknowledging that the 'problem' can partly be a social structural issue. Professional social work academics and activists made feeble attempts at understanding the implications of structural social work and at 'deconstructing' the notions of 'state', 'national interest', 'eminent domain' and 'development' with the help of social scientists. This marked a shift. Formal professional social work discourse explicitly emphasized the profession's commitment to addressing the problem of structurally caused poverty and to nudge the state to espouse policies to arrest the drift. This manifested in the development of professional ethical codes which have been reconfirmed during the last few decades. Given these manifestations of professional commitment in the declared modes of social work discourse, it was expected that one would find 'social justice-aware social work'.

Rise of Radical Political Social Work

The 1980s was the golden era of professional social work. More than 70 schools of social work proliferated in some of the rural and/or smaller cities of western, northern and southern states. Most of these centres were private entities founded by MPs and MLAs in their respective constituencies charging high fee and affiliated to respective state universities. In order to maintain their university affiliation and to be viable, these centres admitted Scheduled Caste (SC) and Scheduled Tribe (ST) candidates and produced "trained" social workers in adequate numbers.

Some of the rural "trained" social workers gained entry into state sponsored welfare system via large multi-laterally funded poverty reduction projects. The SC and ST rural "trained" social workers availed government employment opportunities through civil service utilizing preferential treatment policies. Having entered 'government service', the SC and ST rural "trained" social workers did not feel the need for statutory recognition of social work as a profession (like Medical Council of India, Bar Council etc.); all they were interested in was to be part of patronage distribution system and cash in on the status and power accruing from 'government service'. Beginning from the 1990s, many professional social work educational centres were established in north eastern states also; though they were part of the government university system, the story of 'trained' social workers repeated itself in these states also.

Most of the new professional social work educational centres replicated the curriculum in vogue in some the older well-known institutions. Gap between what was in the syllabus and what was taught left the students confused and unprepared for the world of work. During the 1980s, there was no effort on the part of the profession to ensure that positions involving social work functions in the state and national governments were open to 'trained' professional social workers alone. As a result, 'trained' social workers fitted themselves into whatever positions were available in whichever government or non-government establishments.

In search of newer arenas of engagement, professional social work engagement had expanded into new arenas such as medical social work within municipal hospitals and social work in industry in the 1980s. Especially social work in industry, corporate social responsibility indicated ideological deficit and conservatism. Huge arenas of rural, urban, forest, environment, management of common natural resources, local self-governance, malnutrition and other sustainable development agendas remained largely untouched by professional social work. Inadequate role definition, means-ends dilemma, lack of clear ideology, conceptual clarity and middle – class value orientation prevented professional social work from taking up rights based approach in letter and spirit in these arenas of study and professional practice, and continue to prevent it from being an agent of change.

The ruling class using a predatory state had started working covertly against equality, social justice, citizenship rights, democracy, secularism and other Constitutional principles in the name of democracy and development. With the increasing demand for rights from nebulous fragmented marginalized groups, rise of identity politics, poverty was rediscovered. And popular buzz word "rights based approach" had caught on in the late 1980s at international and subsequently percolated to national levels and to professional social work. Espousal of "rights based approach" placed professional social work in a dilemma being statist and conservative—whether to protect the rights of their clientele or serve the interests and the rights of the ruling class. Professional social workers' divided loyalties and ambivalence about rights based approach were exposed and their double speak was not missed by beneficiaries, general public and the political class. Rhetoric of 'rights based' approach was not helpful in increasing the credibility of professional social work.

The streak of reformist force within professional social work took active change agent form beginning from the early 1980s. Out of this was born the *radical political perspective* within professional social work. *Radical political perspective* within professional social work attacked the very system out of which it was born. *Radical political social work* was not just suspicious but was resentful of the feudal and capitalist forces that were perpetuating status quo of which professional social work was part. *Radical political perspective* accused professional social work of pandering to the ruling class and their hegemony. According to *radical political perspective,* professional social work, even by adopting 'rights based' approach, in any welfare oriented system only legitimized the existing oppressive capitalist processes and acted as an institutional buffer to absorb potential revolt against the status quo. Rather than tinkering with the norms and/or the processes of the existing system, *radical political social work* emphasized the need to question the state's choice of development model and strategies, and to hold the state accountable for depriving the people of their life and livelihoods of citizens in the name of development. *Radical political social work* activities ranged from client advocacy to civil disobedience, confrontation and demand for people's participation and consent as necessary step for introducing new policies, changing existing policies, establishment of large development projects, etc. by state. This bottom-up approach was premised on the belief that people's consent is mandatory in an open social democracy in which citizen's authority is sovereign and state derives its authority from peoples' consent and cooperation.

Professional social work in India having had conservative origins and having pragmatic outlook, initially rejected *radical political social work* as unsuitable and/or impractical. Not many professional social workers took to *radical political social work* because it is extremely demanding on their personal integrity. Abrogation of democracy and use of Emergency powers in 1975-76 by Indira Gandhi and many of the development policies adopted by government thereafter had inspired many non-party political formations. Activists like Medha Patkar, a professional social worker adopted *radical political perspective,* began using Gandhian non-violent civil disobedience methods to question the state, its policies and its strategies for development; and suggested that state change the development model and strategies adopted by it. *Narmada Bachao Andolan*, a peoples' movement led by her put several issues related to the rights, entitlements of the vulnerable sections and role of the state in guaranteeing basic human and fundamental rights, management of common natural resources, environment versus life and livelihood of the voiceless citizen displaced and deprived in the name of "development" on the political agenda beginning from the early 1980s. Inspired by Patkar and other activists, few young professional *radical political social workers* started fighting for land, forest and water rights of involuntarily displaced development project affected indigenous people in different parts of the country.

In 1984 when the Bhopal tragedy, a man-made disaster took place, many professional social work educational institutions were mobilized to carry out relief work. During the following decade many professional social work educational institutions were engaged in relief work for the victims of natural and man-made disasters. These engagements, apart from opening up new arena for professional social work practice—'disaster management', also contributed to questioning the state and its choice of development model. In addition, involvement in disaster relief also contributed to redefining 'community organization' and 'community development' in the context of a developing country.

Consequences of Insulation

These developments also enabled professional social work to understand poverty in a broader political economic structural context rather than as personal pathology in the early 1990s. Two approaches divided the poverty discourse within professional social work: one view perceived poverty as a phenomenon resulting from individual traits, values, moral standards, choices and behaviour, while the other saw poverty as a social structural issue linked to a range of policy, structures and institutions resulting from political economy of democracy. Poverty-aware professional practice stemmed from the latter perception of poverty and viewed people living in poverty as struggling with limited social and economic opportunities in major aspects of life, such as food security, livelihood security, access to housing, education and health care. Poverty-aware professional social work sought to increase social and economic opportunities and realize the social rights of those who live in poverty, rather than (implicitly) blaming service users for their poverty and perceiving change in personal conduct as the main way of improving their situation.

While poverty may sometimes be a *result* of behavioural problems (such as addiction or substance abuse), poverty was more often seen as a *cause* of problematic situations and behaviour. Primary assessment of clients' situations included an assessment of their economic status. However, poverty-aware professional social work was not content with a narrow definition of economic distress as only a lack of money, but extended it to include a severe lack of social opportunities (in health, education, livelihood or housing) and of symbolic capital (as manifested by exclusion, stigma and lack of voice) (Lister, 2004). It was necessary precisely to evaluate how poverty affects the availability of resources in everyday situations, as well as the feelings and experiences of service users. Thus, the primary assessment process in poverty-aware professional social work practice was required to include availability of food, livelihood opportunities, educational resources, specific conditions of employment, housing and health, the level of personal security as well as experiences of being stigmatized or marginalized due to poverty.

Poverty-aware professional social work practice positioned the clients' lack of material, social and symbolic resources as a target for change and action; similarly, the way in which other problems such as domestic violence or parental malfunctioning were defined. A poverty-related intervention purpose was to be achieved both by individual strategies, such as empowerment, advocacy for individual's rights, procuring necessary resources and active assistance in finding employment, as well as through social strategies, such as social advocacy, policy practice and community economic development.

While *radical political social work* involved all of the above, professional social work, especially urban professional social workers most of whom had nothing to gain or lose, were ambivalent about their ability and willingness to engage at these different levels. They extended episodic solidarity with *radical political social work* selectively. Rural forward caste professional social workers most of whom happened to be stakeholders in the issues related to land, water and forest in their respective locations were vary of extending support to the issues raised by *radical political social workers*. Rural backward dalit and tribal professional social workers were also skeptical about extending support to the people's movements led by *radical political social workers* because there was no consensus among the *radical political social workers*. Taking a stand and extending support to the issues related to access and management of common natural resources meant that rural professional social workers had to be part of the solution, not just be part of the problem. They acknowledged that they were not against development and industrialization; they were keen that development should not deprive basic life/livelihood and impoverish people.

Although the Indian Constitution was committed to ending caste system, to guaranteeing equality and social justice to one and all, to majority of educated, English speaking middle-class urban professional social workers, reservation perpetrated caste system, amounted to defeating the vision of the Constitution. Majority of them even today maintain discrete silence on caste and identity politics lest they are politically misunderstood. Maintaining discrete silence is often interpreted as covert support to status quo and denial of citizenship rights, equal opportunities and social justice to those who are in no position to assert their rights in a neo-liberal milieu.

On the whole, though professional social work continued to see itself as the vanguard of the rights of the excluded, urban professional social work came to be seen as an instrument in the hands of dominant sections to exclude or include different sections in the process of development and democracy as per political expedience. And a section of rural professional social workers came to be seen as genuinely adopting rights based approach to promote the rights of the rural poor and deprived. In view of the divide between rural-urban, backward-forward, *radical political social workers* believe that people should be mobilized along class lines not along caste and ethnic identities that divide and fragment people. To them, the need was to organize and unify the rural and the urban exploited labouring industrial-agricultural working classes to be able to negotiate from a position of strength in a neo-liberal milieu and to be able to resist the processes of exclusion.

In the 1990s, professional social work found itself unprepared to foresee the consequences of economic reforms, information technology revolution or globalization for the marginalized sections whose rights it was committed to protect. Education and health services became increasingly inaccessible to the socially excluded despite proliferation of educational and health facilities in the private sector. Land acquisition by government for large development projects was not new. Liberalization and privatization policies in the 1990s gave a fillip to land acquisition, involuntary displacement of people and corruption. But people's awareness about their rights and their strategic political competence was a new phenomenon. Once again, the *radical political social work* activists were quick to recognize the mood of rural masses and take the lead to articulate the implications of the economic reforms on governance, on the citizens' basic human rights and for the poor. As the imported variety of professional social work discipline was groping for a suitable ideological perspective to adopt, there was a brief period of disengagement. And eventually this variety of professional social work meekly followed the lead of the *radical political social work* activists.

Either way, professional social work found itself in a catch 22 position until a handful of Indian political scientists and few *professional radical political social workers* helped differentiate between 'electoral politics' and 'party politics' from 'development political processes' conceptually in the early years of the 21st century. This conceptual clarity reassured professional social workers' hope that their participation in 'development politics' on behalf of the excluded could lend credibility and legitimacy to the profession, and that they indeed should actively highlight the plight of the marginalized both from within and outside government in some way on behalf of the voiceless excluded sections.

Till this point in time, majority of professional social workers appeared to be helplessly supporting status quo rather than challenging the hegemony that traditionally excluded poor, dalits, minorities, tribes, women, persons with disability and other marginalized vulnerable sections. In an endeavour to institutionalize professional social work, it had insulated itself not only from relevant social sciences theoretical knowledge which had made great strides in understanding contemporary Indian society, state and analyzing the centrifugal and centripetal forces unleashed by LPG but also from the resulting changes in socio-political reality. Professional social work had become parochial in the absence of research based empirical evidence about the causes, measurement, processes and manifestations of poverty, impoverishment and marginalization within social work and due to its ambivalence about politics and politicization of welfare issues. Professional social work methods such as case work, group work and community organization continued to be taught without adequate linkages to thc changing socio-political realities and plausible solutions.

Till 2005, professional social work continued to treat mental health, domestic violence, atrocities against SC/STs as pathological conditions or as crime, deviance, a law and order issue, an aberration or as a personal problem rather than looking at these from the Foucauldian perspective – as structural processes of social construction for domination and exclusion. This also contributed to the creation of an impression that professional social work's disengagement with reality as being manipulative and strategic on behalf of the capitalist ruling classes. Without an understanding of social sciences theoretical knowledge, just being engaged in delivery of a variety of social services implied that it was engaged in remedial activities and was not able to bring about social change towards a vision of equality and social justice. This raised the question of relevance of professional social work.

Rural Urban Divide

At no point in India, state social welfare services was charity oriented in approach or was about handing out "doles" except in the cases of destitute and totally dependent individuals and families. Due to heightened and intense political competition between regional political parties, between regional and national political parties and between coalitions ruling at the national, state and at local self-government levels beginning from the mid 1970s and the 1980s, highly politicized means-tested populist charity oriented welfare programmes were introduced in some of the states. Despite the fact that public allocation and expenditure on these populist welfare programmes did not exceed five per cent in a year in any state, the media hype drummed up by competing political parties gave an impression as if the state had transformed itself into a truly welfare state. In fact, social welfare had become a hand-maiden of political class. These initiatives created a number of government positions although entry into these positions was only through civil service and were open to anyone who could clear civil service examination. Rural oriented sons of the soil professional social workers managed to entre government service at state, district levels and the rural/urban local self-governments. Occupying positions at the cutting edge, rural professional social workers implemented most of the area and target oriented and/or integrated poverty reduction and development programmes introduced by national and state governments in the 1970s, 1980s and the 1990s.

Rural professional social workers, especially forward caste trained social workers took full advantage of these openings. Though the excluded sections benefitted from these programmes to some extent, both rural forward caste "trained" social workers and the beneficiaries saw these programmes as palliatives. Non-government voluntary organizations continued to be used as launching pads for political careers for local petty leaders with political aspirations despite the fact that the relationship between government and non-government organizations was ambivalent. As such government, these leaders in collusion with the forward caste "trained" social workers distributed the grants to voluntary organizations as political patronage; these grants were/are meagre, sporadic and thinly spread to achieve maximum coverage with a view to gain and retain the support of "vote banks". In this way, a good number of astute rural professional social workers belonging to land-holding upper forward castes were able to take advantage of the opportunities presented by expanded role of government in social welfare, rural development and democratic decentralization. They were/are in a position to continue to control the distribution of public welfare entitlements/benefits on behalf of the local petty political leaders as patronage in return for political support; and were/are able to retain their dominant socio-political status and/or improve their status. Both forward and backward caste rural professional social workers consider politicization of poverty reduction, welfare and development programmes as legitimate and a necessary evil in a social democracy. It was/is not unusual to find some rural professional social workers acting as conduits for receiving bribes on behalf of their political patrons, gaining benefits for themselves in the process of implementing the pro-poor policies and programmes.

Professional social work academia, on the other hand advocate keeping religion and politics out of professional social work as the profession wanted to portray a 'secular' 'non-partisan' image to its advantage. Beginning from the mid 1980s, faith-based voluntary organizations also proliferated in rural areas. Few professional social workers were attracted to these entities. When policy of positive discrimination (reservation) for Other Backward Castes (OBCs in the process of what is called Mondalization) was adopted by national and state governments in the late 1980s, some welfare benefits were conferred on the OBCs; some of the OBCs who were Muslims also were to benefit from these programmes. However, subtle religion based discrimination by rural professional social workers working at the grass-roots level in government deprived the Muslim OBCs of their entitlements. Flow of bi-lateral and multi-lateral, government and non-government, sectarian and non-sectarian foreign development aid funds to NGOs was all time high during the 1980s and the 1990s. NGOs received these funds either directly or through the government. Some of these NGOs were mainly engaged in capacity building and perfunctorily reforming the way government welfare services delivery system functioned. The other kind of NGOs implemented 'given' government schemes on behalf of governments to reach the unreached.

Majority of the urban professional social workers established themselves in the non-government sector in urban areas as innovative service providers, activists and/or as functionaries in grant making non-government agencies including corporates. Urban professional social workers were loath to working in the government because of its restrictive environment. Urban professional social workers were loath to working in the rural and tribal areas earlier took to work in these areas because such employment offered stability and career advancement after receiving foreign development funding. They were associated with NGOs in the capacity of CEOs, managers, programme officers, researchers, trainers, makers of documentaries and consultants but rarely were they involved in direct service delivery. While urban professional social workers working in government or non-government voluntary organizations tried to insulate themselves from local politics to a large extent, they were strategic in cultivating the top ruling elite at the state and national levels as they considered politicization of welfare programmes as subversive but wanted to influence and persuade the elite politicians to adopt pro-poor policies.

On the whole, by the 1990s, professional social work had come to be accepted as credible source of 'employment' for the rural and urban young middle-class educated genext. But, at no point rural professional social workers either felt the need to form and/or institutionalize a statute backed professional association to gain job security and benefits accruing to members of professional associations; but a section of the rural and urban professional social work educators deprived of benefits coming with employment in recognized educational institutions were keen to have statutory recognition of social work 'profession'.

By the 1990s the divide between rural and urban professional social workers had become pronounced and blocked certain career opportunities for both. The rural and urban oriented professional social workers, though miniscule in number (compared to the total number of local, state and national government employees), were working at cross purposes. One was working towards a vision of equality and social justice goals and social change; the other was working towards maintaining the hierarchical social structure and status quo. This divide helped maintain caste, community hierarchies and patriarchy intact instead of bringing about structural change. And, this divide has not helped increase legitimacy of social work as a profession; in fact it prevented social work secure full statutory status as a profession backed by legislation.

Relevance of Professional Social Work

Looking back, it is now realized that these developments, the national commitment to and consensus on national unity, integrity, democracy, secularism, equality, centralized state, federal system, planned change, social justice goals and concern for freedom have had visible impact on the development of social work as a discipline and as a profession. Today professional social work stands co-opted by the same forces that reinforce capitalist, neo-liberal tendencies. It has become an object of change rather than being an agent of change.

Far from being neutral, the state has come to represent the interests of the elite, and has at its disposal the instruments necessary to keep the elites in power. Confronted by the need to create a new social order and to promote development with social justice, professional social work is now slowly realizing that active people's participation is necessary to bring about social change, but has no leverage to mobilize the masses. In exceptional isolated localized instances, *radical political social work* has been successful in demanding and obtaining efficient and just delivery of the entitlements for the poor, deprived, displaced and exploited as a matter of inalienable right by mobilizing support of the masses.

Over the years, with increased social mobilization and political contestation, state has been facing crisis of governability. There is a vast difference between the state of the 1950s and as it is today. Analysis of the changes in the party system and the federal system shows that there has been erosion of the Nehruvian centralized state. Multi-party system, strong regional parties, market ideas and practices have displaced central (national) planning and controlled economy in the last two decades. States (provinces) are increasingly becoming power centres. Interventionist state has become increasingly decentralized regulatory state. And the balance of power has shifted in favour of the Supreme Court, the Election Commission and the President at the expense of the Parliament, the Prime Minister, the Cabinet and the elected representatives. Professional social work generally interacts with state – local, district, and state levels—only when state's action or inaction affects the people with whom social workers work. But professional social work has never sat back to look at the features of the changed nature of the state; professional social work as a discipline has never articulated what kind of state is acceptable.

Sociologists A R Desai and P C Joshi unfailingly exposed class interests that the state development policies were serving and the hiatus between lofty policy and actual implementation of plans. P C Joshi warned of inherent danger of statism in social sciences and social scientists becoming mere tools of the government. These observations are equally applicable to professional social work in India today. Practically every decision taken by the government has had implications for the common person in terms of the degree of equality and liberty available to her/him and in terms of what s/he gets and how much of it s/he gets. Policy questions such as whether to subsidize the big farmers or the small, whether to set prices of public corporations at the levels that tax or subsidize rich consumers, whether to build roads for private motor vehicles or for mass transportation, to improve quality of education in rural or urban government or private schools etc. affect the common person. In such a context, professional social work is in a position to analyze the nature, role and function of the state because it functions in the interstitial spaces between the people and the government. But near absence of theory in social work research and emphasis on dealing with immediate practical problems has prevented professional social work from asking fundamental questions about the role and functions of the state and urging the state to take pro-poor, pro-people decisions. Neither academics nor practitioners have articulated their assessment of the Indian state in systematic organized manner because professional social work considers itself to be apolitical, though social work in fact is political and cannot avoid being involved in politics of development as an agent of change.

At the implementation level, professional social work has not been officially systematically involved in large development programmes of the government such as the NREGA, NRHM, Bharat Nirman, SSA, Micro-finance and other poverty reduction programmes in different parts of the country. Organizing the people at the grass roots level to ensure proper maintenance and utilization of public utilities, explaining the norms for equitable distribution, interpreting government's mission and policies are the some of the tasks that professional social work is equipped to perform. In the absence of professional social work acting as the bridge between the people and the state, traditional caste and patriarchy continue to deny entitlements to the marginalized sections. Where the state is slow in taking action against unjust, unfair, inhuman practices, professional social work can act as watchdog and bring the state agents to book. But, involvement of professional social work in politics of development has been patchy, episodic and person-dependent.

Four modes of professional social work response in India can be delineated: (1) concentrate on what one is doing, (2) produce reports but remain indifferent about its utilization by policy makers, (3) lobby vigorously and get policy recommendations accepted, and (4) critically evaluate policies as complementary to effective governance. To work at these four levels, subjects like democratic decision making, social action for social change, rural development and community work, development and environment, disaster management, management of income and employment generation programmes, etc. were incorporated into the curriculum of professional social work education. Despite late recognition of the importance of these subjects, there was no clarity about the theoretical framework or ideological perspective that these 'new' subjects ought to have.

Invisible Yet Influential Professional Social Work

Various political processes that were unleashed from the mid 1970s onwards resulted in the creation of new smaller states; insurgency raised its ugly head with menacing frequency in some of the north eastern and western states; communalism and identity politics became issues around which politicians mobilized people; and because of state-sponsored violence against its own people to put down fissiparous forces, the viability of the idea of nation-state and nation-building efforts of the ruling elite has come to be questioned.

Role of Indian state has been determined by its structural and functional evolution. As a conceptual entity, the state is based on universally accepted moral principles, humanism and democratic ideals. Gradually one-party dominance paved the way for polarized pluralism, and more and more elements have entered the state system through free and fair elections. The Indian Constitution has become the principal site for the elaboration of political discourse of the state and has become central to an analysis of the changing role of political and bureaucratic structures.

State led development strategies have made all kinds of demands on the discipline of professional social work in India. Concepts like 'urbanization', 'industrialization', 'tribalization', 'criminalization', 'driving individuals mad within the family' as macro social exclusionary processes entered the parlance of professional social work academia after 2000 for the first time. Professional social work was by and large overwhelmed by these concepts and processes, and the need for structural change. Professional social work did not have adequate sociological or political or economic theoretical knowledge based analytical skills to comprehend these forces and the implications of these processes on the oppressed and exploited, let alone intervene based on critical analysis of empirical evidence. Despite the fact that professional social work as a discipline had been preoccupied with the micro-level remedial work for too long, donor agencies – government and non-government local, national and international—have been promoting linkages between the professional social work educational institutions and their NGO partners in order to keep both afloat and competitive in times of cutbacks.

Professional social work was/is expected to critique state policies as an act of representing the perspectives and voices of the marginalized. Relationship between professional social work and social policy offers an opportunity to assess social utility of the social work discipline. Whether the state and other users have been making increasing demands on the expertise and insights of professional social workers? What have been professional social workers' attitudes and responses towards the task of policy making, planning and implementing development and poverty reduction programmes of the state? What is or would be the long term impact of that engagement on professional social work as a substantive, theoretical academic discipline? To identify modes of responses of professional social workers to growing demands for producing social knowledge relevant to changing contexts, one must look at where professional social work is situated in society, social structure, in the processes of domination and marginalization in terms of ideology.

Professional social workers are not called upon to formulate development policies or to advise appropriate means for direct intervention these days. Yet, in the last seventy odd years of its institutional existence in Indian academia, professional social work in India has managed to carve out a niche for itself. Their influence permeates social policy issues more indirectly than directly because professional social work, it is assumed, is unwaveringly committed to certain social values and value premises. While it adds to their credibility, the influence of professional social work is "ideological" because the discipline helps to deconstruct ideas with facts and appeal to people's rationality and sense of justice and fairness. The end result and the extent to which professional social workers are able to engage in policy processes, and contribute to the processes of structural change has depended on its ability to identify the object of its intervention and the establishment of its moral purpose.

It was in the late 1980s that professional social work grudgingly acknowledged that social work is political in nature. This realization was significant and a change from remedial and residual orientation of social work and social welfare to 'rights based' approach has taken place, though not uniformly in all sections of professional social work academia and practitioners. This shift – a shift from residual to rights based developmental social work was paradigmatic. There is some acknowledgement that professional social work has had a role in converting private personal problems into social public issues and in putting them on the political agenda.

Notwithstanding the vicissitudes of its flourishing creativity and recognition, discussions about relevance of professional social work continue to take place among professional social workers themselves even now. These discussions have streaks of introspection that prompt questions—whether professional social work has a body of knowledge of its own; if yes, as a body of knowledge, has professional social work proved its utility; is professional social work's ability to generate knowledge about social reality adequate? Does the relevance of professional social work knowledge require endorsement by administrative and political elites who usually author social policy statements and design social welfare programmes?

The health of the economy has become the priority for the government. Governments have shown a depressing lack of compassion, courage and vision about inclusive growth and development. For example, militarization against its own people demanding development as citizenship right does not inspire public confidence in the government's ability to govern in socially just manner. Beginning from the 1990s, professional social work began to see the Indian state as being predatory acting against its own people especially in the context of unfolding of large scale corruption. It was during this period that a section of rural and urban professional social workers associated with voluntary organizations began to openly express solidarity with small mass based social and peoples' movements in different locations of the country when they raised issues pertaining to right to food and livelihood security, right to health and education, right to access and manage common natural resources, etc.

What professional social work has learned in these seventy five years is just how complex is the interaction between the economic growth and social development policies. Professional social work is now better aware of the scale and complexity of what once seemed fairly straightforward issues. As an applied science, professional social work has had to remain committed to the canons of objectivity and empirically verifiable facts. As a social theory, it is expected to offer universalistic explanation. And professional social work theory, it is assumed, would act as a guide to social policy options. Though social theory and social policy are inseparably intertwined, some tensions have persisted between social theorists, be they sociologists, economists, psychologists or political scientists, and professional social workers throughout the development of professional social work as a discipline in India because social scientists lack practical knowledge and professional social workers' theoretical knowledge is weak.

The territory of professional social work has greatly widened with mixed results. Ironically at this juncture, with neo-liberal forces gaining in strength in the 1990s, the international trend of looking at the voluntary sector as the substitute for state welfare percolated into social work academia. As a profession, social work has become more interested in organizational and management issues because of perceived shortcomings in delivery of public welfare services. And, with the rise of terrorism, interest in organizational management is justified because state started regulating NGOs and the need to safeguard NGOs' autonomy became necessary. Willingness to evolve management of NGOs as a new discipline within professional social work got strengthened by this developments. Seizing the opportunity, social work academia took to NGO management, but somewhat reluctantly. Once again, the lead to building the knowledge base for NGO management came from some of the 'corporate NGOs'.

Although, so much was happening, scholarly writing on changes taking place and their implications for professional social work education and practice have been and continue to be a mere trickle. Some of the elite sections of professional social workers who were part of women's movements and succeeded in getting women's policy adopted by state and national governments also have not contributed much to professional social work literature. Even among the few who have contributed to some extent, there continues to be hiatus between the writing of those "activists" who had taken up issues pertaining to poor, dalit and Muslim women's rights and those who had taken up issues about status and rights of women in general. It is not as if few academically oriented professional social workers with social science and law background were not sensitive to the issues concerning dalits, tribes, Muslims, migrant labourers, displaced persons, mentally ill vagrants, homeless destitute persons, persons with disability, single women, domestic violence, human rights violations, victims of mass violence, victims of natural/man-made disasters and issues pertaining to victimization, exploitation, oppression and marginalization. But they were totally engrossed in activism; and their writing and contribution to knowledge building has not been visible in the mainstream social work literature. But their writings have been mainly for the purposes of presenting their side of the story and argument to the policy makers or to the courts.

Sociologists like Radhkamal Mukherji and DP Mukerji believed that policy, planning and social justice were not merely technocratic exercises, but stressed the importance of integrating economy and culture, as policy making, planning and social justice are essentially cultural tasks. If policies and plans have to reflect peoples' aspirations, drives, motivations, capacities, then, Mukherji believed, these inputs could be provided better by professional social workers and social scientists other than economists.

Professional social work educational institutions were traditionally the centres for knowledge production in the early decades. Since the 1980s, there has been gradual emergence of research and knowledge production outside professional social work educational institutions. NGOs have contributed a great deal to the production of social work knowledge. The emergence of new modes of knowledge production, for example various tools used for assessing social impact, vulnerability, organizational strength of NGOs, SHGs, protection of human rights, gender justice developed by other than professional social work academia and practitioners, was expected to alter the discourse about the perspectives and substantive contents of professional social work education in India. However, professional social work education and practice is lagging behind even in using the tools developed by others. What this will do to professional social work as a discipline in India remains to be seen.

Professional social work educators and practitioners have very little political perspective about the role of opposition in a democracy. Activism is often equated with street politics by conservatives among professional social workers who did not acquire the ability to engage in mainstream democratic politics of development through incisive writing and analysis. When one looks at the institutionalized professional social work, somewhere the real concept and vision of the social justice and equality appear to be lost. Search for relevance of social work continue to this day.

Where does this leave professional social work? Professional social work has to learn from experience, to experiment and evaluate, to stand firm and initiate possible visible political action. These are some of the key challenges to which professional social work in India has to rise up to. The future challenges for professional social work is certainly daunting. It is necessary to decolonize the profession. Inter-disciplinary theoretical inputs ranging from biographies to agriculture, social psychology to information technology, political science to climate change must inform practice, research and education.

Anti Oppressive Social Work

Under pressure from left of centre political forces, professional social work slowly realized the adverse impact of neo-liberal policies such as the SEZ and hollowness of Constitutional amendments to decentralize governance to give more powers to local self-government bodies for managing common natural resources without dismantling the edifice of caste and patriarchy. It was during this period that professional social work started looking at theoretical knowledge about democracy, state formation, linkage between ideology and governance, marginalization processes, loss of control over the common natural resources, etc. Knowledge based analytical skills are required to engage meaningfully in facilitating sustainable development and to engage the state in a meaningful dialogue to achieve the vision and mission of the constitution. Gandhian and Ambedkarite thoughts continue to inspire *structural social work.*

It was in the 1980s that Indian state started facing flak from the development project affected persons and families who were promised adequate resettlement and rehabilitation packages that was not kept. Professional social work, that was merely a spectator in the initial stages, availed the opportunity presented by state-sponsored development projects that involved involuntary displacement and deprivation of livelihood security, and began to look at its role in the context of development and democracy.

Extending relief to the victims of man-made or natural disasters also facilitated professional social work to reflect on the roles of and relationship between state, civil society and market vis-à-vis its own role. As long as professional social work continues to consider politics as 'dirty' because it believes that compromise on social work 'values' and principles is inevitable in the processes of electoral politics, not only will relevance of professional social work be questioned, but professional social workers, both practitioners and educators, have to clarify their stand regarding democracy and development by asking "whose development, and at whose cost?"

Partly as a result of this reflection and praxis, professional social work hoped to regain some of its past glory. It is at long last realized that emphasis on 'service delivery' alone would amount to piece-meal approach; and if the Constitutional goals—equality, social justice, secularism and democratic governance – are to be achieved, and if professional social work would want to contribute to the nation-building, development and democratization efforts, it has to learn necessary skills to engage effectively in the processes of development, democratic politics and become an agent of social change – learn to do what is now known as 'structural social work'.

Professional social work also realized that if it has to empower the vulnerable and the marginalized sections to assert their human and citizenship rights to be able to ensure that the state, government and dominant ruling elite are responsive to their changing aspirations and needs, in the wake of economic reforms, liberalization, privatization and globalization, then, it is not only necessary to understand how government is organized and democratic institutions and processes function, but also it was necessary to participate in these processes by acquiring social advocacy skills to be able to politically influence social policy and justice processes in the government at all levels and stages, from formulation to implementation and evaluation stages through democratic institutions prescribed in the Indian Constitution.

3

Social Work Education in India

Transition from Westernization to Indigenization

Suresh Pathare

The history of social work education in India is about eight decades old. The individuals from America sowed the seeds of social work education in India. However, its roots are deeply connected with the local social service organizations. The social service organizations in India played important role like the early educational development of social work education in the United States of America, where the first schools were part of private social services (Trattner, 1989). Even, the history of social work education in Asia begins with social work education in India. The leadership involved in establishing social work education in India has also been instrumental in promoting social work education in Asian countries (Luke, 1985). Therefore, the development of social work education in India occupies prominent place in the history of social work education in Asia. The social work education in India has celebrated its platinum jubilee with Tata Institute of Social Sciences (TISS), the first social work institute in Asia completing its 75 years in 2011.

In this context, it is significant to explore the nature and process of establishing social work education in India. It needs to be understood from socio-economic and cultural context of the country. India is one of the oldest civilization in the world (Wright: 2010), spanning more than 4000 years and witnessing the rise and fall of several empires. The end of the British colonial rule in 1947 was the landmark dividing the history of the country into pre- and post-independence era. The transition from colonial rule to self has added the developmental challenges to the existing socio-economic problems of the country. The country had a culture and tradition of voluntary social work, social reform and philanthropic work. The community living, mutual aid, cooperation: these have been the cardinal values of Indian society. In the post-independence era, the country has achieved high growth rate and development on some of the indicators. However, it continues to struggle for wide sharing the fruits of development. It is due to the plague of social inequalities based on caste, gender, ethnicity, religion and language. As a result, India's performance on Human Development Indicators continues to be very poor. India being a developing nation and having rural base has issues concerning groups and community rather than individuals. The issues include poverty and population, illiteracy and education, food insecurity and hunger, ill health and malnutrition, poor habitat (sanitation, drinking water, housing, etc.), low productivity, unemployment and underemployment, inequity and the exploitation of the vulnerable and weaker sections of the society. Social work education introduced with western perspective has been trying to address these contextual issues and concerns in India.

The growth and trends of social work education has been reviewed and discussed at various forums and subsequently published in the form of books or papers in national journals (Wadia, 1968; Mehta, 1986; Ramchandran 1957; Pawar, 1999; Kumar, 2002). The University Grants Commission (UGC), the regulatory body of higher education in India has also reviewed social work education and prepared a model curriculum for social work schools to adapt from (UGC, 1965; 2001). There has been conferences and seminars that deliberated and debated on the westernization of social work education in India. The need for indigenization has been lamented from time to time throughout the history.

Development of Social Work Education and Institutions

Social work education in India started with beginning of the Sir Dorabji Tata Graduate School of Social Work in 1936. The professional education since then is developing. The development of social work education has been clearly classified into stages. Mandal (1995) grouped it into three stages. The first stage in the pre-independence period (1936-47), he labeled it as 'a period of relatively indigenous inception of professional social work education'. The second phase was the post-independence period (1947-48), when social work education in India was shaped under American influence. And the third phase Mandal labeled as 'a period of suggestions for reforming social work education emerged as sporadic reactions to the inadequacies of the curative model of social work education adopted from America'. Bhatt and Pathare (2004) have classified significant stages of growth of social work education as initiation phase during 1936 to 1946; experimentation phase during 1947 to 1956; expansion phase during the period of 1957 to 1975; stagnation phase during the year 1977 to 1986; and explosion phase from1987 onwards. The present status of social work education is more ambiguous. There is proliferation of institutions and university departments offering social work education, however, there is no availability of reliable data and details of these institutions. It has been estimated that by 2003 there were 260 institutions and as on 2013 while there is no real count on the number of institutions; educators put the number at around 650 (Bodhi and Tripura, 2013).

At the first stage, Sir Dorabji Tata Graduate School of Social Work was the only institution of social work education for initial eleven years. In the second stage which began in 1947 when India got its independence, eleven new schools came up till 1956. All these schools had some specific characteristics. Delhi School of Social Work, Rajagiri College of Social Science and Indore School of Social Work were started by Christian Missionaries. Kashi Vidyapeeth and Gujarat Vidyapeeth were based on Gandhian principles, and schools of social work at Lucknow, Baroda and Agra as departments at universities were experiments without orientation. They started these schools with photocopied courses with minor changes (Bhatt and Pathare 2004). They even had different nomenclature for their academic degrees like Master of Social Applications (MSA), Master of Social Techniques (MST), Master of Social Administration (MSA), Master of Arts in Social Work (MASW) etc.

During this period as a result of agreement with the US Government, the Technical Cooperation Mission Programme was formed with the Council on Social Work Education and the Government of USA in 1950. This event brought in the faculty and institutions from the USA who influenced the social work curriculum of social work education in India.

After 1957 in the phase of expansion, social work education spread to other parts of the country, increasing its number to 35. Except one or two, most of these schools were located in urban areas. During this period universities opened separate departments of social work and introduced, by and large, the American or British model of social work education. The year 1960 was landmark as the UGC appointed the first review committee on social work education in India. The committee submitted its report entitled "Social Work Education in Indian Universities" in 1965. The committee in their report emphasized the need for para-professional training, recognition to the social workers qualification for jobs, and made recommendation with regard to instructional material for social work education, library facilities and teacher-students ratio (UGC: 1965). During the same period doctoral programmes in social work were introduced in Lucknow University in 1960, Andhra University in 1962, Delhi University in 1965, TISS in 1969 and at Kashi Vidyapeeth in 1969.

The decade of 1977-86 was a stagnation period for social work education as there was no addition to the number of schools concerned. However, there was much reflection on the pattern and nature of social work. While advocating for making the curriculum more relevant several schools undertook review of courses and curricula. In 1980 the Second Review Committee appointed by UGC on Social Work Education submitted their report. The scope of this Committee was wider than the previous committee. The committee was to review the content of social work education and give recommendations for making it relevant to the needs of the country, setting up programmes at Doctoral, Masters and Bachelor's degree.

The country witnessed phenomenal quantitative growth of schools of social work after 1986 as the figure of social work institutions increased to 152 in different parts of the country. There is proliferation of institutions and university departments offering social work education; however, there is no availability of reliable data and details of these institutions. It has been estimated that by 2003 there were 260 institutions and as on 2013 while there is no real count on the number of institutions; educators put the number at around 650 (Bodhi and Tripura, 2013). Regarding the quality of proliferation of social work colleges and schools Srivastava and Singh (2003) remarked, 'deteriorating academics, stagnating curricula, superfluity of field work, absence of creditable profession-sustaining research output, shopping out of traditional territories of employment for professionally trained social workers, moribund and virtually ineffective functioning of professional organizations, became issues of fierce and fiery debate and critical writings surfaced the scene, demolishing euphoria and causing despair' (Srivastava and Singh, 2003: 72).

The Levels of Education

The first educational institute in India—Tata Institute of Social Sciences (TISS) was conceived and established in the general pattern then prevailing in the system of professional education in the USA. that is, essentially a post bachelor's two year degree programme. Today, this trend continues as most of the institutions are offering education at the post graduate level although, it is not necessarily the most appropriate level for the needs of the country. While offering post graduate education presently there are three models of education i.e. generic course, generic course with provision for electives or special papers as areas of special interest and practice and specialization course.

It is interesting to note that postgraduate level programme in social work education started first and programmes at under graduate level later, however, the reverse is normal practice in university system. The beginning of undergraduate education in social work in India was made in 1956 by the Department of Sociology and Social Work, Lucknow University, with the introduction of social work as one of the subjects of the degree of B.A. The Lucknow University simultaneously made provision for the degrees of Ph.D., and D.Litt. in Social Work. Thus it took twenty years, from 1936 to 1956, for social work education for having a complete sequence from the Bachelor's to the Doctoral degrees in India (Hasan: 1967). The Doctoral programme in social work was initiated by Lucknow University in 1956, Andhra University in 1962, Delhi University in 1965, TISS and Kashi Vidyapeeth in 1969.

The need and relevance for social work education at undergraduate level has been reiterated repeatedly from time to time. The first Review Committee on Social Work Education while recommending for the undergraduate programme observed that such a programme intended not only to meet the needs for trained personnel in field and at intermediate fields but will also help to strengthen the existing training programme at post graduate level. Social Work graduates were required to meet the growing demands of welfare personnel due to expanding social welfare programme (UGC Report: 1965, p. 54). The Study Team on Social Welfare, after examining the requirements for welfare personnel and the training facilities available in India, recommended that undergraduate training programmes should be organized on a two-year basis and that, "The undergraduate and graduate training programmes should be linked together so that experienced welfare workers could qualify themselves for higher responsibilities on the completion of suitable training courses" (UGC, Report of the Study Team: 1959).

Armaity Desai while analyzing the different aspects of social work education pointed out the weakness of the present pattern of social work education at the postgraduate level without a broad undergraduate base because even beginning skills have to be taught at the level when professional education should be advanced. There have been experiments of linking undergraduate programme with the graduate programme and offering five years integrated course. The social work department at Assam University of Silchar runs Five Year Integrated Course in Social Work which leads to Bachelor of Social Work (three years) and Master of Social work (two years) Degrees. Tata Institute of Social Sciences in 2004 experimented B.A. in social work with specialization in Rural Development, however this programme has recently been changed to B.A. in social Sciences and linked it to master's programmes.

Thus the current trend of social work education in India continues to focus on the Masters level education. Most of the universities have introduced Ph.D. programme whereas M.Phil in social work is offered at few schools.

Focus of Training and Curriculum

Social Work education everywhere is to bring improvement in quality of life and in human society. The effectiveness of a profession depends on the quality of training of its practitioners. In preparation of the professionals, training objectives, the curriculum and the entire training methodology are central. In India, Dr. Manshardt suggested the social work education programme as he was not able to get trained staff for community work. His job oriented education programme was considered innovative and pioneering and the Trustees of Sir Dorabji Tata Trust accepted to support the establishing of Graduate School of Social Work. The objectives of this school then were to: a) providing those students, who desire to work with either public or private agencies, a sound professional education, including training in practical work; b) providing social workers (now engaged in social work) opportunities for advanced study, which will enable them to be efficient administrators of social service enterprises; c) stimulate an interest in social research with the end in view of enabling students to carry on independent social investigations and to evaluate and interpret their findings; d) assist in establishing Indian social work on a scientific basis.

The first Review Committee on social work education was of the view that social work should concern itself with providing welfare of people from weaker and vulnerable sections of society, and that the solution of mass problems was beyond the preview of social work intervention (UGC 1965, Hasan 1971: 212-20). The second Review Committee (1980: 41-42) identified that the major goal of social work is to enhance the well-being of people, ensure social justice and opportunities for people to develop their capacities to become participating and contributing citizens…. It should have developmental thrust but should also not ignore rehabilitation and remedial tasks.

The University Grants Commission of India has provided the structure for social work education in the form of a model curriculum. It was developed in 2001 by the UGC Panel for Social Work Education convened by N.A. Gokarn. The Figure 3.1 below indicates the curriculum frame and influences on social work profession in India:

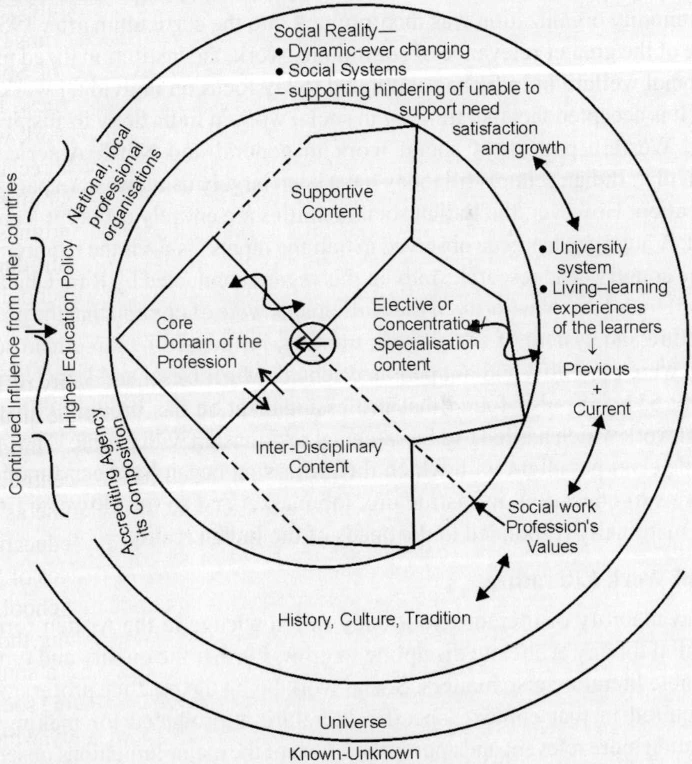

Fig. 3.1: Social Work Profession Curriculum Frame and Influences
Source: UGC, Model Curriculum on Social Work Education, p. xiv.

The figure above indicates the continued influence from other countries on higher education in general and social work education in India in particular. Especially the core domain of the profession has been influenced with American design. The content in the model curriculum is in three domains and the fourth set is that of elective content. The domains are: the core, the supportive and the inter-disciplinary. The elective content has few courses given as illustration. The given curriculum framework demands educators to identify knowledge, values and objectives, very similar to the format in US curriculum design.

Thus, similar to social work education in the U.S.A., there has been a greater stress on developing skills to address the problems arising from maladjustment. Therefore, the preferred method of work was social case work. The other primary methods of social work namely, group work and community organization as evolved much later in the U.S.A., were introduced in India many years later. Group Work, in its elementary form, appeared in the curricula with the emphasis on recreation rather than task or therapeutic orientation. Community organization was incorporated into the curriculum after 1950. In spite of the greater relevance of community work, the institutionalized model of social welfare in India has continued to lay focus on individual work.

It is accepted fact that training in social work in India drew its inspiration from Western pattern of social work in general and North American in particular. Indian schools till today have been largely using western pattern of education. However, the Indian social realities are entirely different from the West. A huge gap has been observed in training inputs vis-à-vis the requirements of the country. The research study in this regard conducted by Ram Chandran (1986) found that a majority of the participants were of opinion that the present structure and system of social work training, influenced by American social work were pro elitist and not people oriented. Murli Desai and Lata Narayan (1998: 531-558) also found that professionalization has brought elitism in social work which has led to a hierarchical relationship with people. The urban middle class paradigm with which the profession began has been functional in terms of education, infrastructure, job market and so on. However, it has only marginally responded to the needs of the Indian reality.

Social Work Literature

The availability of literature as a body of knowledge in the written form is essential for any academic discipline to grow. Further the quality and type of available literature also matters. Social work being the practice profession, it is required in that context, specific literature is produced for making the education more relevant and appropriate. One of the major limitations observed by several scholars is the lack of adequate indigenous literature. Nagpaul (1993) has presented detailed analysis of Social work teaching materials in

India and concluded that there is great need for indigenous literature. He observed 'even today, there is no basic textbook on Indian social work which takes into consideration indigenous elements of social, economic and political life. India has found a readymade body of formulated concepts, principles, theories and techniques in US social work literature (Nagpaul 1993, p.211).

However, Bhatt and Pathare (2004) noted that there is a plethora of literature available on social work education in India. It is available in the form of seminar papers, proceedings of conferences, case studies. The review of the available literature shows that the significant problems and issues of social work education in India have been identified, analyzed and to some extent conclusions have also been drawn. Though the literature has been published in various forms it has not been disseminated for wider use and it remained inaccessible for wider use by faculty and students. There are efforts to indigenize the social work profession by bringing about literature in the Indian context (Thomas, 2010).

In this regard good news is that School of Social Work, Indira Gandhi National Open University at New Delhi has substantially produced indigenously developed material for social work education. Gracious Thomas, the Director of this school has been involved in this venture for about a decade and played very instrumental role in engaging Indian social work educators and practitioners from across the country in developing social work material suitable to Indian context.

Professional Associations and Journals

The Indian Journal of Social Work (IJSW) published by the Tata Institute of Social Sciences is the oldest and uninterrupted publication of the social work profession in India. The first issue of the IJSW was published in June 1940. As the perspective of professional social work is changing from welfare to developmental, the language of the IJSW is shifting from that of social problems to that of issues of the marginalized groups. The Indian Journal of Social Work, over the years, has worked towards the objectives of catering to the need for literature on social work, and being a medium of dissemination of indigenous work being carried out in the country (IJSS). The Indian Conference of Social Work (ICSW), was the first attempt in 1947 to establish national level professional organization of social workers in India. The first real initiatives and movement to more organized social welfare by state were greatly envisioned, influenced and channelized by the ICSW through agencies it conceptualized and planned (Bodhi and Tripura, 2013).

In 1957, Delhi School of Social Work (presently Department of Social Work, University of Delhi) had initiated the publication of a series 'studies in social work' with intention to study social problems and to foster the development of an efficient system of social welfare services, social work and social work education in the country. The same school later published an annotated bibliography of articles/papers/books published on issues related to social work under the title 'Welfare and Development Bulletine'. Both these publications eventually stopped. In 1960 Association of Schools of Social Work in India (ASSWI) was formed which made significant contribution on professional matters till 1986. It brought out about a dozen books, seminar reports and conference proceedings. A year after ASSWI was formed, the Indian Association of Trained Social Workers (IATSW) came into existence in 1961 with the purpose to provide a platform to the practitioners of different fields. The IATSW had started the quarterly 'Social Work Forum' in 1962 and it continued till 1974.

The Indian Society of Professional Social Work (ISPSW), is another association of professional Social Workers in India which was established in 1970, then known as Indian Society of Psychiatric Social Work. This association primarily focuses on uniting the professional social workers to debate, discuss and develop conceptual frameworks and feasible indigenous interventions of social work for practice in India. In order to facilitate this purpose, the Society has so far conducted 24 annual conferences and many seminars and symposia on various social issues, all over India (http://ispsw.wordpress.com). This association have their annual national conference every year and they also have been bringing out a biannual journal titled 'National Journal of Professional Social work' since the year 2000.

The alumni association of Department of Social Work of Lucknow University started a journal called 'Lucknow University Journal of Social Work' later renamed as 'Contemporary Social Work'. The college of social work Nirmala Niketan, Mumbai brings out a professional journal namely, 'Perspectives in Social Work' for the advancement of perspectives on social issues and social work intervention. In 1994, the National Institute of Social Work and Social Sciences, Bhubaneshwar started a publication called, 'Fourth World—the journal of marginalized People'. Another publication titled, 'Journal of School Social Work' is published by Madras School of Social Work since 2004. Centre for Studies in Rural Development Institute of Social work and Research, Ahmednagar has rejuvenated its 'Journal of Development and Social Justice' since the year 2011. It is biannually published journal with multi-disciplinary approach connecting social work with other disciplines in social sciences (csrd.edu.in).

There are a few regional and state level organizations active in profession. To mention a few are: Association of Schools of Social Work in Kerala (ASSK), Bombay Association of Trained Social Workers (BATSW), Karnataka Association of Professional Social Workers (KAPSW), Kerala Association of Professional Social Workers (KPAS), Maharashtra Association of Social work Educators (MASWE). Besides this there have been several sporadic attempts to establish professional organizations or start journals, however, only few sustained for over a period.

As the latest developments, National Association of Professional Social Workers in India (NAPSWI) established in 2005 is the only national level association with largest membership in India. The NAPSWI had organized first Indian social work congress in 2013 on the similar line of the Indian Conference of Social Work (ICSW), which was established in 1947. Recently, the Indian Journal of Dalit and Tribal Social Work engaging with Dalit and Tribal Social Work in Indian Social Work Education and Practice is started by social work educators, and practitioners together in 2013. Its primary goals are to bring to the public social work domain research papers and articles by social work educators and practitioners working on Dalit and Adivasi/ Indigenous people's empowerment in South Asia with a special thrust on India (daltrijournals.org).

Thus, as discussed in the foregoing paragraphs, social work education in India has gone through various stages. From the single institute offering graduate diploma course it expanded to the highest level of education and the numbers multiplied manifold. There have been experiments and explorations with regard to focus of the training. The influence of American model of social work education is evidently visible. There are a number of journals and regional level professional associations operating in the country. Although the impact of these associations and journals is limited, they have potential to make profession relevant to the local context.

In the preceding pages we have discussed the process of origin and development of social work education in India. It is evidently clear that social work education in India has been initiated and shaped under the patronage of American social work education. It can be observed from the documentary evidences on how social work education has been greatly influenced by American model of social work education. Social work educators and scholars from India have argued about this influence and expressed from time to time need for overcoming the legacy of American influence by indigenizing the social work education. Prior to making any conclusive comment about the positive or negative impact of American Influence, we would like to consolidate some of these observations to build upon the suggestions for future direction.

The historical development of social work education in India shows that establishing social work was in response to the emerging needs of trained personnel to address the social welfare and development programmes. However, there was no academic need assessment study for social work education in the country rather it was more of individual or organizational initiative based on their conceptual belief and understanding of Indian context. The history of social work specialization in India shows that setting these up was in response to government programmes and highly influenced by American social work education in the beginning (Desai, 1990). There were considerations and efforts to apply American social work knowledge to the Indian situation.

In India the evolution of social work education has been quick but fragmented (Bodhi, 2013). The significant stages of growth of social work education can be classified into significant phases. The first phase is a period of relatively indigenous inception of professional social work education in the pre-independence period (1936-47). The second phase is the period after independence (1947-48), when social work education in India was shaped under American influence. The third phase is a period when suggestions for reforming social work education emerged as sporadic reactions to the inadequacies of the curative model of social work education adopted from America. The present phase of social work education is more ambiguous. There is proliferation of institutions and university departments offering social work education, however, there is no availability of reliable data and details of these institutions.

The growth and trends of social work education has been reviewed and discussed at various forums and subsequently published in the form of books or papers in national journals (Wadia, 1968; Khinduka, 1965; Mehta, 1986; Ramchandran, 1957; Pawar, 1999; Kumar, 2002). The University Grants Commission (UGC), the regulatory body of higher education in India has also reviewed social work education and prepared a model curriculum for social work schools to adapt from (UGC, 1965; 2001). There has been conferences and seminars that deliberated and debated on the westernization of social work education in India. The need for indigenization has been lamented from time to time throughout the history.

Manshardt (1967, p. 9) the founding father of social work education in India, had visualized an indigenous model of social work education. Referring to TISS, the first school of social work India, he wrote, "While the school, as a graduate institution seeks to maintain high academic standard, it also seeks to be eminently practical, applying the best of modern social thought to the solution of our present-day social problems. It believes that scholarly activities are not incompatible with simplicity and common sense, and that the test of the professional social worker is his ability to give himself an intelligent, skillful and disinterested service to others. The school recognizes that the cultural, economic and social conditions of India differ from those of the West and make every effort to adapt its materials to Indian condition, and to interpret Indian problems in the light of the national heritage." Thus the need for indigenizing social work was emphasized right from the beginning.

Several scholars have observed the outcome of American influence and expressed the need for indigenization of social work education in India. The early scholars like Pathak (1975: 178), noted that American influence 'led to the curtailment of the social science content inadequate emphasis on social action, alienation of a group of trained social workers from the *Sarvodaya* social workers and neglect of social reform'. Gore and Gore (1977: 265-6) pointed out that the American influence made social work education in India more concerned with method and techniques of work. It deemphasized the needs of social and economic development, promotion of preventive services and social action – the prime need of the country in the post-independence era.

Nagpaul (1980: 222-4) observed the inappropriateness of the American model of social work education for India and other south Asian societies. Similarly Desai (1985) expressing the inappropriateness of American model asserted that the social work education in India has followed largely the Western social work model, which is mainly pre-occupied with the problems of urbanization and industrialization. 'And the consequent residual problems of the socially abandoned, especially the women, children and the aged; the physically or the mentally handicapped; the criminal and the delinquent; the problems of adjustment to the new institutions of industry and education – all these have remained the major pre-occupations. In a country where the majority of the people are rural, where exploitation and injustice leave the majority in a state of poverty, social work has remained, to a large extent, peripheral to the root causes of the problems of a non-industrial and rural society' (Desai, 1985, p.44). While analyzing teaching material in India, Nagpaul (1993) noticed that 'US social work education is highly ethnocentric, and its essential elements are inappropriate and irrelevant for India and other developing societies where not only social structures and social problems are different but even human needs, beliefs, myths, values, traditions, goals, roles and aspirations of people are so divergent that new strategies and solutions need to be developed (Nagpaul, 1993, p. 215).

Indian schools of social work largely followed the curricula and the pattern of education borrowed from the West. Desai commented that these schools mostly aimed at helping people adjust to an industrial, postindustrial, urban and city dominated social environment (Desai, 1981). 'Social work was established to help the deviants of the system, to adjust to it, and to provide remedial services to those who become the victims of the new social system. The tasks were those inherent in services provided by labour welfare officers, probation officers, medical and psychiatric social workers, community workers in welfare centres, and child and women welfare workers. Our curricula were thus derived from the remedial, rehabilitative, residual model of practice in the West' (Desai, 1981).

In continuation to this debate Alphonse *et al.* (2008, p. 155) considering the contemporary social issues in the current global context calls for a paradigm shift in the social work curriculum in India from its current emphasis on clinical or generalist practice, including the person-in-environment fit, to more critical theories. Singh (2010, p.863), noted that the latest course descriptions from various departments of social work from India, reflect global terminology and priorities, and are parallel to courses taught in Western and American universities. 'To date, the indigenous content in the curriculum remains the smallest part of the social work curriculum.' In order to address the contemporary socio-economic issues in India, Alphonse, George and Moffatt (2008) calls for a paradigm shift in social work to a more politically aware definition of the profession.

The evidences from the existing curricula of the prominent schools that reviewed for this study show the changing pattern of social work education. The restructuring of TISS and the updated curriculum focus of social work school is very contextual. The design and content of the courses are in response to the contemporary socio-economic and political context of the country. The school has introduced the foundation courses that focus on the developing societies, economies and polities with emphasis on experiences of societies, economies and polities, rather than focusing on theories. The courses like M.A. Social Work in Dalit and Tribal Studies and Action; M.A. Social Work in Livelihoods and Entrepreneurship; M.A. Social Work in Public Health; M.A. Social Work in Women-Centered Practice, are having strong indigenous content and to the large extent departure from the so called Western model. Regarding the restructuring of TISS, Bodhi and Tripura (2013, p. 1) observed that "restructuring opened the doors for formulation and articulation of a distinct anti-oppressive perspective that has now been incorporated into the teaching curricula". Further the teaching at Centre for Studies in Rural Development, Institute of Social Work and Research with its rural base and teaching methods combined with participative rural community development makes it indigenous model in true sense.

As a way forward it would be appropriate to mention some of the challenges that social work education in India is confronting today. Having a long history of eight decades of social work education, the profession continues to struggle with its identity as academic discipline and as a profession. As of date the expedition for national council for professional social work continues. As a result issues like national standard and parity in curricula, standard code of ethics, licensing for practice, bringing coherence in practice with education, accreditation and regulation of social work education and practice continues to invite considerable criticism by the social work fraternity at the local and international level. The passage to getting dignified positioning for social worker at par with other service professionals in India seems far away. Except the sporadic attempts in the country, social work in India continues to strive for a robust national level organization bonding the schools, educators and practitioners of the country. In view of the globalization process and internationalization of social work while indigenizing its education for local needs, Indian social work education has to develop adaptive capacity and competence to appropriately respond to the global challenges.

While concluding on a positive note, the profession of social work in India has been making substantial contribution and impact on the development of the country. There is growing acceptance and appreciation for the contribution made by social work education. As stated by Palattiyil and Sidhva (2012), social work "strives to alleviate poverty and empower marginalized and oppressed people in order to realize their true potential. As such, social workers can be described as change agents in a society that is marked by caste and class divisions and structural inequalities". It is a known fact that social work education in India established on the American model, however, there has been a constant efforts and experiments to indigenize the profession taking into account the social and cultural diversities that are part of Indian society. Moreover, the profession developing radical intervention strategies in order to address the issues of masses that emerged due to onslaught of globalization.

4

Social Work Education through Distance Learning in India

A Reality

Gracious Thomas

Professional social work education through distance learning mode is five decades old on our planet. In India the first Bachelor Degree Programme in social work through open and distance learning (ODL) was launched by me from Indira Gandhi National Open University (IGNOU) in 2004. As on date about twenty universities are offering social work education through ODL in our country. The ODL system is not just a multi-media approach to teaching a distance learner, but a professional concept of providing open access to higher education to all those deprived and disadvantaged groups who are unable to continue education due to restrictions of age, geographical locations and economic situations. For people in a vast country like India with about 1300 million people of which about 70 per cent continue to live in rural sector, ODL is one of the best means of pursuing a recognized university degree, diploma or certificate programme. When over 90 per cent of Indian Universities are urban based, the community needs an alternative mode of education such as the ODL, to fulfill the long-cherished constitutional obligation of providing equal opportunities for the masses to pursue skill oriented professional programmes of study. The Government of India directed every state government to establish state open universities while its own Ministry of Human Resource Development (MHRD) established IGNOU by an Act of Parliament in 1985. As on date there are 14 State Open Universities in India.

The Open and Distance Learning (ODL) System

ODL system is a philosophical concept of providing education to all disadvantaged groups who could not join the formal streams. We know the story of Ekalavya in Mahabharat who could learn archery from a distance without a teacher. The disciples of Jesus taught the teachings of Jesus Christ initially through writing letters. We find in the Bible several letters written by Paul, Peter, James etc. to the Romans, Corinthians, Galatians, Philippians and so on. Later we have witnessed correspondence education from the second half of 19th century with the launching of postal system. The ODL System is borderless in concept. It provides equal opportunities for socially relevant education for the masses and is a cost effective system of education. ODL uses principles of modern learning pedagogy and reaches the unreached – rural, tribal and the marginalized everywhere including far flung areas.

Armaity Desai (1994) stated that there is need to visualize distance education to cover the length and breadth of this country for workers, who have no certification in social work, and are scattered in numerous organizations of NGOs and the Government. This visualization of Desai is blocked by some, rejected altogether by some others, postponed by some others with a view that "we are not yet ready for it", several others might not have thought about it and some academics in India continue to simply question this visualization (Pawar, 2000).

In an interview to Indian Journal of Social Work (2000), Prof. Desai spoke at length about social work education through ODL. She said: "In distance education, field work could be where the students are located. Videos will have to be developed for teaching social work methods and skills of intervention. There can be study centres in various parts of India. Distance education is an alternative which implies restructuring of social work education. Distance education in social work education can be used also for the regular MA (Social Work) programmes. IGNOU says that they are much more scrutinized because their courses are in written form. They are open to the public unlike a closed-door classroom. Thus, quality can be maintained. TISS is in an ideal position to start distance education in social work. If you do not, somebody else will start". And that is exactly what happened when I launched the first Bachelor Degree Programme through ODL from IGNOU in 2004.

The NAAC Manual (2005) states: "If the social work education programme uses the distance or the mixed mode of education, it collaborates with an open university and makes provision for adequate infrastructure, computers, texts, audio-visual equipment, community resources for field work education, and on-site instruction to facilitate the achievement of its mission, and programme objectives". The UGC, NAAC, TISS and other responsible bodies are fully aware of the need and importance of implementing social work education through ODL.

Correspondence vs. Distance Education

Correspondence education in India and elsewhere in the world has a reasonably long history and tradition. During the first half of the 19th century, when postal system was used for educational purposes for the first time in England, the conventional educational system brought correspondence education within its gambit, as one of its sub-domains. To all intents and purposes this new addition remained unnoticed for years, though the proliferation of courses given through correspondence went on unabated. It is with the beginning of the British Open University in England, that distance education emerged as a concept different from correspondence education. Distance educators themselves took more than ten years to finally realize that they were more than correspondence education. It was during the Twelfth World Conference of the International Council for Correspondence Education (ICCE) held at Vancouver in 1982 that the council was renamed as the International Council for Distance Education. Very often, distance education and correspondence education are seen as synonymous. However, the scope of distance education is much wider than correspondence education. Distance education differs from correspondence education in its purposes, orientation and media through which education is imparted.

Let us first see, how correspondence and distance education vary in their objectives. For long, correspondence education as an appendage of conventional educational system has had its main purpose as preparing students to appear for regular board or university examinations. Whereas correspondence education becomes an extension of conventional education as far as its imparting of prescribed knowledge for issuing of certificates is concerned, distance education aims at more varied goals. These include personal growth, training for better job prospects and job enhancement, i.e., in-service training, lifelong and continuing education, a change in attitudes in addition to imparting of knowledge. Above all, distance education has a social purpose, which the correspondence education has ignored throughout. By tradition, higher education has been the privilege of a few. Education has been an elitist pursuit, with only a few belonging to higher economic and social class having access to it. Distance education is a means of education for masses. At the same time it tries to fulfil the constitutional obligation of equal opportunities to all. Distance education promises much more by way of educational opportunities by extending its reach to one and all, undoing all the traditionally known constraints-non-availability of seats in educational institutions, non-availability of such institutions in geographically difficult terrains, poverty of aspirants, etc. Not only does distance education make education accessible to masses, it also makes education more socially relevant. It offers the types of courses and programmes that people need, not only in order to become better in their professions, but also better citizens and human beings, aware of their rights and duties. Distance education by virtue of what it does and can do is an important means of democratizing education.

Correspondence and distance education differ in their orientation also. Correspondence education is, essentially, based on the mode of the distribution of didactic materials, simply oriented towards imparting of information. On the other hand, distance education is oriented towards pedagogy that is, affecting the process of learning/teaching. It tries to build the teacher in the course material itself. Through various means, effective academic communication takes place between the teacher who is away from the learner in physical terms and the learner. No such communication is envisaged in correspondence education. As far as the means of imparting information are concerned, correspondence education refers to traditional type of education given mainly through printed materials, by the postal system. On the other hand, distance education refers to non-traditional innovative type of education that uses all the possible means of communication, that is, a multi-media approach including the human contact. The other media involved in a multi-media package in addition to print are audios, videos, radio and television broadcasts, computers, etc., as well as face-to-face sessions. With the advances in communication technology, distance education has tried to incorporate advanced strategies and technologies of communication. However, this is not to mean that electronic media can be used indiscriminately, just because the system accepts and follows a multi-media approach. What has to be done is to make optimum use of each medium. What goes best through print should be necessarily imparted through print only. Similarly, for certain concepts that can be put across through audio or video only, audio/video may be used.

Open Education

Often 'distance education' is confused with another term, that is, Open education. Open education refers to that kind of non-conventional education which has been weaning away from the conventional constraints that characterize the traditional university education. Certain features associated with open education are non-restrictive admissions, multi-point entry, no age and qualification restrictions, no attendance restriction, teaching at a distance in a non-continuous manner, no restrictions on the period of time devoted to a course, no restrictions on the number of examinations given and taken in a year, no restrictions on subject combinations for a particular degree, credit accumulation, learner autonomy, etc. The larger the number of above features incorporated in a particular system of education, the higher the degree of its openness. It should be clear that Correspondence Institutions or even Distance Education Institutions may or may not be Open Institutions, or may be so only to a limited degree. And at the same time, even a traditional college/university may become 'open' to a recognizable degree. It should be clearly understood that there can be various degrees of the 'openness' of education. However, at the moment, it is difficult to say as to which level of 'openness' may legitimize the nomenclature 'open university' for a university but the relationship between distance education and open education is increasing progressively. Open education can be effected easily through distance education systems on the one hand, and on the other advances in the practice of distance education help and encourage education to become more and more open. The distance mode allows the educational systems to be 'open' and the openness of the educational systems suits the promotion of distance education. That is why the two go together so well.

Social Work Education through Distance

While in the United States, Canada and Australia, distance education has been a feature of social work education since the early 1970s in the United Kingdom teaching of social work through distance learning for social work education and training has grown particularly within universities covering smaller, but widely spaced communities in rural areas and has not just been in qualifying programmes, but also at the level of continuing education (Avril Osborne, 1985). Using distance learning techniques to deliver continuing education in rural areas has been occasioned not just by obstacles of distance, but also by staff limitation and insufficient funding (Clark *et al* 1982).

The James Madison University, Virginia, and the University of South Dakota, USA, began social work education through distance learning in 1977 in consultation with the Council of Social Work Education—the accrediting body. Similarly, the University of Moncton and the Maritime School of Social Work in Canada began to work jointly on a project aimed at decentralizing social work education. The project was government funded and started teaching social work through distance learning with its first intake in 1976. The Association of Social Workers has appointed delegates to their advisory committees. Australia also has substantial experience in distance education in Social Work which exists within a national framework of educational policy. Four main institutions were set up for social work education through distance learning during 1972-75. Since 1978 academics have started supporting distance materials by travelling to these centres regularly and holding tutorial meetings. In UK distance learning in social work was first introduced in the Caledonian Certificate in Social Service Scheme in 1980-81 which was supported by six colleges and universities. Most of the materials used for this programme were developed by the Open University (Avril *op. cit.*). While a number of Schools of Social Work now are offering social work education through distance mode, a new trend has emerged wherein Social Work Education is being offered on-line by several universities. Some of them are the Monash University, Australia, Hong Kong University, British Open University, Victoria University, Canada, and University of South Carolina, USA.

Like distance education in general, distance education in social work developed as the result of advances in technology. Wilson (1999) reports on three distinct phases in the development of distance education in social work. The first phase witnessed the development of off campus programmes, whereby social work classes were taught at a distant learning site by faculty travelling from a main campus of a university or by local adjunct instructors. The second phase ushered in the use of distributed education in the form of technology such as interactive television (ITV). And the third phase is what we are in now—a period in which computer-mediated education is becoming increasingly popular. Each of these phases has required innovation and caution when it comes to the quality of social work education.

Distance learning models developed in the West originated in the Open University in Great Britain. Initially resisted as a "gimmick", the techniques have since been widely embraced, and emerging outcome evaluations have generally supported the usefulness of distance learning techniques. Overtime, social work through distance learning progressed from off campus programmes with live instructors to distribute education using interactive television, to the current computer-mediated models. These have been increasingly dependent on advanced technology, posing problems in both cost and access (Vinton & Neil 2010). Detractors raised numerous concerns, emphasizing the importance of face-to-face learning opportunities, particularly in social work practice classes where opportunities for interactive role-play were viewed as essential. Though outcome studies show that there are many similarities in learning outcomes, development of critical thinking skills, and satisfaction with the learning experience, questions remain regarding the degree of interaction afforded students. In general, distance learning models have become increasingly favoured by programmes seeking to help students pursue their educations while managing limitations in their locations and challenges relating to coexisting work and family responsibilities (*ibid*).

Significant Features of Distance Education Programme Collaboration

It is noticed that almost all universities implement their distance education programme in collaboration with other organizations, namely, social service agencies, government bodies, social work institutions and professional social work community. Collaboration helps the service providers in many ways, these include:

Implementation of Field Work

It is a fact that in the conventional system, there is collaboration between the school and field work agencies. However, in distance learning the responsibility of the field work agency is even more. For example, in UK Open University, the employing organization of the students serves as the field work agency too. It also plays a major role in assessing the student's performance. On the other hand, conventional universities do not delegate such responsibilities and limit the role of the agency only to provide training to students. IGNOU has a massive network with social service agencies across the country and beyond the boundaries in several countries.

Provision of Teaching Faculty and Tutors

Many universities use locally available professional social workers working in various sectors as teachers for the students. Others use their own faculty members who travel to the communities while community based social workers are used to provide tutorial assistance. Apart from the regular faculty of social work at the headquarters, IGNOU gets the assistance of about 1500 professional social workers as academic counselors, tutors/field supervisors.

Provision of Teaching Facilities

Many universities use the facilities of the local colleges/institutions and other resources to teach their courses. In return, the university provides the college, academic resources and in many cases affiliation as well.

Broadcasting Distance Education Programmes

Many universities have contracts with television channels and radio broadcasters for airing their programmes. In case of government universities, many have links with government broadcasting agencies. For example, UK Open University has a tie up with the BBC. IGNOU has its own Television Channels and Gyan Vani Radio stations across the country.

Need to Offer Social Work Education through ODL

There are several reasons for launching social work education through ODL in India. ODL makes it possible to train/educate large number of persons while they continue their vocation, i.e. provide an in-service educational opportunity. We find concentration of Schools/Departments of social work in south and western regions. There is acute shortage of trained social workers particularly in rural areas as pointed out in UGC Review Committee reports on social work education in India. Private universities in India charge exorbitant fees—in some cases over Rs.100,000/- per annum. The ODL system provides an opportunity for the employed to study. It enables to train large number of social workers who would stay back in the country and bring the much needed change among the service providers in social and welfare service sectors.

The Reality in India

Social Work Education in India through ODL has become a reality today. This has created many questions, fears, inhibitions, reservations, doubts and concerns in the minds of some professionals. Time has come to address these concerns. Over 20 distance education (or better to call correspondence education) programmes in Social Work in India are on record today. Most of them do not fulfill the ODL criteria just as the conventional system which violates UGC/NAAC norms. The IGNOU model needs a careful consideration and must be treated as role model.

Table 4.1: Spread of Schools of Social Work in India

Sl. No	*Name of the State/U.T*	*IGNOU Regional Centres*	*Total No. of Social Work Institutions*
1.	Andaman & Nicobar Islands	1	1
2.	Andhra Pradesh	3	39
3.	Arunachal Pradesh	1	1
4.	Assam	2	10
5.	Bihar	4	7
6.	Chandigarh	1	1
7.	Chhattisgarh	1	3
8.	Goa	1	2
9.	Gujarat	2	15
10.	Haryana	1	5
11.	Himachal Pradesh	1	3
12.	Jammu and Kashmir	2	4
13.	Jharkhand	2	4
14.	Karnataka	2	45
15.	Kerala	3	45
16.	Madhya Pradesh	2	10
17.	Maharashtra	3	62
18.	Manipur	1	4
19.	Meghalaya	1	3
20.	Mizoram	1	2
21.	Nagaland	1	1
22.	New Delhi	3	8
23.	Odisha	2	12
24.	Puducherry	-	3
25.	Punjab	1	2
26.	Rajasthan	2	5
27.	Sikkim	1	1
28.	Tamil Nadu	2	92
29.	Tripura	1	1
30.	Uttar Pradesh	4	19
31.	Uttarakhand	1	2
32.	West Bengal	3	6
	Total	56	418

* IGNOU has established at least one regional centre in every state and union territories which offers social work programmes through several study centres. The table presents total number of Schools/Departments/IGNOU Regional Centres offering social work programme in India as on January 2013.

Indira Gandhi National Open University (IGNOU): A Role Model

Indira Gandhi National Open University was established by an Act of the Parliament in September 1985, as an instrument for democratizing and augmenting opportunities for higher education, and widening access and providing a flexible and cost effective system of education. The University has carved a niche for itself in a short span and was conferred the honour of "Centre of Excellence in Distance Education" by the Commonwealth of Learning (COL). The COL has also conferred "Award of Excellence for

Distance Education Material" to IGNOU. Some of the features of the University are: (a) National jurisdiction, (b) Flexible admission, (c) Individualized study centre, (d) Use of modern education and communication technologies, (e) Student support services, (g) Modular programmes, and (f) Resource sharing.

Academic Programmes

The University offers several programmes (228 in 2013) leading to certificates, diplomas and degrees of professional, vocational, technical and awareness generating areas. IGNOU is also offering BSW, MSW, PGDSW, M.Phil and Ph.D in social work. In fact, IGNOU is the only University in India to have indigenously developed text books on social work, supplemented with audio and video programmes both in English and Hindi. There is also interactive radio counselling and teleconferencing sessions for social work students, which no other university in the country could provide.

Instructional Material

IGNOU follows a well-organized plan of course development to ensure quality and effectiveness of the study material. It draws on nationwide talent to support the core academic staff. The headquarters of IGNOU is at Maidan Garhi in New Delhi. In 2013 the University has 67 regional centres, about over 3000 study centres, about 30 international study centres and has over three million students on the roll making it the world's largest University.

Given the kind of nation-wide network supported by the multimedia components and expertise from the conventional system in the country, IGNOU has become an alternate model to launch quality programme of study in social work for the wide variety of student population across the country from Kashmir to the Andaman and Nicobar Islands.

IGNOU has perhaps the unique status of employing maximum number of professional social workers at its headquarters as well as the regional centres. While the school of social work alone has eleven faculty having post graduate degree in social work, the university has employed several academics in its other schools, regional centres as well as study centres. Almost 1500 academic counselors having MSW support the teaching and supervision of social work students both within and outside the country. IGNOU provides research scholarships to about one dozen scholars from social work to pursue M.Phil/ Ph.D Programmes.

The School of Social Work at IGNOU

The School of Social Work (SOSW) was established on August 16, 2007 with the approval of the President of India who is also the visitor of the university. The school currently offers eight programmes of study in social work and two on HIV and family education. Over 30,000 students currently pursue these programmes of study through ODL from within India and twelve countries from India's neighbourhood and African continent. This makes SOSW the largest School of Social Work. SOSW gives utmost importance to research and has about 60 students pursuing M.Phil/Ph.D currently. The school also recognizes Rajagiri College of Social Sciences, Kalamassery as a Research Centre for research work.

SOSW is known for developing indigenous material on social work keeping in view the core values of competence. The school has produced over 200 titles with ISBN numbers and offers over 60 courses on social work and closely related topics both in English and Hindi. Apart from high quality print materials, the school`also has produced about 75 video programmes which are on regular telecast and most of them are available in YouTube. The school also has direct interactive teleconferencing sessions and interactive radio counseling for social work students within India and for the students covered under Pan African–e-network.

Keeping in view the recommendations of the First and Second Review Committee Reports of UGC on Social work Education, the SOSW has developed its programmes of study addressing the issues of the rural and tribal population of the country. The school also revises its programmes at least once in five years. The school has field action projects in open community setting as well as in Tihar Jails. The school organizes one Annual National Seminar on Social Work every year since 2004. It also organizes State level seminars all across the country. The faculty frequently travel across the length and breadth of the country for orientation programmes of academic counselors and field supervisors.

SOSW has a 100 million project through the CBCI Chair. The school also houses the Mother Teresa Chair and the Centre for Tibetan Studies. SOSW extensively participates in extension activities including reaching out to the homeless/flood victims/earth quake victims and victims of natural calamities all over the country. The school has the distinction of launching the first MSW programme with specialization in Philanthropy and another one on Counselling specialization. These programmes originally started as on–campus programmes have now became part of the ODL programmes of the school.

Social Work Practicum

The social work practicum components in all the programmes of study being offered by IGNOU comprise 40 to 50 per cent of the total weightage. While NACC and UGC criteria for practicum range from 33 to 40 per cent, IGNOU has gone beyond those minimum standards to ensure that the social work programmes through ODL is well designed and strongly founded to be professional in nature. For each programme, separate field work journals have been prepared giving objectives and targets for each year. The practitioners guide and programme guide spell out every detail to help out both the student as well as the field supervisor. Every student is being guided by a professionally qualified supervisor having postgraduation in social work.

Perhaps IGNOU is the only university offering Doctoral Programmes in Social Work with compulsory components of field practicum. The school does not admit graduates from other disciplines to its doctoral programme which is otherwise a practice even in central universities located in Delhi. Hundred per cent attendance is mandatory in field practicum for all social work programmes of IGNOU.

Establishment of School of Social Work at IGNOU

Experts who proposed that establishment of School of Social Work (SOSW) at IGNOU in 2007 include renowned social work educators and practitioners such as Prof. Surendra Singh, former VC, MGKVP, Varanasi; Prof. Sanjai Bhatt, Head, DSSW, Delhi University; Prof. Anjali Gandhi, Head, Jamia Milia Islamia; Prof. G.C. Khan, Head, Visva-Bharati, West Bengal; Prof. Thomas Kalam, Director, St. John's, Bangalore and Prof. Gracious Thomas, Director, School of Social Work, IGNOU. The Board of Management, Academic Council and Planning Board of IGNOU had/have social work educators and practitioners including Dr. Armaity Desai, Fr. Jose Alex from Rajagiri College, Smt. Ruth Manorama, etc. The Doctoral Committee as well as Board of Studies of SOSW have at least five each experts from TISS, DSSW, JMI, and other central universities who meet at least half a dozen times every year. Curriculum designing committee and faculty selection committees have experts from TISS and several Central and State Universities. Course preparation team including chapter writers, editors and translators are from conventional system having postgraduation in social work. Paper setters, moderators, and evaluators of social work programmes are from conventional system. Academic counselors and FWSs are also from conventional system. Several study centres are located in conventional Universities and colleges of social work. Experts for audio/video programmes as well as interactive radio counselling and teleconferencing sessions are from conventional system.

The SOSW and its social work programmes are fully designed, developed and supported for maintenance by social work faculty from conventional system comprising over 160 experts which include academics and practitioners. Most university departments and schools of social work across the country extensively use IGNOU materials for class room teaching. Perhaps IGNOU has the best of network with other schools of social work.

Bhatt states that the country's biggest National Open University, named Indira Gandhi National Open University (IGNOU), has set up School of Social Work with undergraduate to Doctoral level courses. Though IGNOU has produced good quality of study material, which is being used by conventional university students also, other distance education universities could not match with requisite standards of practice oriented course especially in field work. While IGNOU took all possible care to monitor structured field work essentially to be supervised by a professionally qualified social work graduate with field work manuals, other distance education institutions could not maintain any standard with respect to field work programmes through distance mode. Since distance education council has not prepared any guidelines for field work programme, there is no control of any national or professional body in this regard (Bhatt, 2012).

Summary

The advent of IGNOU in launching social work programmes through ODL has provided for the first time indigenously developed print, audio and video programmes both in English and Hindi. IGNOU has reached out to the far flung areas where other schools of social work could not do for the past eight decades. The involvement of IGNOU in social work education has also provided wisdom, knowledge, and understanding about diverse population of India and the variety of problems that they confront. In order to address those issues the SOSW has added six more methods of social work being presented by its founder director namely, advocacy, strengths based practice, public interest litigation, networking, awareness campaign and resource mobilization. Similarly the six additional core values of social work being taught by SOSW include: patriotism, hard work, teachership, cultural sensitivity, and commitment and responsibility to the profession.

5

Bridging Gaps in Professional Social Work Education in India

Teddy Andrews J.

Social Work Profession has completed 70 years of its existence in India, however, it is still way behind attaining the full recognition. At the wake of various newly emerging social issues due to globalisation, people are realising the need for Social Work Professionals to provide and strengthen the human services. Therefore, it is becoming increasingly significant for the Social Work professionals to look into the gaps that exist between the training provided and the skills required for actual practice. Besides this gap, another issue that concerns is the quality of training provided. At present, in many training institutes, the theory courses and field work training are the main core components of the Social Work training in India with few add-ons including research, rural camp, study tour, summer and block placement. On the other hand, the literature concerning the various components and its effectiveness in Social Work training is limited, particularly in India, hardly any studies are carried out. Certainly those are important components, however, the quality of those components needs to be strengthened significantly and, in addition, novel training practices also need to be identified and practised.

Considering the need, this paper aims to look at the strengths and gaps in social work training and also attempts to suggest strategies to bridge the gaps. Therefore, the paper is of discussion in nature based on selected literature, author's experience and MSW trainees' feedback through focus group discussions at Manipal University. The issues and strategies discussed in the paper include well planned orientation programme in the beginning, making the classroom instructions participatory and transformative, field work training more structured and focused, bridging and strengthening partnership between field work agency and the institution, developing strategic collaborations, journal club discussions on a weekly basis, addressing community needs through extension activities and specific capacity building sessions.

The core and the add-on components to strengthen the social work training are discussed below under various heads:

Orientation Programme

The Masters' programme in Social Work attracts trainees from different disciplines and for them to obtain a deeper understanding on the nature of Social Work programme, its concepts, theories and the field work practice usually takes more time. Depending on individual capacities, some trainees pick up clarity early and others take more time, particularly when it comes to field work practice requirements. Even trainees from Bachelor of Social Work background sometimes find it hard to catch up with the standard that is maintained in Masters level. In order to facilitate the students understanding and start working towards the field work requirements, a structured and tailor made orientation programme for a week or 10 days would help build their confidence and basic capacities that are required to start their field work training in the first semester. The orientation programme could focus on trainees' values and attitudes, self-awareness, self-esteem, working in teams, social consciousness and relationships, motivation, leadership, reaching out to vulnerable population, stigma and discrimination. Making the sessions of the orientation programme in a participatory mode will enable the trainees to start thinking critically, creatively and rationally, overcome the inhibitions they have and to open up, which will boast their confidence. Faculties at Manipal University are in the process of experimenting the orientation programme covering the issues highlighted above and noticing positive results, however, more rigorous evaluation of the same needs to be done to show the results scientifically.

Participatory and Transformative Classroom Instructions

Theoretical teaching, as part of classroom instructions is highly significant to impart concepts and build the knowledge base and aims at enhancing the skills of the trainees too. At the same time, one should check the methodologies adopted for teaching and how far the learning objectives are accomplished using those methodologies. The Social Work trainers/educators need to reflect on their teaching engagement and assess, is their classroom instruction a traditional monologue or an interactive dialogue or a live theatre performance with a space in between to discuss, debate and clarify doubts, which triggers the critical and creative thinking of the trainees. Certainly the teaching session should be a right blend of lecturing, power point presentations, role-plays, group activities, individual exercises, documentaries followed by discussions and creative group games. Laying more stress on or using more of any of the above mentioned modes might hinder the optimal learning experiences of the trainees. In other words, use of multiple teaching-training strategies would enhance trainees' engagement in the learning process which, in effect, would provide an effective learning experience. So the faculty member is not the key player, being an information giver, rather, both the trainees and faculty is engaged in teaching learning process. Boyer T (2006) and Wren J and Wren B (2009), in their papers, have highlighted the significance of multiple teaching practices in social work education.

Boyer T. (2006), in his paper presented at a NACSW (North American Association of Christians in Social Work) National Convention in the US, highlighted that he plays the role of a group facilitator using small group activities, films, guest speakers and students presentation to keep it interesting and offer a variety of learning experiences. He has assessed the effectiveness of multiple training strategies through exam scores and pre-test and post-test scores.

Wren J. and Wren B. (2009) found that learning is best achieved when students are actively involved in a cyclical process that includes observing, applying, reflecting, and sharing their experiences. From the social and pragmatic constructivist literature, we see that students learn best as active learners who integrate thinking and acting, who reflect on the act, and who share their reflections and observations with others. Active and constructivist learning models also stress multiple teaching modalities, including learning by doing and having the student serve as a teacher of what they are learning. Therefore, the social work educators need to be open for learning from the trainees.

MSW trainees at Manipal University also have given their opinion on the same as below:

> "Lecturing with power point slides improves learning and acts as a main tool of learning through auditory and visual sources"—2nd Year—MSW trainee (2011), Manipal University.
>
> "Use of role-plays enhances our confidence levels and clarity over the concepts and provides an experience to get a feel how it is to be a social worker and also as a client"—2nd Year—MSW trainee (2011), Manipal University.
>
> "Role-play increases our abilities to analyse situations and find out alternative ways of handling issues"—1st Year—MSW trainee (2011), Manipal University.

Wilson G. and Kelly B. (2010) have obtained comments from the social work students that "Role-plays were useful in identifying and developing communication skills/weaknesses".

> "Group activities help us to build our skills in working in teams, interpersonal relationships, coordination and overall leadership abilities"—2ndYear—MSW trainee (2011), Manipal University.

In addition to making the classroom instructions more effective, the kind of assignments given for continuous assessment need to be relevant and provide an experiential learning, rather than on writing up an assignment on a given topic. In order to optimise the trainees' learning through this work, the trainers need to do a lot of home work in planning and assigning tasks to the trainees. For example one type of assignment could be to provide a problem situation at the individual level or group level or community level, ask the trainees to explain how, as a social worker, they would approach this issue. They can be guided to refer available literature, access other resource materials and consult social workers and other professional, if available and required.

Wilson G. and Kelly B. (2010) also have received recommendations from the social work students in the UK that more explicit links to application of knowledge in practice; more experience of observing social work practice; more teaching from social workers engaged in current practice; more in-depth training on social work theory and methods and skills for social work practice. The MSW trainees from Manipal University highly appreciate the inputs of the external experts from the respective fields. These recommendations also could be understood in a different way, which is applicable perhaps to Indian context, in some places it is difficult to get practitioners to conduct guest lectures, may be due to financial constraints of the institution or difficult to get experts itself. In such situations, it very much helps that the academicians are also involved in practising social work alongside.

Field Work Practice and Guidance

Wilson G. and Kelly B. (2010) in their evaluation of the effectiveness of social work education in the UK found significant level of disjunction between academic and practice learning and suggest that better integration between these two domains of learning is needed if social work students are to be more effectively prepared for the challenges they are likely to encounter in practice. One of the ways to integrate academic and practice learning is through academicians going to the field along with the trainees and along with the field supervisor train them. The educators need to model the trainees in the beginning and demonstrate the application of social work knowledge and strategies in helping the people. It helps in both ways, one, in training the trainees more effectively and two, these experiences will aid the faculty members in making the classroom instructions more effective.

The faculty members accompanying the trainees to the field work is greatly valued by the trainees and found very useful and beneficial.

> "You came to the field and explained to us the application of theory into practice which helped me to get more clarity on approaching and intervening with client's difficulties"—2nd Year—MSW trainee, Manipal University (2011).

The sustained effective guidance in field work by the faculty supervisor helps the trainees' polish their skills. In addition to the guidance provided in the field, the faculty supervisors also need to provide guidance based on the report that the trainees submit on weekly basis. The guidance sessions need to be done in groups and also at the individual level to optimise trainees' learning. As reporting is one of the important skills, the trainees need to be guided through in building their skills in writing reports of good standard. The guidance on reporting need to include all the dimensions of the report like, language, content, structure and the overall evaluation of the report.

Field work training needs to be more focused with more intensive and relevant work. Usually, the trainees are expected to practise casework, group work and community organisation methods and other activities of the field work organisation. Learning the direct methods of Social Work is important but how far it is being used in the actual practice after completing Social Work programme is a concern to be thought about. Just having an understanding and field exposure in practising the core methods of Social Work is not adequate, importance needs to be given to research, administration and advocacy based practices as well.

The field work training requirements stipulates that the trainees need to do a particular number of case work, group sessions and community programmes. In addition to the traditional stipulations, criteria including conducting a small study, designing some Information Education Communication (IEC)/Behaviour Change Communication (BCC) materials, developing short videos or documentaries and designing training modules and conducting short training programmes would certainly strengthen the field work training and in turn build trainees' capacities matching the demands of potential organisations.

In Manipal University, taking up intensive study of a particular social concern in the field work organisation and mobilising resources for the field work agency are pen down as some of the desirable requirements of the first year field work practicum. In the second year, through various forums, the trainees are provided opportunities to develop training modules, develop short videos and evaluative assignments. Through these experiences, trainees become more competent and able to face up to the expectations and requirements of the assignments that take up in their career.

Bridging and Strengthening Partnership between Field Work Agency and Institution

IASWR - Institute for the Advancement of Social Work Research (2007) states that the challenge for social work education is to become a knowledge translation and implementation enterprise, building on existing field/academic partnerships to bring existing science to "real world" practice. There is still a long way to reach that stage in India. In Social Work training, learning experience in class and in field are meant to go hand in hand and integrating both is highly imperative. One of crucial factors in optimising this integration is through establishing strong partnership between the institution and the field work agencies. IASWR (2007) has emphasised in its report that there should be a focus on communication between the academic institution and the field placement agency to develop a mutual understanding of the needs. In a way, it could be understood that the field work practicum needs to be designed not just by the institution but in consultation with the field placement agencies.

In the process of discussion, the Social Work institutions need to enter into a professional dialogue on the guidelines and requirements of the field work training with an aim to clearly inform the agencies about the same. Also they need to be open for the comments from the agencies to what extent they will be able to provide training opportunities to the trainees in building the required skills. This helps both the institution and the agency to have a clear understanding on the nature of exposure that the trainees would get in the field work agency and the social work educators can be prepared to guide and support the trainees accordingly. The discussion between the field supervisors and faculty supervisors needs to be held on a regular basis to maintain the right kind of partnership required for more effective field work training.

Strategic Collaborations

The Social Work training institutions need to enter strategic collaborations at different levels, including International, National, State and District, depending on availability of resources and strengths. The collaborations can be in any form or nature like students exchange, faculty exchange, running online courses across countries, between institutions and organisations, initiating online journals, grant writing assignments and conducting workshops, symposiums, conference, etc. Certainly, gaining different perspectives through various collaborative initiatives would empower the trainees with knowledge enhancement, skill building and attitudinal change. In the present day context, establishing a platform where the trainees can interact with experts and experienced practitioners, academicians and researchers in the field nationally and internationally and also with trainees from other institutions in India and overseas, would be of great value addition to the Social Work training. These can be worked out through personal participation and through online mode.

Continuing Social Work Education (CSWE) for trainers aimed at strengthening the capacities of the trainers could be designed and conducted by different institutions and organisations jointly. The areas that can be covered in CSWE may include emerging social problems, updates on novel social work interventions in different settings, grant writing skills, innovations in social work research and scientific paper writing.

Journal Club

Weekly journal club meeting is one of the very useful platforms that provides opportunities to the trainees to review literature, do a critical analysis of a paper, obtain new ideas, clarity over designing research methodologies, understand theories developed out of systematic studies, presentation of study findings and writing up of a scientific and theoretical paper. These forums may consider reviewing both conceptual and scientific paper or an article for using certain standard framework.

> "The journal club activity helps us to think critically and find out appropriate ways of designing and conducting studies"—2ndYear—MSW trainee (2011), Manipal University.

Journal club meet also enables the trainees and the faculty members to upgrade the knowledge on the latest evidence based practices in social work. The evidence base for social work interventions is scarce in India, yet this activity might ignite the thinking and motivate the trainees and the faculty members to strengthen the scientific evidences on best practices in social work. Even if a literature from the West is reviewed, it gives lot of insights on novel intervention techniques and strategies that could be tested out in Indian context.

Addressing Community Needs as Part of Extension Activities

Social Work training involves generating professionals to work in development and service sectors, a great deal of experience can be provided to the trainees by engaging them in community extension activities. In the process, the trainees are equipped with skills in understanding the needs of people with difficulties, design relevant intervention packages and evaluate the interventions. It is highly imperative that the faculty members, as a department, take up need based community extension initiatives to cater to the felt and implied needs of the society. These activities provide an opportunity for all the faculty members and trainees to sharpen their skills and abilities.

Social Work Administration is an area of exposure that is given the least importance in field work training in India. Rutgers University Centre for International Social Work in their report (Dec. 2008) has recommended that the social work curricula could be expanded or a separate track could be created to address administrative and management skills such as needs assessment, programme development, strategic planning, and programme evaluation. Similarly the Department of Public Health, Manipal University, takes up health programmes and evaluation studies as part of the community extension projects. Since the start of the course in Sept 2009, the MSW trainees at Manipal have been involved in seven such projects including:

1. Evaluation of pulse-polio immunisation in collaboration with National Pulse Polio Surveillance Programme, WHO.
2. Evaluation of mass drug administration for filariasis supported by Ministry of Health and Family Welfare, Government of Karnataka.
3. Social Auditing of Mahatma Gandhi National Rural Employment Guarantee Scheme as a joint venture with Udupi Zilla Panchayath.
4. Performance evaluation of solar home lighting system in a rural community funded by Bharatiya Vikas Trust, Manipal.
5. Annual Status of Education Report (ASER) Survey in Udupi District, Karnataka.
6. Health seeking behaviour of a tribal (Koraga) community in Udupi District, Karnataka.
7. Mental health status and social networks of older people in Udupi District, Karnataka.

Chui EWT *et al*, (1997) in their attempt to evaluate the community work education through skills laboratory, they found that the acquisition of interpersonal and communication skills was particularly prominent as students had the opportunity to meet real clients. MSW trainees at Manipal University are regularly provided with opportunities to interact with different population through community extension activities on a range of purposes. They have collectively reported that their engagement in such activities build their confidence and skills in programme planning, organising and overall management of the projects.

Specific Capacity Building Sessions

Presently the issues in Social Work profession that stands in the way of attaining complete recognition is the benchmarks and competencies that need to be developed in the trainees during their training. Due to various reasons, the usual experiences like classroom instructions, field work, research, camp, tour etc., that are provided in the institutions are not adequately capacitating the budding professionals to develop the required competencies. Therefore, having fortnightly or monthly capacity building sessions on various issues and skills required would provide an additional opportunity for the trainees.

One of the activities for the trainees in Manipal University is skill development sessions wherein they will be provided with opportunities to work in teams to run participatory training programmes with the structured modules and also resource materials in the beginning. The sessions are supported and supervised by the faculty members. Gradually once the trainees gain confidence and develop skills, they are guided to design such training programmes in a planned and systematic fashion on their own in small teams with different population and for different issues.

> "One thing I learnt from these sessions is managing time efficiently"
> —2nd Year—MSW trainee, Manipal University (January 2011).

These sessions enable them to practise group work interventions in a systematic and organised fashion. In turn, it also makes the field work practice more meaningful and relevant.

Role of a Social Work Educator/Trainer

Major contribution in strengthening the social work training lies with the Social Work trainers. One is that the social work trainers themselves need to be equipped with adequate potentials to render the quality field work guidance and supervision. Second, some of the field work agencies are busy with their regular work and find the trainees placed with them as a burden or additional responsibility to assign them work and guide them. As a result, the trainees do not get the optimal learning in field work training. The social work trainer's role in this context could include:

- Making the classroom environment an 'experience of transformation' for the trainees by using multiple training methodologies.
- Faculty members in social work should be a 'field trainer' as well. At least once a fortnight or once a month the faculty supervisors need to go along with the trainees to the field and train them by showing how the theories and concepts learnt in the classroom can be applied in field practice.
- Academicians need to be 'practitioners'. Besides being an academician, they need to practise the social work methods and intervention techniques by being associated with an organisation or through community extension activities.
- Being an active 'researcher' is significant by studying social phenomena and testing novel interventions for its feasibility, acceptability and overall effectiveness. It should not just stop with conducting studies, they should go further ahead to publish their learning and experiences so that the theory derived could be tested in other settings as well.
- 'An innovator' – in terms of building knowledge and skills of trainees not only in the regular methods of social work but also on developing IEC/BCC materials, documenting and recording specific social work interventions, guiding the trainees to take up small studies in their field work agency and so on.
- On the whole, social work trainers need to be the 'role models' to the trainees in practising social work values and ethics. Thus, by observing, the trainees also internalise those values. Congress E P

(no date) expressed in her paper that the teachers should also serve as role models for professional practice.

Conclusion

It is high time that the Social Work fraternity should introspect on the kind of training being provided in the social work training and explore ways of bridging the gaps and strengthen the training in India. Perhaps, all the factors that are highlighted in this paper may be relevant to certain context and may not be applicable to some, but on similar lines, the Social Work trainers need to think and open opportunities to maximise the learning experiences to the trainees. One of the significant areas that the Social Work trainers need to work on is evaluation and documentation of the various training components, therefore, certainly this applies to the kind of training experiences provided to the trainees. It is just not evaluating but also identifying the areas to improve and keep upgrading the training components. Evaluating and updating the social work training components is not adequate, the experiences and expertise need to be shared across institutions so that an overall growth and development of the profession can be witnessed. The professionals who are practitioners and researchers also can contribute enormously in this effort of upgrading the social work training in India.

6

Development of Social Work as a Profession in India

Challenges Faced by the Social Work Fraternity

Kaivalya T. Desai

Many people in the social work fraternity share the opinion that, social work geminated from voluntary and charitable work that finds its roots in philanthropy. This slowly gave way to training in social work practice, which has evolved into a profession. The development of social work as a profession, like other professions, has been supported by the development of Social Work[1] as an academic discipline. Social Work builds the knowledge base of social work profession and trains people in becoming professional social workers. However, since its infancy, there have been many discussions and debates about the purpose for which Social Work trains human-power.

Purpose of Social Work

Many educators and students of Social Work, when asked about the role of social workers, rhetorically reply: '*to help people so that they can help themselves*'. This suggests that social workers are supposed to work within the established system and its norms, and help the 'troubled' or 'deviant' people to adjust within the larger society. Thus, it is assumed that social problems are located in the individual inadequacies of the people and that the norms of the given system are accepted as social facts that exist irrespective of the individual consciousness. Senior educator, Ms. Subhramaniam of the Nirmala Niketan, Mumbai said,

> Social Work trains students to help individuals and families who are not able to cope with the accepted norms of the society. Although the process of helping begins with charity, but the final aim is empowering these individuals and families so that they are able to utilise their full potential and lead functional lives in the society.

This highlights that the purpose of Social Work is micro-oriented and that it trains human-power for individualistic field interventions. However, in order to work at the individual level, it is necessary to understand a problem at both micro and macro-level. According to Ms. Bose of the Visva Bharati,

Sriniketan, Social Work inculcates in the students values of commitment and dedication towards social care through knowledge of theory and fieldwork training. In doing so, it develops in them an understanding of discrimination and troubles that individuals face due to economic, political, psychological, or social reasons. This was confirmed by Mr. Thomas of the Madras School of Social Work, Chennai:

> A social worker is expected to understand those aspects of human behaviour and social environment that might make a person vulnerable, and after developing the understanding of these factors, develop the skills to: (i) influence and direct the individual behaviour on the one hand, and (ii) alter her/his social environment, on the other, in a positive direction to empower that person and make her/him self-reliant.

Many students from different institutions of Social Work also confirmed to this viewpoint. The reflection of Ms. Shilpa from Assam University, Silchar, highlights this: "*The purpose of Social Work is to develop capacities in individuals who are committed to social causes, so that they can enhance the social functioning of individuals, groups, and communities by creating favourable societal conditions*."

As different from this, there were others who reflected on the purpose of Social Work as being more radical, a purpose which supports interventions at macro-level and pushes for systemic changes. For example, according to senior educator Mr. Sinha of the University of Delhi, the purpose of Social Work is to enkindle in the students as well as the educators, the understanding about the oppressive structures of the society and then to develop strategies to alter them by looking at the macro-system in an unorganised context.

A close look at the above mentioned purposes of Social Work highlights two important points: (i) diversity in viewpoints with respect to the purpose of Social Work, and (ii) common understanding that the purpose of Social Work is connected to the concept of social justice. It is probably the strategies for interventions, being suggested, that are diverse. According to Ms. Vashi of TISS, Mumbai, "*Social Work aims at social justice. In order to fulfil this aim, social workers need to work closely with the people and represent their voice in the process of development*." This also highlights that the purpose of Social Work can only be met if there is consent of the people. Therefore, it is clear that the approach of the social workers is one of working with the people and not for them.

The History of Social Work

From the time when Social Work emerged in Victorian England to the current post-modernist times, it has come a long way. With the move from charity organisation and service-delivery to organised social work practice, different methods of social work practice emerged. As the origins of Social Work are located in the West, the western line of thought has had a strong impact on the development of Social Work in India. Even the literature that was and is referred to in teaching students in India was borrowed from the West (Nagpaul 1972).

In India professional social work began with the establishment of Sir Dorabji Tata Graduate School of Social Work (now known as the Tata Institute of Social Sciences) in the year 1936 under the leadership of Clifford Manshardt, an American missionary. The curricula of the earlier institutions of Social Work were patterned after the social work institutions in USA; rather, many of the teaching staff in Social Work were trained in the West (Moses 1961; Yelaja 1969).

> ...the philosophy, theories, methods, principles of social work as prevalent in the Metropole were diffused to India and our educational system adapted itself and created the necessary mechanisms to accommodate and integrate this innovation (social work profession) into itself. It is natural for India (sic) social work to have all the major traits of American social work (Siddiqui 1984: 55).

However, the westernisation of Social Work in India was met with some resistance by many Social Work educators. Not only did they try to contextualise Social Work with respect to the Indian situation, they also raised doubts about the urban orientation of social workers. This critique received thought and attention as large masses of Indian population resided in rural areas. People involved in working with the communities were more receptive of this critique and consequently, they started to raise concerns about the role of social workers in community development programmes in rural areas. According to K.D. Gangrade,

> Indian society is characterised by and has a tradition of corporate life, with such traditional institutions such as the joint family, caste and community. Interdependence of individuals through help and co-operation within these institutions is much more part of their daily existence than individualised and independent existence. In the light of such a cultural background we have to consider the application of community organization to the Indian scene (1971: 24).

Thus, one can see that, although the content of Social Work was largely borrowed from the West, critique with respect to the rural context of India came to influence its development. Then, the difference with regard to the predominant ideology in the West and in India again came to influence the development of Social Work; individualism based on a capitalist ideology in the West was in contrast to the community-oriented living in India.

Community organisation in India was dormant during the first phase of development of Social Work. A major shift in focus took place when the Government of India launched the Community Development Programme (CDP) in 1952: the focus of CDP was on rural communities. But, still, most of the professionally trained social workers concentrated on the practice of casework in urban areas. Thus, although the focus of community organisation was rural, the major thrust of Social Work remained urban in character (Siddiqui 1997). The post 1970s, when community work in the West was experiencing a radical shift towards conflict-oriented work, the focus of community work remained welfare-oriented in India. Post 1980s, there were a few isolated cases of educators in Social Work, especially in the field of community organisation, who advocated for collective resistancc against the state. These educators critiqued the community development programmes of the state and the apolitical stance of the social workers. Drawing from the social movements and the grassroots initiatives entailing collective assertion, they started advocating for a change in the community organisation perspective (Andharia, 2007). In addition as Grace Mathew (1992) notes, in India many clients were involuntary, who were compelled to receive the attention of social workers. This highlights that Social Work does not enjoy as much societal recognition in India as in the West. One possible reason for this is that, in India, an institutionalised system of social work practice with government support did not exist, and therefore, professional social workers had to approach the clients for individualised practice rather than the other way round.

Another sharp contrast in the development of Social Work has been that, in America, the focus of Social Work has been on specialised training in methods of social work practice. Whereas, in India, the focus of Social Work has been on an integrated approach that is based on a generic model. Even in the institutions of Social Work that follow a specialisations-based model, the focus has been on areas and fields, and not on methods of social work practice. The reasons for this are: (i) plurality in the purpose of Social Work, as envisioned by the people in the Social Work fraternity, and the absence of a continuously functioning professional body that can define the ambit of social work activities, (ii) social work activities being considered as voluntary and, therefore, lack institutionalised support from the government, and (iii) the multiplicity of problems in the India that calls the attention of the social workers who are limited in number, who therefore need to possess the knowledge of all the methods and intervention strategies.

Social Work as a Profession in India

The development of social work as a profession has been under debate both within the social work fraternity and outside of it. Over the years, the definition of a profession has undergone change and new vocations or semi-professions have come to be accepted as professions. Meher C. Nanavatty (1952) has cited four characteristics of a profession as enumerated by Carr-Saunders in the *Encyclopaedia of the Social Sciences*: (i) the development of the body of knowledge upon which the skill rests, (ii) the reservation of functions to the qualified by means of licensing or the restrictions of the professional bodies, (iii) the development of the professional consciousness amongst the practitioners, and (iv) the contribution of the specialised skill and viewpoint to appropriate problems in the surrounding society. As regards development of social work profession in India, currently it is weak with respect to the first three characteristics. The first characteristic is weak as many educators and students complain that most of the knowledge base of social work is borrowed from the West and is not of much relevance in the Indian context. Till now, the professional bodies of social work have not been able to ensure licensing of social work practice in India. Also, there is not much professional consciousness among trained practitioners.

In his lecture, Abraham Flexner (1915), *Is Social Work a Profession*?, delivered at the National Conference on Charities and Corrections, examined the characteristics of a profession with reference to social work. The characteristics of a profession, as listed by him in 1915 are still relevant for social work in India, as it is still struggling to establish a professional status for itself. Firstly, professions are intellectual in character, a professional assumes responsibility for her/his decisions, and there is a considerable degree of originality in the decisions that are made by the professional. Secondly, professions are learned in character, that is, they involve a steady stream of ideas. Thus, every profession involves the borrowing of ideas from either natural or social sciences which need to be learnt in order to become a professional. Thirdly, every profession involves the component of practice. The knowledge that is learnt needs to be applied by every professional having a definite and practical objective to her/his work. Fourthly, a profession needs to possess an educationally communicable technique which can be imparted through a professional course (hence the importance of an academic discipline for every profession) that involves a component of field-based training as well. Fifthly, every profession should have its own professional body which advocates for a common social interest. Thus, professional bodies are assigned the task of establishing a code of ethics for every profession. Lastly, every profession has a definite social status attached to it (*ibid.*).

If we examine social work as a profession in India with respect to the characteristics given by Flexner then social work might qualify as a profession. For example, the learned character, the practical purpose, a professional course, professional bodies/organisations all exist in India but still many do not accept it as a profession. Many social workers advocate that, it will require organisation and lobbying on the part of the social workers, for the attainment of a professional status for social work in India. However, there are contrary views both within and outside of social work fraternity on the acceptance of a professional status for Social Work.

Challenging Views from Outside

The biggest challenge that social work faces for being recognised as a profession is the haziness of its social status. It is still assumed that social work is voluntary in nature and any individual (with a kind heart) who wishes to pursue social work can do so. In India, the lack of governmental support compounds this problem. Many social work educators have sought to organise a 'National Council for Social Work Profession' that would be recognised by the government. But, so far their efforts have not been successful. Some would argue that social worker's efforts are limited to identification of a problem; solving that problem requires the services of other professionals such as doctors, lawyers, bureaucrats, and teachers. To counter this observation, social workers argue that their work involves intellectual power of analysis and discrimination, breadth and flexibility of sympathy, sound judgement, skills in utilisation of available resources, etc. These tasks cannot be performed by people who only voluntarily assume to help the people in need. Thus, there is a distinction between social-service delivery and professional social work activities.

Then others also emphasise that social workers in India are involved in multiple activities and there are no distinct fields of social work. Professions need to be limited and definite in scope but the high degree of specialised competency required for action cannot possibly go with social work. Lack of specificity in aim adversely affects the training of social workers in a specialised area. The occupations of social workers are so numerous and diverse that no compact and specialised educational discipline is feasible. Therefore, most of the institutions of Social Work in India offer generic training programmes for social workers rather than specialised ones. People within the social work fraternity, who promote the development of social work as a profession, argue that the reason behind this is not the inability of social work to organise specialised training programmes, but it is the multiplicity of problems in India that calls for a generic training programme. In India, they point out, well-informed, tactful, judicious, sympathetic, and resourceful people are needed more than specialised personnel. Another major hindrance for social work to attain professional status is the job factor. There are hardly any practice areas in the fields of social work that are reserved for social workers. In addition, the concept of receiving payment for doing social work is far from being accepted in India.

Also, people from academia raise issues about the quality and quantity of the publications that have been produced in social work. There is dearth of literature that has been produced by the social work academicians and practitioners. To this critique, the social work fraternity responds that there are social work journals that have been continuously publishing articles and research papers pertaining to social work practice and it needs to be taken into consideration for recognising social work as a profession.

To the challenges that are raised against calling social work a profession, social work fraternity has tried to produce contrary arguments in its favour. But social workers in India are of the view that lack of organised lobbying on the part of social workers is the major reason for the non-attainment of a professional status. As mentioned earlier there are oppositions not only from outside but within the social work fraternity itself for calling social work a profession. This issue has been debated by Social Work educators for some time now and the irony is that the involvement of practitioners in this debate has been found to be minimal.

Debate within Social Work Fraternity

Educators who argue in favour of professionalism in social work highlighted three important points. Firstly, if social work gains professional status then the quality of Social Work education could be maintained uniformly throughout the country. Secondly, with professional recognition, societal recognition with respect to the importance of the work done by social workers will improve. Lastly, it will provide security to the social workers in terms of their employability. Senior educator, Ms. Bhatnagar of the University of Delhi said that social work as a profession is weak in India due to the absence of a professional council of social work. Mr. Pandey of the University of Delhi was of the opinion that the absence of a professional council for social work has been the biggest hindrance in attaining a professional status. If there is a professional council then like the West, social work will be licensed, elevating it to professional status. He further added,

> Licensing not only guarantees a permission to practice, but also helps in developing an organised system of practice. In addition to this, under an organised system of practice, job opportunities can be created for trained social workers. Once the jobs are created then they start influencing practice and consequently the development of the profession. After a continuous development slowly the concept of private practice also emerges in a profession. The absence of a strong professional body created the hegemony of TISS which, by many, is referred to as the gatekeeper of social work profession in India. Even the premier journal of social work in India, the 'Indian Journal of Social Work' is published by TISS instead of a national level professional body.

However, Ms. Vashi of TISS, Mumbai was of the opinion that the absence of licensing in social work is beneficial as it provides flexibility in terms of visualising the philosophical base (social justice) of social work from a radical angle. It also facilitates the politicisation of social issues which is important for a macro-approach in social work. Mr. Sinha of the University of Delhi said that licensing of social work will create a hierarchy between the trained social workers and the para-professionals. Currently, the para-professionals constitute the bulk force of social work practice, and the licensing system will create a sense of insecurity in them. Senior educator Ms. Kriplani argued against this viewpoint by drawing an analogy with the medical profession. According to her, para-professionals are the appendices to the main professional. As far as the hierarchy is concerned, it exists even without licensing. This view was confirmed by Surya, a student of the Karve Institute of Social Service, Pune who has three-year experience of working as a para-professional. He said, "*I joined MSW because in the organisation where I was working I realised that I could only get a further promotion (irrespective of my field knowledge) or a higher position (with a better salary) in any other organisation if I pursue a MSW degree.*"

In brief, those who support the view that social work in India should aim at professional status, identify four important requirements for realising it: (i) creation of an independent identity for social workers, (ii) maintenance of uniform standards for social work education and training, (iii) provision of security in terms of the employability of social workers, and (iv) formulation of a code of ethics for social workers. However, those who are against calling social work a profession argue that the professional status will limit the scope of social work within the boundaries set up by the state and its policies. Ms. Vashi of TISS opined that, in India, social work has the potential to create an alternative voice for the people outside the boundaries of the state. Mr. Sinha of the University of Delhi was of the opinion that social work should not strive for professional status as it is a western notion that defeats the very purpose of social work, namely, social justice.

Some educators also expressed the concern that professionalization of social work will also shift the focus of social work more towards jobs and employment. Mr. Khan of the Jamia Milia Islamia, New Delhi observed that institutions of Social Work, on the demand of the students, now focus on job placements, because of which other aspects of social work profession such as maintenance of ethical standards becomes a problematic as then the focus is more on higher salary packages and market demand. Professional status carries with it an understanding that social work education and training prepares the students to take up certain jobs in the society, but the market has its own demands; it wants social workers to take up already laid down tasks in the voluntary sector. As a result of the market demand, social work needs to incorporate more skill-based training courses in the curriculum rather than focussing on the intervention strategies based upon a sound understanding of the theoretical concepts.

One of the central features of any profession is the existence of a professional body that directs its growth and development. For the social work profession, at the international level, there are professional bodies, such as the International Federation of Social Workers, that direct its growth and development internationally. In the developed countries like UK and USA, there are national level professional bodies of social work that are active. But this is not the case in India. Let us, therefore, discuss the roles of and the challenges faced by professional bodies of social work in India.

Professional Bodies of Social Work in India

In India, many efforts have been made to come up with national and state-level professional bodies of social work to foster the development of social work as a profession. Some of these include Association of Schools of Social Work in India (ASSWI), National Association of Professional Social Workers in India (NAPSWI), Indian Association of Trained Social Workers (IATSW), Maharashtra Association of Social Workers Educators (MASWE), Bombay Association of Trained Social Workers (BATSW), and Karnataka Association of Professional Social Workers (KAPSW). Meher C. Nanavatty, in his analysis of the literature on professional associations of social work highlighted,

> Coming to the promotion of professional associations. They have remained as peripheral activities. Though during the seventies and the early eighties, the professional associations had shown some signs of growth and vitality, due to internecine conflict arising out of individual motivation versus social motivation as well egocentric leadership, the IATSW ceased to exist. In spite of some efforts at revival a new spirit could not be infused. This is one of the most important handicaps of the profession of social work in India (1997: 298).

One of the primary roles of a professional body is to maintain a minimum standard and quality of education and training of social work in the country. Ms. Bhatnagar of the University of Delhi, opined that, as supervised fieldwork training is one of the core components of Social Work, therefore professional bodies should ensure that distance learning in Social Work is abolished. In the distance learning programme, fieldwork training is fragmented and unsupervised. She further added that, like other professions, education and training of Social Work should be done through a regular five-year integrated programme of Social Work and this is something that should be ensured by the professional bodies. Senior educator Ms. Jhunjhunwala of the

M.S. University, Baroda, strongly expressed that, in the current scenario, the primary role of a professional body is to stop the commercialisation of Social Work education and curtail the mushrooming of self-financing institutions of Social Work that collect capitation fee from students. Senior educator, Ms. Thadani of TISS was of the view that commercialisation of education is rampant in almost all the professions and, in the current globalised times, under the auspices of neo-liberalism, it will be hard to control this phenomenon for Social Work. Therefore, the attempt should be to find out ways of enhancing the quality of education in the new institutions so that they are able to meet the minimum standards of education and training. According to Armaity S. Desai,

> ...a School [institution of Social Work] not meeting standards could be given a specified period of time, such as two years, when it could be given professional membership, and the School assisted to reach this objective through consultations and loan of faculty from other established schools, or assistance from a school in the same area. Only as we do this vigorously, we will be able to turn out a professional social worker, who is well equipped and whose knowledge and skills are relevant to our society's needs. To achieve tasks, the Association [ASSWI] needs a standing committee on curriculum, and another on minimum standards and accreditation of Schools (1973: 10).

Senior educator Ms. Pinto of Nirmala Niketan, Mumbai said that, apart from ensuring minimum standards, professional bodies should maintain the academic rigour in social work profession. This can be done by creating a common platform for social work academicians and practitioners to come together in conferences and seminars to up-grade their knowledge and skills. Ms. Wankhede of the Karve Institute of Social Service, Pune said that, professional bodies need to promote research on Social Work education and training so that the knowledge base of social work can be up-graded, based on evidence and observation. S.R. Mohsini, in reference to IATSW, stated,

> There is a dearth of indigenous literature on Social Work in India. There is an urgent need to develop indigenous literature on different fields of social welfare. The Association has a plan to select different papers and articles pertaining to various fields for welfare from various Social Work journals and to publish them with a exhaustive introduction after getting them to be roughly edited (1973: 21).

Ms. Kriplani of TISS was of the opinion that, apart from focussing on the higher education in social work, professional bodies should focus on the training of para-professionals through field exercises for skill development. Ms. Swamy of the Karnataka University, Dharwad further added, apart from training of para-professionals, professional bodies should organise refresher courses for trained practitioners so that they can regularly up-grade their knowledge. These issues and concerns have been raised for long but little has been implemented. For example, the role highlighted by Ms. Kriplani and Ms. Swamy above has been discussed by K.N. George more than three decades back,

> Preparing auxiliary personnel and offering orientation, refresher and other types of in-service training programmes to different categories of personnel of Government and voluntary sectors including those occupying developmental positions at higher levels in Government and non-government agencies are the responsibilities of the Association and the Schools (1974: 61).

Professional bodies are often referred to as the gatekeepers of a profession. As social work is struggling to attain a professional status in India, many educators expressed that one of their primary role is to give professional legitimacy to social work, to ensure recognition of social work education as a pre-requisite for social work practice and improving the working conditions of the social work practitioners (Mohsini 1973). For this, professional bodies need to push for a national council of social work on the one hand, and lobby for getting recognition for Social Work as a professional course on the other. In addition, the professional bodies also need to ensure that the national council (if it comes into existence) should be controlled by them rather than being dominated by bureaucrats (Nanavatty 1993).

One supposed role of professional bodies of social work, which had the consensus of most of the Social Work educators, was the formulation of a code of ethics for social work. Ms. Kriplani of TISS, Mumbai observed that currently many social workers are engaged in profit-making activities in the voluntary sector. Such practices are creating a bad name for the profession as well as for the non-government organisations. The professional bodies should develop a code of ethics which should be mandatory for the trained social workers to follow.

Challenges Faced by Professional Bodies of Social Work in India

Most of the professional bodies of social work are either limited to the Social Work educators or are dominated by them. Bodies like ASSWI and MASWE are meant only for academicians and are concerned only with Social Work education and training. Other bodies such as NAPSWI and BATSW are open to social work practitioners as well, but are still dominated by academicians. Senior educator Ms. Pinto of Nirmala Niketan, Mumbai said that the practitioners, especially the para-professionals, feel left out and think that their concerns are not given importance by the professional bodies.

On the other hand, Ms. Wankhede of the Karve Institute of Social Service, Pune said that no regular dissemination of academic information takes place on the part of the professional bodies, and, therefore, educators have lost interest in the activities of the professional bodies. This has fragmented these bodies and rendered them dysfunctional. Senior educator, Ms. Swamy of the Karnataka University, Dharwad said that the challenges faced in the establishment and functioning of professional bodies of social work were neither addressed by the pioneers of Social Work and TISS nor was the authority and responsibility of the leadership passed to other institutions of Social Work. Similarly, senior educator Ms. Bhatnagar of the University of Delhi observed that, as social work was a growing profession, many educators competed to occupy key positions in the professional bodies, and, therefore, the more important roles that these bodies should have taken up got lost in the politics of power. This resulted in a lack of solidarity and the professional bodies became dysfunctional in the course of time.

Ms. Swamy of the Karnataka University, Dharwad and Mr. Gangte of the Assam University, Silchar also raised the concern with respect to the cultural diversity of India and the location of institutions of Social Work in different parts of the country. According to them, the cultural differences and the diverse environment of social work practice did not give way to a common understanding of social work and the people could not come together in a national-level professional body. Consequently, they could not arrive at a consensus with respect to the roles of these bodies; different regions came up with state level professional bodies to address their specific concerns, rather than looking at some uniformity at the national level. However, senior educators who have been involved in the professional bodies argue that professional bodies have become dysfunctional because of lack of financial support from anywhere and lack of political support from the government. In addition, social work fraternity is so scattered in the country and they are so busy in their individual work that there is no time for them to come together and promote the growth and development of the professional bodies.

From the above discussion on the development of social work as a profession and the different viewpoints on the professional bodies, two points of consensus among social work educators, whether they support a professional status for social work or not, can be highlighted. Firstly, there is no objection on the development of a code of ethics for social work fraternity. And, secondly, the need for maintaining quality education and training of Social Work is widely recognised. But one point that did not emerge clearly from the reflections of the educators on professional aspect of social work was clarification in terms of the practice component. A strong critique that senior educators (who view social work as a profession) have against radical social work is that students, even if they are influenced by the radical perspective, do not end up practising the same after the completion of the master's programme. If the question is about a job in the end, then the professional status can facilitate that process. In case some students do want to take up activism, they are free to do so as citizens of the country; the social work profession, thus, only sets boundaries for the profession and not for individuals. The educators who oppose professional status for social work counter this critique by saying that it is the irony of our time due to the extremely powerful role of the market: the framework that we oppose ironically becomes the framework of our operation!

Summary

The case for professional status has been perennially debated on in social work, especially in India. This debate is rooted in the different viewpoints that exist vis-à-vis the purpose of social work practice and the role played by Social Work education and training in developing different perspectives on it. Of late, these viewpoints have at least converged on one point, that is, the promotion of social justice. Therefore, the International Federation of Social Workers has come up with an all-encompassing definition of social work that has been widely accepted by the social work fraternity all over the world.

Historically, after social work started to emerge as a scientific activity, it developed different methods of intervention. The theoretical domain always played a supportive role in providing an understanding of the different situations that social workers encountered in practice. The dominance of a particular ideology and forms of society during different points in time has influenced the development of social work whether it was the functionalist perspective in the Victorian England, or community living in India, or the individualistic spirit in USA, or the plurality propagated by postmodernist ideologues in current times. Social work fraternity being a part of the larger society has time and again adapted to the changes in the existential conditions. One of the perennial concerns for the social work fraternity that has been under discussion over the decades is the professional status of social work. In the West, social work is recognised as a profession, which permits only licensed practice in limited boundaries for professionally trained social workers. This growth of social work as a profession has been supplemented by the professional bodies of social work that are responsible for maintaining the ethical standards for social work practice.

However, in India social work is not yet fully recognised as a profession. Different people share different opinions with respect to the professional status of social work. But, despite this, efforts have been made to establish professional bodies of social work to promote the growth and development of social work as a profession. The different roles of these professional bodies have been identified as follows: (a) maintaining and enhancing the quality of social work education in India, (b) promoting the establishment of a national council of social work, (c) developing a code of ethics for the professional social workers, (d) facilitating training of para-professionals, and (e) creating employment opportunities for social workers. Simultaneously, these bodies have also faced numerous challenges, as there are many people who do not support the view of developing social work as a profession. Some of these arguments or apprehensions include: (a) creation of hierarchy among educators, trained practitioners, and para-professionals, (b) lack of space for creativity and innovation in social work as professionalization would set boundaries for social work practice, (c) professional bodies catering more to individual interests rather than promoting the goal of social justice, and (d) lack of rigour in these bodies to promote academic interests of the educators.

NOTES

1. Social Work spelt with capital 'S' and 'W' refers to social work education and training, that is, social work as an academic discipline.

7

Social Work Education

Educating for Social Change

Namita Jainer

Social work profession emerged in the context of western society as a response to industrialisation. It is being argued by a section of academia that the development of the professional social work education and training has been imported from western universities. The landmark that marked this development was the establishment of the first School of Social Work namely Sir Dorabji Tata Graduate School of Social Work (now Tata Institute of Social Sciences) in Bombay in 1936. It was established under the leadership of Dr. Clifford Manshardt of the American Marathi Mission. The vision for the institution was to prepare trained manpower which was properly equipped with the knowledge and skills of social work required to bear varied kinds of responsibilities in the field of social welfare. The School was primarily based on the pattern of Schools of School Work in the United States of America and the American influence still pervades the social work education in India (Mandal, 1989). The model of Social Work that was imported was the individual oriented professional model (Pathak, 1981a, 1981b; Mandal, 1989). This was found to be highly unsuited to the needs and conditions of Indian society (Khinduka, 1971; Nagpaul, 1972, 1993; Bose, 1992; Hall & Midgley, 2004). Thus, there was a need felt in India for developing indigenous literature on social work (Nagpaul, 1972, 1993) so that social problems and social issues in India can be addressed in a contextualised way.

The second social work education institution was established in 1946 almost a decade after establishment of the first school. It came up in Lucknow under the auspices of the National YWCA. Later, it moved to Delhi and was named Delhi School of Social Work, affiliated as a graduate school to the University of Delhi for the Masters of Arts degree in social work. In 1979, it merged with the university as one of its departments for administrative purposes. There has been no looking back since then. Numerous educational institutions have opened up to provide social work training and education in order to prepare social work professionals for social work practice ad research.

In order to ensure quality standards among these proliferating social work education institutions, the Association of Social Work in India was established in 1959 by drawing parallels with the American model and its Council of Social work Education (CSWE), with the object of establishing and enforcing minimum standards of social work education (Singh, 2004). Social work education has received the attention of University Grants Commission (UGC) twice till date. This has led to the appointment of two review committees on social work education in the 1960s and 1975 (Pathak, 1981). The latest of UGC's endeavour in enhancing the quality of social work education has been the preparation of UGC model curriculum, 2001.

Thus, it can be noted that Schools of Social Work are increasingly being recognized and held responsible for training and preparing social work professionals. In this context, the role of social work education in training of social work professionals is of utmost significance. It needs to be understood that social work education is a broad and comprehensive concept that encompasses theory, classroom teaching, field work, research projects, term paper assignments, co-curricular activities, individual and group conferences etc. Rather, it can also be taken as a sum total of all the activities aimed at training students to become social work professionals to do social work practice and also research.

According to the joint statement of the International Association of Schools of Social Work (IASSW) and International Federation of Social Workers (IFSW), "the social work profession promotes social change, problem solving in human relationships and the empowerment and liberation of people to enhance well-being. Utilising theories of human behaviour and social systems, social work intervenes at the points where people interact with their environments. Principles of human rights and social justice are fundamental to social work (IASSW-IFSW, May 2001)." This definition brings forth the agenda of "social change"- both for social work practice as well as social work education. It is this agenda of "social change" (Hudson, 1985) to meet the ideals of "human rights and social justice" that must guide schools of social work to prepare social work professionals by transmitting requisite social work knowledge, skills, values and ethics. Social work values, professional standards and curriculum guidelines (UGC model curriculum for social work education, 2001) bestow schools of social work with the responsibility of teaching students about racism, sexism, hetero-sexism and other forms of oppression as also values of social justice (Raske, 1999). These perspectives are an essential ingredient in the training of social workers for professional practice to aid the empowerment of marginalised and oppressed groups.

Much of the social change that needs to be brought in our society pertains to the discriminatory social cultures due to certain attitudes, prejudices and stereotype towards certain groups like women, dalits, Tribals, persons with HIV, persons with disability and religious groups like Muslims. Most of the times social work students who come to the programme for training are very much a part of the same social structures and discriminatory social cultures. Entrants to social work may carry with them stereotypical responses on gender issues, caste and religious groups and may become perpetrators of the same oppressive structures which social work profession works to change. We as educators must recognize that organizing for social change reflects the connection between the classroom and the world outside it (Vinton & Nelson-Gardell, 1993; Taylor, 1994).

Social workers, thus, must be trained to put aside their biases. Yet, they are at risk of holding on to their previous held beliefs, until exposed to concerted training which enables them to question discriminatory and oppressive structures. Exposure to philosophy and ethics of social work, coupled with human right perspectives, may generate in students a process of introspection (Gandhi, 2004). So, Social work education needs to also focus on lot of "unlearning" rather than learning. This has to do with unlearning the discriminatory of seeing, unlearning the discriminatory ways of understanding and unlearning the discriminatory ways of living in the society. Consequently, they will weigh field experiences against their own socialization.

In this endeavour, the most important and challenging task at this stage of training and educating in social work knowledge, values and skills is to develop critical thinking and reflective thinking among the students so that students develop the ability to question the discriminatory structures which they were part of by questioning the discriminatory status quo. Developing critical thinking is the only means to initiate students into process of introspection and reflection. Critical thinking also provides an ongoing opportunity to social work students and practitioners to refine their skills and rectify their own biases. As a result of such intense training their biases may be located and rectified say for example by engaging students through intense dialogues. It should be noted that in order to aid in the empowerment of others, social workers must feel empowered themselves. Dore cited in Taylor (1994) identifies the parallels between student learning and social work practice. There are important research questions here—if students are empowered in their practice learning will they practise in an empowering way?

Critical and reflective thinking cannot be achieved in a traditional classroom where teacher adopts "banking model of education" and denies accepting students as possible resources for knowledge generation. Freire (2007) pointed out that 'Without dialogue there is no communication and without communication there can be no true education' (pp 92-93). Thus, the right kind of pedagogic approach is central to evoking critical thinking among the students. Feminist Pedagogy and Critical Pedagogy is the prerequisite to initiate students in critical and reflective thinking (Taylor, 1994; Pennell & Ristock, 1999; Madan, 2011). Ledwith (2001) defines 'Critical pedagogy is that form of education which emerges from critical compassion; a transcendence of emotional and the intellectual; the heart and mind learn to see and know in new ways. It requires liberation of the mind, the courage to act and the confidence to connect-autonomy, agency and alliance; and the beginning of this transformative project lies in simply 'extraordinarily experiencing the ordinary'.

Critical pedagogy can also be considered as 'that particular type of pedagogy which is concerned with issues concerning social difference, social justice, and social transformation' (Mayo cited in Ledwith, 2001). The three primary goals of feminist and critical pedagogy, of empowering all participants, developing a classroom community, and enhancing leadership capacities, provide a framework for teaching and learning social work practice (Dore cited in Taylor, 1994). Students also have the realization of the capacity to take responsibility for one's learning.

Kevin Harris in the book titled "Education and Knowledge: the structured misrepresentation of reality" provides a good account of how influences of ideology on knowledge framework perpetrate themselves, ways to attack such ideology if it is not in line with human rights values and also possibilities for consciousness-raising through education to promote social justice in its introductory chapter, Harris emphatically questioned that is 'knowing and interpreting the world' gives out a 'detailed examination of what is involved in coming to know the world' and the role of formal education in provision and structuring of our knowledge. In this deliberation, the author dwells on various debates in the realm of knowledge. The first debate is at the philosophical level about the nature of relationship between the *knower* and the object to be *known*. The author puts forth two extreme philosophical positions of idealists like Plato, Leibnitz, and Berkeley and Kant and that of extreme materialists like Bergson in the western philosophical thought about the nature of this relationship. The author calls both these positions as untenable. The second debate is about the predominance of empiricist-intuitivist model of knowledge generation of science and its application to social science. The author questions this positivist culture of knowledge generation and shares the view that "there is no such thing as 'given non-theoretical knowledge'. In line with this discussion the author presents his views about how theory and concepts always precede investigation. According to him, "each method of investigation is theory-laden". The conception of nature of reality and our belief systems (ontology) guide our study of knowledge (Epistemology), influence our investigation and also our methodologies of investigation. Thus, the gathering of the data is theory dependent and not theory free. The author further questions the empiricist and positivist regard for "sensory experience" by bringing to attention the various ways in which our sensory experience is filtered like flaws in sensory perception, bodily adaptations, selective noticing, delusions, prejudice, previous conceptions, experience and mental sets. These filtrations mechanisms are directly related to historical and social circumstances that guides a person's interaction with the world. At the end of chapter the author poses a very significant question, "If instances or phenomena can be picked out by many theories (even competing and conflicting one), and so be interpreted in many different ways, on what grounds can we judge any particular interpretation to be the best or correct one?" According to the author, the best possible is the best interpretation of any phenomenon is that which is given by the best available theory and thus in the next chapter the author sets on to the task of charting out the criteria for a good theory.

The second chapter is "Theory and critical preference". In this chapter the author emphasises that in an attempt to choose the good theory, "we must necessarily adopt a theoretic stance ourselves". Further the author using ideas of Lakatos on fitness of scientific theory delineates criteria for selecting a good ideology as follows—

(i) Ideologies are not be judged with regard to their 'fit' with observed instances
(ii) Ideologies can be judged only in a historical context with reference to their preceding and contemporary rivals
(iii) Ideologies can be judged by or in terms of other ideologies
(iv) Ideologies deserve our favourable judgement to the extent that they are progressive

The author further builds on this framework using Marxian historical materialism. This analysis emphasises on the social dimension of knowledge production and calls this entire engagement as 'Knowledge as Production'. The third chapter of the book is 'Ideology'. This chapter details the ways in which ideology functions and discusses the ways in which structured misinterpretation of reality is carried out. Ideology is defined by the author as a perception of the world as seen from a particular from a particular standpoint. The authors makes an effort to bring the ways in ideology can be misrepresentative, thus needs critical judgement. According to the author, one of the reasons for this misrepresentation is selfdelusion and acceptance of this delusion by means of behavioural defence mechanisms. Another important reason is the power structure and ruling interests which exert control over knowledge communities and all public knowledge. The role discusses the role of institutions which strengthen and legitimise the status quo as also the role of supportive rhetoric in maintaining the received view. In the end of the chapter the author describes ideology as a context of lived experience within the ideological matrix which determines consciousness of the person. Ideology is described as historical, theoretical and political production.

In the fourth chapter that is 'attacking ideology', the author discusses options to counter ideological motives. The first step is to have orientation to begin with by recognising the ideological and by being critical off the ideological. Mystification and false consciousness are the tools and ways in which ideology perpetrates. Mystification is an instrument of disguise and to cloak relationship between people and people as people and the world. False consciousness is about living with a distorted view without questioning it. The next step to attacking ideology is giving space for internal contradictions and dialectics. Both these are powerfully counter-ideological.

The next chapter in the book titled 'education' discusses how education is a tool for political manipulation and serves the ruling interests. This book mentions this particularly in relation to school education. Thus we all must recognize education both as a site for struggle and as a tool for change-making (Madan, 2011). We must acknowledge that the classroom is a site of gender, race, and class inequalities, and simultaneously a site of political struggle and change. But it is also true that teaching and learning have the potential to bring about liberation (Briskin & Coulter, 1992; Taylor, 1994)

'Possibilities', the last chapter of the book, the author uses Freire's ideas about consciousness-raising. The role of education and liberatory pedagogy are also discussed to look for possibilities of change. This is of particular relevance to social work. Say for example, a proposed task to students in the form of written assignment can be given to students where they develop acceptance of difference by exploring their own ethnic, social and culturally determined beliefs and values, and compare these with other students from a different ethnic origins. It may reveal how relationship barriers can be culturally driven. Embracing narrative, by the exchange and validation of individual stories and voices has the potential to broaden the educational field for social work students. Students can reflect through narrative forms of inquiry as such platforms can provide platform to reflect on their biases, prejudices, needs, values, and life experiences and how these affect their work. It is clear that postmodern emphasis on selfreflexivity would translate into a greater emphasis on social worker's development of self (Pennell & Ristock, 1999; Brown, 2012).

This book in essence serves as an eye opener to ideological formulations 'legitimise the ways and perspectives by which and from which we shall come to know the world'. It lends us an understanding that there is requirement to emphasise the need of a clearly stated value framework for social work education bereft of dehumanising ideological influences-both stated and hidden in order to promote values of human rights and social justice. We must provide an environment conducive to fostering reflective and critical thinking to counter oppression, discrimination and subjugation (Morley, 2008; Redmond, 2010).

8

Field Work Practicum in Social Work Education

Atul Pratap Singh

Social work is the applied social science which prepares students for achieving its objectives through interventions in real life situations involving class room teaching and field work practice learning. Thus, field work is an integral part of social work education. It is a closely supervised educational internship programme in social work education that provides planned opportunities to apply theory taught in class room to actual field situations which in turn enhances the learning of students. In field work, theoretical understanding is increased and translated into practice. Since, social work is a practice profession, hence the contents offered are of vital significance in practice learning opportunities. In fact, field work practice learning is the back bone of social work education. It is a dynamic process of creative and innovative ideas, devices and techniques. It fosters the development of professional attitude of students.

In the last two decades, a sea of change has taken place in the economic, political and social realities across the globe. The social work profession could not have remained unaffected by these changes. The increasing complexities of life today have compelled us to hunt for new ways to help the needy and strife ridden humanity. Professional social work is gradually enhancing its boundaries to include new and challenging areas of practice. With the changing socio-economic realities, the functional role of social workers is now seen in new dimension. The field work practicum in social work education has not been developed as it should have been. In fact, it should have earned the status of an independent profession because of its specialty, i.e. concurrent field work training. But, unfortunately the social work educators seem to have failed in reaching the core of the training. Though, theory classes in certain fields are well organized and comprehensive but practical experience offered in these fields is very elementary. So, it suffers from the lack of integration between theory and practice.

Different schools and departments of social work have developed their own programmes of field work depending upon the kind of agencies and opportunities available in the area and the differences in curriculum and fields of specialization. If we compare the field work requirements of different schools and departments of social work, we find a wide variation not only in terms of focus, organization, structure, approach, but also dissimilarity in commitment, operationalization, training duration and expected output. Moreover, it seems that sufficient efforts have also not been made by the concerned persons to develop it according to the needs of the society and also for making the students perfect in their chosen profession. Relevant and sufficient practical-oriented literature on field work has not been produced by the educators in our country. However, some of them have made attempt in this area.

Therefore, the students are unable to understand the proper use of social work methods, skills, techniques, principles and values in the actual field settings. Even most of the time, faculty members, especially those who have been in the newly established Universities and/or departments are confused about the modalities related to field work, such as—How to begin the field work? How to complete it? How to supervise the students? What should be the criteria to evaluate the students? This paper presents SMART objectives for field work practicum in order to answer all such questions.

Social Work: A Distinct Discipline

Social work is the applied social science of intervening into social problems at individual, group, and community level to achieve an effective level of social functioning and wellbeing of people and bringing about social change for social and human development through empowerment, advocacy and social justice in order to reduce dependency of people (Verma and Singh, 2011). As a professional discipline, social work prepares its students for achieving the objectives through interventions in real life situations which are dynamic in nature and therefore, demand an individualized attention, keeping in view with peculiar characteristic features. For the purpose of preparation of trained man power for social work profession, formal education and training, like other various human service professions such as—medical, nursing, education etc., are being imparted through the network of educational institutions created at higher level in Universities and Colleges. In other words, social work education is formally provided either through independent schools or colleges affiliated to the Universities recognized by the UGC or through the specially created departments of social work functioning as a part and parcel of the University system. Social work education is provided at Under-graduate, Post-graduate, M. Phil., Doctoral and Post-doctoral levels. Social work education is comprised of class room teaching and field work practicum. The class room teaching is directed towards familiarizing the students with principles and skills required for social work intervention and developing students' personality through inculcation of democratic and humanitarian attitudes and values. Field work practicum is agency based as well as community based practice in which students are engaged in different types of work relating to the rendering of remedial and rehabilitative services and promoting development with justice. The curriculum in social work with regard to field work practice is assigned to both under-graduate and post-graduate students with more or less same objectives.

There are several distinct features, which make social work profession a unique type of assistance aiming towards solving the problems of individuals, families and groups and communities through enhancing social functioning, which are as follows:

- (i) It has a unique educational programme involving classroom teaching and field work practice learning.
- (ii) Relationship is the key in the social work intervention process.
- (iii) It has an orientation in psychiatric concepts and has taken much from psychology and sociology. Besides, it is also indebted to economics, political science, public administration and law etc.
- (iv) It emphasizes on social interaction and resultant social functioning and malfunctioning.
- (v) Its aim is to help individuals, families and groups and communities to help themselves.
- (vi) It believes in the basic worth and dignity of every human being.
- (vii) Supervision is the tool for developing professional attitude, skills understanding of social phenomena.

Field work is an integral part of social work education. It is the field training that differentiates social work from other social sciences. Field work practice learning helps the students to put theory into practice. In other words, what is learnt in the class room could be verified in practice through field work. The goal of field work is to help the students to acquire skills of working with people in problems besides enabling them to integrate theoretical learning in the class room with field work practice. In the field, students are helped in developing the understanding of issues, problems, various situations, causative factors and interventions towards solution of the problems and fulfilment of needs of the people.

Meaning and Definition of Field Work

The field work may be defined as a planned educational experience in a social welfare, social service and social development settings, which provide for practice component of the field education curriculum. Two definitions of field work in social work are as follows:

1. According to Brown and Gloyne "Any kind of practical experience in a social organization or agency if this experience has been

deliberately arranged for the education of students who are undertaking courses partly or wholly designed for those who intend to become social workers" (1966).

2. According to R.R. Singh "Field work in social work education is a guided interaction process between a student and the actual life situation in which social work as a profession has an abiding and deep concern and which needed to be remedied, improved or changed for a fuller development of human-environmental potential" (1985).

Nature of Field Work

Field work training started as field instruction with apprenticeship in social agencies. The tasks given then were similar to the craftsman's task and there was a dichotomy between administrative and non-administrative skills. Field work has been seen as an integrating factor, which acts as a balancing force between the theory and practice. The blend of theory with practice, facilitates fusion of thinking with doing, combines philosophy with action, integrates understanding about people and methods of helping them. Its techniques draw heavily on scientific knowledge about people and social phenomena. It is functional in nature and technical in process. It involves an educational process that fosters learning in students. It is an integrated approach that goes concurrently with the classroom instructions (Maurya, 1962).

Field work programme provides an opportunity to the learner to apply his/her theoretical knowledge taught in the classroom appropriately in different practical situations. It serves a kind of social laboratory where a student is taught to test his/her theoretical knowledge and skills against practical situations of social living. Therefore, field work is a way to translate knowledge through certain skills and techniques into action. The importance of field work training in professional social work education is consequential because of its nature of dealing with the problems practically. Field work training is always imparted under the able guidance and supervision of faculty member and also under the supervision of experienced professional social worker in the agency. The student is helped through supervision to help himself for working in a complex, intricate and composite social environment. It would defiantly be unwise to think of theory as being taught only in the classroom and practice of theory as being done only in the field.

Field Work Practicum: Core Competencies

All professional trainings require standardization in terms of knowledge and practice learning of skills besides ethical commitments. Professions are normally regulated by mandatory requirements either by law or through professional organizations or both. Standards issued by Council on Social Work Education on Educational Policy and Accreditation (2008) in US require developing some core competencies. It is expected that upon completion of the social work course, students will be able to demonstrate the integration and application of the following competencies:

Identify as a professional social worker and conduct one-self accordingly: Social workers serve as representatives of the profession, its mission, and its core values. They know the profession's history. Social workers commit themselves to the profession's enhancement and to their own professional conduct and growth.

Apply social work ethical principles to guide professional practice: Social workers have an obligation to conduct themselves ethically and to engage in ethical decision-making. Social workers are knowledgeable about the value base of the profession, its ethical standards, and relevant law.

Apply critical thinking to inform and communicate professional judgments: Social workers are knowledgeable about the principles of logic, scientific inquiry, and reasoned discernment. They use critical thinking augmented by creativity and curiosity. Critical thinking also requires the synthesis and communication of relevant information.

Engage diversity and difference in practice: Social workers understand how diversity characterizes and shapes the human experience and is critical to the formation of identity. The dimensions of diversity are understood as the intersectionality of multiple factors including age, class, colour, culture, disability, ethnicity, gender identity and expression, immigration status, political ideology, race, religion, sex, and sexual orientation. Social workers appreciate that, as a consequence of difference, a person's life experiences may include oppression, poverty, marginalization, and alienation as well as privilege, power, and acclaim.

Advance human rights and social and economic justice: Each person, regardless of position in society, has basic human rights, such as freedom, safety, privacy, an adequate standard of living, health care, and education. Social workers recognize the global interconnections of oppression and are knowledgeable about theories of justice and strategies to promote human and civil rights. Social work incorporates social justice practices in organizations, institutions, and society to ensure that these basic human rights are distributed equitably and without prejudice.

Engage in research-informed practice and practice-informed research: Social workers use practice experience to inform research, employ evidence-based interventions, evaluate their own practice, and use research findings to improve practice, policy, and social service delivery. Social workers comprehend quantitative and qualitative research and understand scientific and ethical approaches to building knowledge.

Apply knowledge of human behaviour and the social environment: Social workers are knowledgeable about human behaviour across the life course; the range of social systems in which people live; and the ways social systems promote or deter people in maintaining or achieving health and well-being. Social workers apply theories and knowledge from the liberal arts to understand biological, social, cultural, psychological, and spiritual development.

Engage in policy practice to advance social and economic well-being and to deliver effective social work services: Social work practitioners understand that policy affects service delivery, and they actively engage in policy practice. Social workers know the history and current structures of social policies and services; the role of policy in service delivery; and the role of practice in policy development.

Respond to contexts that shape practice: Social workers are informed, resourceful, and proactive in responding to evolving organizational, community, and societal contexts at all levels of practice. Social workers recognize that the context of practice is dynamic, and use knowledge and skill to respond proactively.

Engage, assess, intervene, and evaluate with individuals, families, groups, organizations, and communities: Professional practice involves the dynamic and interactive processes of engagement, assessment, intervention, and evaluation at multiple levels. Social workers have the knowledge and skills to practice with individuals, families, groups, organizations, and communities. Practice knowledge includes identifying, analyzing, and implementing evidence-based interventions designed to achieve client goals; using research and technological advances; evaluating programme outcomes and practice effectiveness; developing, analyzing, advocating, and providing leadership for policies and services; and promoting social and economic justice (CSWE, 2008).

SMART Objectives for Field Work Practicum

The goal of field work is achieved by placing the students under the supervision of a faculty member in the Department as well as professionally trained social worker in the agency. In other words, a student is blessed with two supervisors: (a) Department Supervisor; and (b) Agency Supervisor. A faculty member who provides guidance and supervision to the students at Department level is called department supervisor. He/she normally has the responsibility of supervising field work, developing symbiosis between theoretical knowledge and inculcating professional values and ethics of the practice of social work (Doel and Shardlow, 2005). He/she is in a strategic position to meet students in the field as well as during the supervisory conferences. S/he is also gets in touch with the agency supervisor and other agency authorities when he/she makes field visits. He/she is also expected to give suggestions and feedback to students to improve their performance based on the feedback from the agency supervisors as well as from his/her own observation during field visit and also from the field work reports submitted by the students. He/she has to respond promptly to agency supervisors as well as to students to solve the problems and implement changes in the field work if necessary.

Supervision by the department faculty should not be merely a mechanical and monotonous probing into the work as is done by an inspector, but it is a process of sharing the facts and situations between the two person, as a result of which the student is gradually able to develop and function effectively on his/her own level. A department supervisor should be able to create a sense of trust and confidence in the student towards the supervisor so that the student feels free to communicate and by the recognition of positive factors should be able to eliminate the weak points in his/her functioning. In the course of supervision, he/she should be able to imbibe the qualities of regularity sincerity, honesty, uprightness, etc. and should be able to inculcate these sovereign qualities in the students not by preaching but by his/her own example.

Field work is subjected to continuous process of evaluation in the course of individual conferences between department supervisor and students. The evaluation of field work should be unbiased. The practice principle of objectivity or evaluating students without bias is closely related to non-judgmentalism. To be objective, supervisors should avoid injecting their personal feelings and prejudices into their relationship with the students. Learning of a student does not follow a progressively linear pattern. The tasks assigned should be structured, specific and clearly defined. The student should be encouraged to participate in the planning and implementing of the programme and to acquire certain programme skills. The tasks should be designed for the students around problems requiring exploration, research, surveys, administrative tasks, programme implementation, training, use of community resources and simple problem solving techniques which are related to the programme (UGC Model Curriculum on Social Work Education, 2001).

The student should be evaluated for his/her efforts and progress from one point/one stage to another in the learning process in the field work. In other words, the evaluation should be based on the student's progress and effort towards problem solving. As mentioned earlier, the field work is a planned opportunity to apply theory to actual field situation. The department supervisor is required to prepare a plan regarding the field work of a student, so that he/she could be able to translate theory in to practice in a meaningful manner.

Traditionally, social workers have provided services and therapy for individuals and families. Within the past two decades, prevention has received considerable emphasis and recently a focus on enrichment in living for all people has surfaced. Today, social work is utilized in a variety of setting and agencies. Some of the important ones are—psychiatric, medical, family counseling, school, rehabilitation, correction, work place, drug abuse, women and child welfare etc. Various schools of social work train a student to work in any agency, giving him/her the generic understanding, skills and attitudes that make it possible to function adequately (Farley *et al.*, 2003).

The author has formulated SMART Objectives and an attempt is made to provide at least some basic ingredients along with supportive annexure for generic nature of field work practice learning which can be easily translated into practice. In the term 'SMART objectives', SMART is not used in the context that we might think it is. SMART is actually an acronym that stands for 'S'-specific, 'M'-measurable, 'A'-achievable, 'R'-realistic, and 'T'-timely. It is a little formula to set goals that we can stick with. These objectives can be for managing performance or for developmental purposes. SMART objectives are quite useful for developing core competencies and professional attitudes. The explanation of SMART as an acronym is as follows:

'S'-Specific: Specific means that the objective is concrete, detailed, focused and well defined. The objective must be straight forward and emphasize action and the required outcome.

'M'-Measurable: It means that the measurement source is identified and we are able to track the actions as we progress towards the objectives. It is important to have measures that will encourage and motivate us on the way as we see the change occurring.

'A'-Achievable: It means that objective need to be achievable. If the objective is too far in the future, we will find difficult to keep motivated and to strive to attain it.

'R'-Realistic: It means that we have the resources to get it done. The achievement of an objective requires resources, such as, knowledge, skills, tools, techniques, equipment etc.

'T'-Timely: It means setting a deadline for the achievement of the objective. The deadline needs to be both achievable and realistic. (http://rapid.com/writesmartobjectives)

Increasingly, many organizations are using the SMART acronym in goal setting and performance appraisal or management environments. The use of SMART objective formatting is not limited to business and performance management only. It can be implemented successfully in field work practicum also.

As far as the contents are concern, this paper explores five SMART objectives and their core areas separately. It also offers tasks for each objective that can be assigned to the students. Further, the paper explores the expectations from/of students on each objective. Moreover, this paper also presents some performance indicators and means for evaluation of field work separately for each objective based on tasks assigned to it.

Objective-1: Develop an Understanding about Agency/Community

Core Areas: The core areas are—knowledge about agency and/or community; its structure, functioning, area of operation; policies and programmes, activities, service delivery system, resources available within the agency and/or community, client groups, networking with other organizations etc.

Tasks to be assigned: The tasks include—get a self-orientation about agency and/or community, prepare agency and/or community profile, on-job training at agency and/or community, frequently reporting to agency supervisor and other concerned persons etc.

Expectations from Student: The expectations from the students are—get familiar with the agency functioning, develop maturity in dealing with day-to-day administrative work related to service delivery system of the agency.

Expectations of Student: The expectations of the students may be—some relevant write-ups, tools, time slot to interact freely with agency supervisor and other concerned persons, cooperation at agency and/or community level.

Performance Indicators: The performance indicators are—depth of knowledge about agency and/or community, capability to handle given situations independently, acceptance and popularity among agency staff and/or community people, credibility etc.

Means for Evaluation: The means for evaluation are—clarity in agency and/or community profile, feedback from agency supervisor through periodic meetings, presentation in group conferences, reports, observation during individual conferences etc.

Objective-2: Acquire Theoretical Knowledge and Develop the Capacity to Translate Theory into Field Practice

Core Areas: The core areas are—understanding of fundamental concepts, philosophy, values, principles, methods, skills, techniques etc.; understanding of legal provisions, policies and programmes related to agency's area of working; participation in various service delivery/intervention processes; and use of referrals etc.

Tasks to be assigned: The tasks include—explore, analyze anddeal with needs/problems of individuals, groups and/or community by using theoretical base of social work.

Expectations from Student: The expectations from the students are—learn and practice social work methods, skills and techniques in the field that are taught in class room.

Expectations of Student: The expectations of the students may be—get some case studies based on practice learning model, clarification of each process by relating it with actual service delivery/intervention etc.

Performance Indicators: The performance indicators are—clarity of theoretical concepts; learning reflections; ability to link theory with field practice; ability to affect individuals, groups and/or community etc.

Means for Evaluation: The means for evaluation are—clarity in conversation during individual conferences, records, presentation in group conference, performance appraisal of field work by the agency supervisor etc.

Objective-3: Develop Skills Required for Professional Practice

Core Areas: The core areas are—build rapport; understand social system and realities, human behaviours; observe and analyze human needs and problems; selection of appropriate means to deal with a given situation through planning and decision making and their implementation etc.

Tasks to be assigned: The tasks include—involve in administrative procedures, programme planning and documentation; work with client system and/or community; use of instructions of supervisors (both department and agency); public relation etc.

Expectations from Student: The expectations from the students are—expression of interest, motivation and involvement in various activities of the agency.

Expectations of Student: The expectations of the students may be—demonstration of role play, success story telling, special lectures and workshops for skill building.

Performance Indicators: The performance indicators are—self appearance and presentation; attentiveness and sensitivity towards tasks; organization of information gathered through interaction and observation; changes take place in the student etc.

Means for Evaluation: The means for evaluation are—rationale of using methodologies, principles and techniques; keep a check on regularity and punctuality; communication patterns (both verbal and written); enrichment in professional growth; capacity for selfdirection etc.

Objective-4: Develop Professional Attitudes, Values and Commitment

Core Areas: The core areas are—adjustment and cooperation with clients, agency staff, co-workers etc.; attentiveness in field work, individual and group conferences, workshops, meetings etc.; submission of reports in time; devotion, commitment and sense of responsibility; ability to work within agency limitations.

Tasks to be assigned: The tasks include—learn to be a part of the team of professionals; to be regular and punctual, participate in programme planning and implementation of various service delivery/intervention processes; perform different tasks related to research, surveys, administrative etc.; honour and respect the appointments with others.

Expectations from Student: The expectations from the students are—perform all assigned tasks in hassle free manner with lots of perfection.

Expectations of Student: The expectations of the students may be—flexible hours of field work, individual and group conferences etc.

Performance Indicators: The performance indicators are—application of methods, skills and techniques in to practice; willingness to accept mistakes and ready to remove them with use of practice-learning instructions; ability to mobilize resources etc.

Means for Evaluation: The means for evaluation are—behavioural patterns; respect towards the commitments with agency, clients, staff, supervisors etc.; clarity in activity/term plan etc.

Objective-5: Documentation Practice

Core Areas: The core areas are—dynamics of/in interaction took place, fact finding from different sources, implementation of plan of intervention/ use of problem-solving processes, observation, analysis, self-evaluation, future planning etc.

Tasks to be assigned: The tasks include—prepare report of all the components of field work separately in prescribed/desired manner.

Expectations from Student: The expectations from the students are — complete all written assignments timely.

Expectations of Student: The expectations of the students may be — liberty to submit records as per own convenience.

Performance Indicators: The performance indicators are—narration of incidences, mode of presentation of facts, ability to write relevant points of observation and analysis of given situations, language and style of report writing, etc.

Means for Evaluation: The means for evaluation are—quality of contents of various records and group conference paper.

The above mentioned SMART objectives are fundamental elements to imbibe the attributes required for a good professionally trained social worker. Rests of the other objectives are auxiliary in nature and spin around these SMART objectives. However, the core area and tasks suggested for each objective can be increased by the schools/departments of social work as per their mission, goal and local conditions and accordingly divided in to different semesters. The school/department supervisor is required to select the tasks systematically and help the students in preparing learning plan.

The students should be assessed for their efforts and progress towards tasks assigned from one point of stage to another in the learning process during the field work. Evaluation of the students' performance should be based upon the learning plan which directly correspondents to the core competencies. Here, it is advised that at the time of assessment, the core areas of each SMART objective may be considered as core competencies. Further, it should be expected that upon completion of the semester, students will be able to demonstrate the integration and application of these core competencies. Then, school/department supervisor will assess the students' progress and accomplishment of tasks. The marks or grades should reflect the students' achievements in terms of completion of the tasks and assignments and demonstration of proficiencies in core competencies.

Conclusion

Thus, it can be said that field work practice learning is the back bone of social work education. It is a dynamic process of creative and innovative ideas, devices and techniques. It fosters the development of professional attitude of students. Supervision is a critical and one of the most important aspects of field work as it influences the quality of service received by the client as well as plans a significant role in the professional development of students. Under the supervision, evaluation is also an important obligation of purposeful field work practice and it is done continuously throughout the session. Here, it is suggested that at the beginning of the field work session, department supervisor and student may prepare a learning plan keeping in mind the above mentioned SMART objectives.

Annexure-1
SMART Objectives

Sl. No.	Objectives	Core Areas	Task to be Assigned	Expectation from Students	Expectation of Students	Performance Indicators	Means for Evaluation
1.	**Develop an Understanding About Agency/ Community**	Knowledge about agency and/or community; its structure, functioning, area of operation; policies and programmes, activities, service delivery system, resources available with in the agency and/or community, client groups, networking with other organizations etc.	Get a self-orientation about agency and/or community, prepare agency and/or community profile, on-job training at agency and/or community, frequently reporting to agency supervisor and other concerned persons etc.	Get familiar with the agency functioning, develop maturity in dealing with day-to-day administrative work related to service delivery system of the agency.	Some relevant write-ups, tools, time slot to interact freely with agency supervisor and other concerned persons, cooperation at agency and/or community level.	Depth of knowledge about agency and/or community, capability to handle given situations independently, acceptance and popularity among agency staff and/or community people, credibility etc.	Clarity in agency and/or community profile, feedback from agency supervisor through periodic meetings, presentation in group conferences, reports, observation during individual conferences etc.
2.	**Acquire Theoretical Knowledge and Develop the Capacity to Translate Theory into Field Practice**	Understanding of fundamental concepts, philosophy, values, principles, methods, skills, techniques etc.; understanding of legal provisions, policies and programmes related to agency's area of working; participation in various service delivery/intervention processes; and use of referrals etc.	Explore, analyze and deal with needs/problems of individuals, groups and/or community by using theoretical base of social work.	Learn and practice social work methods, skills and techniques in the field that are taught in class room.	Get some case studies based on practice learning model, clarification of each process by relating it with actual service delivery/intervention etc.	Clarity of theoretical concepts; learning reflections; ability to link theory with field practice; ability to affect individuals, groups and/or community etc.	Clarity in conversation during individual conferences, records, presentation in group conference, performance appraisal of field work by the agency supervisor etc.
3.	**Develop Skills Required for Professional Practice**	Build rapport; understand social system and realities, human behaviours; observe and analyze human needs and problems; selection of appropriate means to deal with	Involve in administrative procedures, programme planning and documentation; work with client system and/or community; use of	Expression of interest, motivation and involvement in various activities of the agency.	Demonstration of role play, success story telling, special lectures and workshops for skill building.	Self appearance and presentation; attentiveness and sensitivity towards tasks; organization of information gathered	Rationale of using methodologies, principles and techniques; keep a check on regularity and punctuality;

Contd....

Sl. No.	Objectives	Core Areas	Task to be Assigned	Expectation from Students	Expectation of Students	Performance Indicators	Means for Evaluation
		a given situation through planning and decision making and their implementation etc.	instructions of supervisors (both department and agency); public relation etc.			through interaction and observation; changes take place in the student etc.	communication patterns (both verbal and written); enrichment in professional growth; capacity for self direction etc.
4.	**Develop Professional Attitudes, Values and Commitment**	Adjustment and cooperation with clients, agency staff, co-workers etc.; attentiveness in field work, individual and group conferences, workshops, meetings etc.; submission of reports in time; devotion, commitment and sense of responsibility; ability to work within agency limitations.	Learn to be a part of the team of professionals; to be regular and punctual, participate in programme planning and implementation of various service delivery/intervention processes; perform different tasks related to research, surveys, administrative etc.; honour and respect the appointments with others.	Perform all assigned tasks in hassle free manner with lots of perfection.	Flexible hours of field work, individual and group conferences etc.	Application of methods, skills and techniques in to practice; willingness to accept mistakes and ready to remove them with use of practice-learning instructions; ability to mobilize resources etc.	Behavioural patterns; respect towards the commitments with agency, clients, staff, supervisors etc.; clarity in activity/term plan etc.
5.	**Documentation Practice**	Dynamics of/in interaction took place, fact finding from different sources, implementation of plan of intervention/use of problem-solving processes, observation, analysis, self-evaluation, future planning etc.	Prepare report of all the components of field work separately in prescribed/desired manner.	Complete all written assignments timely.	Liberty to submit records as per own convenience.	Narration of incidences, mode of presentation of facts, ability to write relevant points of observation and analysis of given situations, language and style of report writing etc.	Quality of contents of various records and group conference paper.

Section II

Social Work Practice Engagement

9

Strengths Perspectives in Social Work Practice in Mental Health

Abraham Francis

Strengths-based practice refers to the identification of strengths within an individual, family, or community. These strengths are then employed to aid in promoting self-fulfilment and healing in a client. This practice demonstrates a deliberate shift away from language and practice based on a client's deficits or pathology, a widespread approach that has dominated many fields within social science for some time. Focussing on strengths is not, however, a new idea and can be found in the writings and practice of many of our past great philosophical leaders and individual practitioners. (Francis and Pulla, 2014, p. 27). The use of strengths-based practice in the social work context has been extensively researched and promoted over the last thirty years and is becoming formalised as a method of best practice across many disciplines and countries, with global cooperation adding depth to ongoing discussion and practice guidelines.

Strengths-based practice in social work has been an area of practice for quite some time now. The application of this approach has been found in many areas, contexts, and countries. The idea of strengths-based practice has found a great place in the area of mental health and among many mental health social workers. While there has been a critique of the use of this concept, there has been a marked interest among social workers to embrace this philosophical shift in their own areas of practice. A recently edited book on 'Advancing Social Work in Mental Health through Strengths Based Practice' by Francis, Pulla, Clark, Mariscal and Ilango (2014) is a true demonstration of the celebration of the concept used across the world. In this paper, the strengths perspective will be discussed with an emphasis on the application of this approach in the mental health field. In recent years, the Strengths Model has been applied to engage with people with a mental illness. "The strength model of case management offers both a theory and a set of tools and methods designed to help people with psychiatric disabilities to recover and transform their lives, by attaining the goals they set for themselves as the needed personal and environmental resources are identified, secured, and sustained. It is a practice theory that contains structural, supervision, and practice elements developed by Charles Rapp and Richard Goscha at the University of Kansas" (Mariscal, 2014). Their model of strengths-based practice is infused with the recovery vision, as "every contact with a person can be an opportunity for building hope, increasing confidence, and taking steps to create a better life" (Rapp & Goscha, 2011, p. 36).

Strengths-based Practice?

The strengths perspective represents a paradigmatic shift in social work practice that focuses on the strengths, assets, and resources that people and communities have to assist people in achieving their goals and realising their hopes and dreams. This perspective emerged in the early 1980s at the University of Kansas under the leadership of remarkable scholars such as Dennis Saleebey, Charles Rapp, and Ann Weick (Mariscal, 2014). They were able to articulate a set of notions that held promise for multiple client populations, in multiple settings and systems, and using a broader range of methods (Saleebey, 1992; 1997; 2002; 2006; 2009; 2013). It has been largely through their initial and on-going efforts that a wide range of applications have been promoted. The book titled "Advancing Social Work in Mental Health through Strengths Based Practice" reflects some of these. A strengths-based practice encompasses any practice that focuses on facilitating the discovery, exploration, mobilisation, development, and use of the strengths, assets, and resources that people and communities have in order to achieve their goals and realise their dreams and aspirations. It is very important to recognise the inherent qualities of people and communities and to appreciate the diversity of strengths that bring possibilities to practice. Strengths-based practitioners therefore bring possibilities, promises and hopes.

> Strengths-based practice is about helping people realize they have the power to affect their own lives and exert some control in carving out their future. This does not mean that people will not have challenges, struggles, or face difficult barriers in achieving the life they want. This is part of the human condition we all face. The identification and use of strengths is helping people change narratives about themselves and their world so they can navigate the difficulties of life like everyone else (Rapp & Goscha, 2014).

It has also been summarised by Gottlieb as follows

> Strengths-based care does not ignore or negate problems; neither does it turn a blind eye to weakness or deficits. Instead, it uses strengths to balance or overcome them. SBC, at its core, is about looking for what is working and capitalising and mobilising those areas within the person, and in the person's life, that are working. In

> SB, the conversation shifts from "What is wrong?" to "What is right?" and "What has happened or is happening?" to "What is working?" This change in thinking places the problem within the context of what else is happening in a person's life that may directly or indirectly affect how the patient and family are responding to and coping with their challenges (2014, p. 24).

Strengths-based practice is gaining importance in contemporary social work practice in India. In recent years, there have been some publications and research papers that reflected this change in the practice context in India. (Ilango, Francis & Udaikumar, 2012; Francis, 2012; Pulla, 2012; Pulla *et al*, 2012, Shekhar, Ilango & Francis, 2014).

Deficits vs Strengths

What is our focus in practice? Do we see the strengths of our clients? What is our assessment method and how do we provide a service to a client? What are some of the theoretical perspectives? are questions that confront the social worker on a regular basis. While there is an emphasis on evidence based practice, not much has been documented about social work practice showcasing the relevance and significance of this approach particularly in an Indian context. However, in recent years there have been efforts by scholars from both India and Australia to bridge this gap. (Ponnuswami, 2012; Pulla, 2012; Francis; 2012; 2014; Pulla & Francis, 2014).

Kisthardt (1997) highlights that the principles of strengths-based helping as the initial focus in the helping relationship is upon the person's strengths, desires, interests, aspirations, abilities, knowledge, resiliency, and ascribed meaning, not on their deficits, weaknesses, problems, or needs as seen by others. Working from a strengths perspective requires a paradigm shift away from a deficit (problem focused) model of practice to one that aligns with possibility, promise and hope for the future. Drawing out clients capacities will foster "…a growing awareness in both the worker and client of the client's strengths relative to their goals rather than the client's deficiencies relative to their problem" (De Jong & Miller, 1995, p.731). Every person, family, group and community has strengths (Saleebey, 1997). Every person contains "…untapped and often unconscious resources" (Stalker, Levine & Coady, 1999, p.470). By analysing the problems through a strengths perspective, a path is created towards the exploration of future possibilities for the client and his/her family (Saleebey, 1997). This is indeed the real task of the social work practitioner which is both a challenge and an opportunity.

In defining the aims of social work in mental health, the AASW (2008) states that "the purpose of practice is to promote recovery, restore individual, family, and community wellbeing, to enhance development of each individual's power and control over their lives, and to advance principles of *social justice*" (p. 8). The AASW (2008) further highlights that "the domain of social work in mental health is that of the *social context* and *social consequences* of mental illness" (p. 8). At the level of 'social context', this means that social workers must seek to understand "the way each individual's social environment shapes their experience of mental illness and mental health problems" (AASW, 2008, p. 8). A concern with the 'social consequences' of mental illness requires social workers to consider "the impact of mental illness and mental health problems on the individual, the family and personal relationships, and the broader community." (AASW, 2008, p. 8). Finally, advancing the principles of social justice requires social workers to be attendant to, and concerned with, "... issues of stigma and discrimination, of political freedoms and civil rights, of promoting access to necessary treatment and support services, and of promoting consumer and career rights to participation and choice in mental health services" (AASW, 2008, pp. 8-9).

However, as Bland, Renouf and Tullgren (2009) clarify, if the above mentioned aims of social work practice are to be realised, social workers must argue for a broader agenda in mental health. That is, an agenda that looks beyond the dominance of narrow, clinical concepts of illness and treatment, to interventions more inclusive of a variety of practice methods, such as individual counseling, community work, group work, social action, social planning, and social policy. Furthermore, realising the aims of social work practice in the mental health sector requires that social workers draw upon the breadth of the profession's knowledge base (for example, various theories of interventions), as well as the variety of social work skills and values (for example, respectful and empathic working relationships) (AASW, 2008). Combined, these features of practice emphasise the centrality of a social justice and human rights approach to mental health. Charles A. Rapp and Richard J. Goscha (2006), in the second edition of the Strengths Model book, entitled 'The Strengths Model: Case Management with People with Psychiatric Disabilities', have established a guiding text for a paradigm shift in mental health interactions toward greater respect and collaboration. As Patricia Deegan, a leading consumer researcher, notes in the forward (p. viii):

> *In this model, strength is not constructed as some superheroic state of invulnerability. Rather, we learn that even when people present with obvious vulnerabilities, they also have strengths. Their strengths are in their passions, in their skills, in their interests, in their relationships, and in their environments. If mental health practitioners look for strengths, they will find them. After strengths have been identified, the practitioner and the service user can begin to cocreate help that is helpful.*

SBP and Mental Health

According to the International Federation of Social Work (IFSW, 2012) the practice of social work is defined as "Social work addresses the barriers, inequities and injustices that exist in society. It responds to crises and emergencies as well as to everyday personal and social problems. Social work utilises a variety of skills, techniques, and activities consistent with its holistic focus on persons and their environments. Social work interventions range from primarily person-focused psychosocial processes to involvement in social policy, planning and development. These include counselling, clinical social work, group work, social pedagogical work, and family treatment and therapy as well as efforts to help people obtain services and resources in the community". (http://ifsw.org/policies/definition-of-social-work). Interventions also include agency administration, community organisation, and engaging in social and political action to impact social policy and economic development. The IFSW proposed global definition of the social work profession highlights a similar vision.

> "Social work is a practice-based profession and an academic discipline that promotes social change and development, social cohesion, and the empowerment and liberation of people. Principles of social justice, human rights, collective responsibility and respect for diversities are central to social work. Underpinned by theories of social work, social sciences, humanities and indigenous knowledge, social workengages people and structures to address life challenges and enhance wellbeing"(2014, http://ifsw.org/get-involved/global-definition-of-social-work).

The holistic focus of social work is universal, but the priorities of social work practice will vary from country to country and from time to time depending on cultural, historical, and socio-economic conditions. It is in this context that this perspective has been discussed, drawing on the literature from the field and the analysis of its importance in the Indian context. As has been mentioned before, working from a strengths perspective requires a paradigm shift away from a deficit (problem focused) model of practice to one that aligns with possibility, promise and hope for the future. Drawing out clients capacities will foster "…a growing awareness in both the worker and client of the client's strengths relative to their goals rather than the client's deficiencies relative to their problem" (De Jong & Miller, 1995, p. 731). Every person, family, group and community has strengths (Saleebey, 1997). Every person contains "…untapped and often unconscious resources" (Stalker, Levine & Coady, 1999, p. 470). By analysing the problems through a strengths perspective, a path is created towards the exploration of future possibilities for the client and his/her family (Saleebey, 1997).

To help a client rediscover his/her strengths and abilities, social workers are encouraged to convey a positive and optimistic attitude and use an approach based on partnership and collaboration. This will increase the resources available to identify creative options and "...solutions developed collaboratively are more likely to be useful to the service user than those imposed by others...." (Healy, 2005, p. 161). As a practice perspective (Sheafor, *et al.* 1996) the strengths approach takes a different look at the client, his problems and his environment, and it requires a different approach from social workers. This is also echoed when Miley, O'melia & Dubois (2004) stress that practitioners need to re-examine their orientation to practice, their views of client systems and the issues clients represent if the strength perspective is to be applied. According to them (2004), the practice of the strengths perspective will prompt social workers to examine three transitions from problems to challenges, from pathology to strengths, and from a preoccupation with the past to an orientation to the future.

Saleebey (2001) states his view very clearly and forcefully: "The strengths perspective is a dramatic departure from conventional social work practice. Practicing from a strengths orientation means this—everything you do as a social worker will be predicated, in some way, on helping to discover and embellish, explore and exploit clients' strengths and resources in the service of assisting them to achieve their goals, realize their dreams, and shed the irons of their own inhibitions and misgivings, and society's domination." According to him, (2002: 1) practice from a strengths perspective demands a different way of seeing clients, their environments, and their current situations. It is thus a practice perspective radically different from the problem-focused approach and it will take time for social work practitioners to change their mindset—moving from the known to the unknown. Saleebey (1999: 16) points out that strengths-based approaches differ from pathology-based approaches in both their language and the principles that guide and direct practice.

While the strengths-based approach to practice in social work is finding its relevance in many parts of the world, scholars have been working on developing a model that can be applied in the mental health field. The Strengths Model has been articulated and refined by Charles A. Rapp, a social work academic from the USA, for the last thirty years (Rapp, 1993; Rapp, 1998; Rapp & Chamberlain, 1985). The Strengths Model is a model of practice for working in collaboration with people experiencing mental illness, to focus with them on their capacities, interests and goals—instead of emphasising their deficits—in assessment and intervention processes. It is a respectful and optimistic model, encouraging curiosity rather than expert distance on the part of the worker. It was first developed by social workers in the United States, and is largely attributed to Charles A. Rapp for his work over more than two decades developing, refining and promoting this approach. It is a model based on some basic principles, summarized by Rapp (1993) as follows below—

The Strengths Model was based on six fundamental ideas or principles:

1. People with Psychiatric Disabilities can Learn, Grow and Change
2. The Focus is on Individual Strengths Rather than Deficits
3. The Community is Viewed as an Oasis of Resources
4. The Client is the Director of the Helping Process
5. The Worker-Client Relationship is Primary and Essential
6. The Primary Setting for Our Work is the Community (Rapp & Goscha, 2014, p. 36).

Application of SBP in Mental Health

This is a question very often asked by practitioners in the field. The demand here is to identify the protective factors and aim to see a future in the midst of all the problems. It is in this context that the skills, knowledge, and values of the social worker play a major role in working with the client. The following are some tips that may be useful for social work practice with clients (Francis, 2012, p.29).

- Actively listening to client's concerns and problems. "Listen to the client's story, instead of zipping through an assessment protocol. Stories and narratives often contain within their plots and characterizations evidence of strengths, interests, hopes and visions" (Saleebey, 2002 p. 88).
- Solution focused interviewing which aims at facilitating hope, belief and agency. Begin with a 'miracle' question to talk to the client to take "…attention away from difficulties and focus on imagining a future when the problem is solved…" (DeJong & Miller, 1995, p. 731). The following question could be used: "Suppose a miracle happens tonight while you are sleeping. The miracle means that when you awake in the morning the problem is solved. What differences would you notice to tell you that a miracle has occurred?" Describing these differences should help the client to focus on identifying solutions rather than problems and "…develop both an expectation of change and a growing sense of the goals toward which to direct effort" (De Jong & Miller, 1995, p. 731). This is the first step in assisting a client to "…change his identity from one who is overwhelmed or disempowered by problems, to one who is capable of facing and solving the problems." (Saleebey, 2009, p. 113). Another way of identifying the client's strengths is to ask a series of 'exception-finding' questions to explore the past and present successes in relation to where there have been exceptions to problems (De Jong & Miller,

1995). For example: "When things were going well in life, what was different?" (Saleebey, 2009, p. 87).

Further options include (Saleebey, 2009; De Jong & Miller, 1995):

- *Coping questions*: "What makes you get up each day?"
- *Support questions*: "Who are the people that you can rely on if needed?"
- *Esteem questions*: "What achievements are you most proud of?"
- *Possibility questions*: "What are your dreams and future plans?"
- *Survival questions*: "How have you managed things in the past?"
- *Change questions*: "What do you think is necessary for things to change?"

These are processes that are not unknown to the social work profession. It is the sequencing and consequencing that we have to regain control of and needs to find a place in our tool kit for practice. "These thoughts, actions and feelings constitute the client's strengths." and formulate the path to "...client-devised solutions" (De Jong & Miller, 1995, p. 734). By harnessing identified capacities, including those developed from adversity, focus is placed on hope and future possibilities. Particular to the strengths approach, *is asking the miracle question.* This question is asked in many ways, but typically a therapist might ask 'if tonight while you were asleep a miracle happened and it resolved all the problems that bring you here what would you be noticing different tomorrow' (Iveson, 2002, p. 150). Iveson (2002) suggests that the practice of miracle questioning allows the person to draw on their creative thinking in order to create a solution.

Are we Ready to Embrace this Shift in Practice?

Clearly, the Strengths Perspective involves an empowering, healing, and completeness process that demands far more than acquiring new techniques, vocabulary, or protocols. This perspective requires a deep transformation of the practitioner's beliefs and worldview; what we look for, and what we listen for, shift as we focus on potential, possibility, promise, skills, experience, wisdom, assets, knowledge, and the smallest sparkle of hope. As Saleebey (2001) asserts, to embrace a strengths-based approach involves "changing one's heart and mind—a personal paradigm shift" (p. 13). The question is–Are we ready to embrace such a shift in practice? This has implications for social work education, teaching and practice.

Recommendations and Tips for Practice

As a practitioner I have been using this framework in my practice and have found it very encouraging and useful. Being prepared to accept this model of practice is a starting point and to up skill and deepen the knowledge base is the second step. But being open to learning, willing to listen, and ready to relinquish the power base is something each practitioner needs to reflect upon, and it is an ongoing process. There is no magic wand that can fix this, but a personal commitment and passion to engage meaningfully with the people is what is required. In this context, it will be appropriate for the practitioner to consider the following before commencing any work with his/her clients or communities.

1. Have a strong belief in the power of people that they can recover/ change and demonstrate a commitment to service. A deeper awareness, sensitivity, commitment and positive attitude to practice which is grounded in reflective practice.
2. Every interaction with a client/community offers us an opportunity
3. Reflect as to how I can turn this opportunity to engage with clients into one which offers possibilities, promises and hopes.
4. Establish a therapeutic partnership with the client, family, and other networks.
5. Develop open communication, and patient listening with the clients, families and communities.
6. Examine your lens of practice—Is this deficit focused? Or….?
7. Have an understanding that recovery is unique for each person and people may be at various stages of recovery. There is no "one size fits all" approach in recovery.
8. Strengths-based practice is based on the foundation of hope and it is also about nurturing relationships.
9. Encourage and celebrate the achievements of your "clients"/ communities with whom you are working even if it is a small step towards recovery.
10. Willing to learn from your clients. You are not the expert but the clients are. They are experts by their experience.

Conclusion

The strengths perspective is not about discounting problems and ignoring the issues. It is not just about positive thinking. According to Saleebey (2001a), "the ideas about healing, wholeness, and wellness that challenge the medical model; the empowerment and liberation movements within and outside of social work; the evolving resilience research and practice; the assets based community building approaches; the power of mind and health organization approaches to individual and community change; solution focused and narrative approaches to therapy; the research on hope, positive expectations and possibility; all of these extend links to, and embolden the strengths perspective" (p. 221). While there are still debates about the application of these concepts, many social work practitioners who have come in contact with me over the years are of the opinion that strengths-based practice models have really worked for them. However, it must be noted that the strengths perspective does not consist of "only a positive reframing" of a problem, "being nice", or compiling a list of strengths (Early & GlenMaye, 2004; Saleebey, 1996). It refers to a "consistent focus on identifying client strengths and resources and mobilizing resources that directly or indirectly improve the situation" (Early & GlenMaye, 2004, p. 123).

Charlie Rapp and Rick Goscha, haverecently stated:

> ...at the same time, a focus on strengths should never ignore that there are economic and social conditions that affect the wellbeing of those with a mental illness. Poverty, unemployment, discrimination, social exclusion, disparities in health care, etc., can be far more disabling for people than symptoms associated with a mental illness. The Strengths Model was never intended to serve as a comprehensive social, economic, and political agenda. Economic and social policy will continuously need to be evaluated to determine its effect on the wellbeing of those with disabilities. But we cannot wait for economic and social justice to occur before we help people use the power of their own strengths and existing strengths of the community to impact their life. This would be an equal injustice (Rapp & Goscha, 2014, p. 3).

It is important to create an environment for practice in social work—"the helping environment" (Early & GlenMaye, 2004, p. 113). Creating a conducive environment, listening to the stories of your clients and identifying the strengths of the clients are paramount in extending a service to the needs of a client. Rapp (cited in Saleebey, 2006), considers an effective helping relationship as "purposeful, reciprocal, friendly, trusting, and empowering" (p. 80), and with positive expectations. Indeed, as Saleebey (1997) states, the role of the social worker is to help to create a dialogue of strength, in which the strengths based practitioner "becomes a translator who helps people see that they already possess much of what they need to proceed on their chosen path" (Weick *et al*, 1989, p. 354).

The strengths perspective demands social workers to change from a pathology-focused paradigm to a possibility-focused paradigm. This shift is more than theoretical; it demands a deep inner transformation (Pulla, 2012). They need to offer hope, promises and possibilities. It is within this context that the social worker is called upon to examine one's own values, aspirations and theoretical frameworks for practice. This critical reflection along with a will to positively engage with people can inspire, and instil hope in people's lives. As Saleebey (2001b) insists, "to embrace a resilience/Strengths Model is not just a matter of acquiring some new techniques or a different vocabulary… it is a matter of changing one's heart and mind—a personal paradigm shift" (p. 13). The real belief in the client's capacity for change is what makes the difference. Indeed, the strengths perspective demands practitioners to adopt a different way of looking at individuals, families, and communities. As Steven Onken says so beautifully "when you change the way you look at things, the things that you look at changes" (2012).

> All must be seen in the light of their capacities, talents, competencies, possibilities, visions, values, and hopes, however dashed and distorted these may have become through circumstance, oppression, and trauma. The strengths approach requires an accounting of what people know and what they can do, however inchoate that may sometimes seem (Saleebey, 1996, p. 297).

This may seem to be a difficult job and one may find it difficult to practice or to embrace this ideological framework. There is no easy solution to this. But one must be prepared to expect the unexpected in practice, especially in working with people and communities that are vulnerable and marginalised. Embracing strengths-based perspectives allows you to see it from a different lens, that focusses on strengths and possibilities that can provide hope to people. This process allows them to take control of their lives. "Social workers interested in the strengths perspective need to engage in a personal process of analysis and transformation, recognizing that this will be a continuous process, recognizing signs of the traditional framework in their practice, becoming aware of themselves and their attitudes, biases, and limitations, and defining a new position for themselves in the helping relationship, that is, removing their "expert" hats and acknowledging the client's expertise, knowledge, and capabilities" (Pulla, 2012, p.15). This shift in focus, practice, and approach certainly has the potential to affect the lives of many people with whom we come in contact in our professional practice. Much is to be done in this area of practice and research and it is our own responsibility to document what we do and share such stories with others so that we can create a helping environment, and develop evidence for practice which will not only be beneficial for our clients but will also enhance the accreditation of the profession.

10

Spiritually Sensitive Social Work

An Emerging Model of Practice

Jaimon Varghese

Spiritual quest is intrinsic to human being. Spirituality is an integral dimension of human life. Men and women across the world spend a considerable time and resources in spiritual endeavours. Besides motivating to form spiritual and religious movements, this quest has enhanced to commitment for just, inclusive and sustainable societies. The recently held international conference on spiritually and social work at Ahmednagar has reemphasized the role of spirituality in enhancing social commitment. Spirituality has ever been the chief motivator for social entrepreneurs who have contributed towards the social, economic and cultural development of various societies across the world. People seek solutions to their problems in spiritual and religious sectors of life. Social work profession which is basically a helping activity cannot ignore these aspects of human life. On the other hand, it is better to integrate the spiritual aspects in their professional practice. It is an emerging model of social work practice. It has almost well established in the west. India, having a rich religious and spiritual heritage, has great scope for developing a new concentration (specialization) of spiritually sensitive social work. This paper highlights various dimensions of spiritually sensitive social work and attempts to frame syllabus for an elective paper on spirituality sensitive social work.

Spirituality and Spiritually Sensitive Social Work

Some literature has been reviewed to convey the significance of spirituality in the lives of human beings. Humans live by ideas and ideals. It can be found that everyone on this earth is in search for some great ideas and ideals to orient their lives. The idea of 'God' has always fascinated people of every nation. *'Millions of people had loved God and have let that love purge their souls, without knowing in the least how to define God. All they have needed is the firm conviction that God is good, and God is love – by no means the kind of concept which a scientist could approve. But our ideals are the jumping-off ground for new adventures in living, not for new discoveries of science. And for that purpose it is enough that we should grasp just a little of the reality which the ideal embraces* (Urwick EJ, 1948). This firm conviction became the basis of human spirituality in the past. Such spirituality is the foundation of the major world religions. Till recently, spirituality apart from the belief in God was seldom discussed. By the turn of the new millennium, spirituality is being considered independent of the belief in God or religion.

Today spirituality is considered as a matter of 'meaning making'. Spirituality is part of our world view and the frame of reference for everything on this earth. Our life is very much influenced by our spirituality. I would like to define spirituality operationally. It is different from the general understanding of the common man. Spirituality is that sense within us which gives meaning to my life, my relationships with everything else in this world. *'It (spirituality) includes our sense of order and chaos, our understanding of good and evil, and our belief in the form of a higher power. It finds expression the way we choose to live our lives. Spirituality takes the form of religious expression for some, but not for others* (Wanda Wagler Martin, 2005: 136).

In this context, we need to differentiate religion from spirituality. Common men use them interchangeably. They share several things in common. However, what makes them different to each other is more important in the context of this paper. There is an intuitive knowledge in both. Both the religion and spirituality involves an experience of the transcendence, something extraordinary. It is important to understand that religion is the institutional aspect of spirituality, while spirituality is the soul of every religion. They are different in the sense that, *spirituality is a personal connection with the universe and religion involves a creed, institution and rituals* (Geri Miller, 2003: 6). Spirituality is the personal connection with the 'transcendent' while religion is a group, rather a mass approach (connection) to experience the connection with the 'transcendent'. Thus we can say that spirituality can have an existence apart from religion, but religion cannot exist apart from spirituality. The organizational and managerial part of religion involves political, economic, cultural, social and ethical considerations.

There is abundant literature available on the meaning and importance of spirituality especially in the context of social work. Spirituality is defined as *'the human quest for personal meaning and mutually fulfilling relationships among people, the non-human environment and for some, God'* (Canda, 1988: 243). Spirituality helps us to establish a working relationship with the universe and find a meaning in such relationship. Such spirituality is essential for cultivating the love of nature, the feeling of belongingness with the nature and above all to strengthen our motivation to protect the nature. Spirituality is sometimes defines as *'the connection to all that is in existence*' (Baskin, 2002: 2). This connectedness is the source of our inner strength, peace and harmony with the universe.

When we realize the benefits of being spiritual, we come to the conclusion that spirituality is one of the fundamental aspects of human development.

Can someone be human without being really spiritual? In that case, can we relate with the humans without taking consideration his or her spiritual aspect. In order to work meaningfully with the humans, the social workers need to consider the spiritual dimension. *'Human beings have longings and aspirations that can be honoured only when the person's spiritual capacity is taken seriously'* (Gratton, 1995). Without inquiring about the spiritual aspirations, we may not be able to work with humans. In simple terms, it is the responsibility of the social worker to take into consideration all that are significant to the individual with whom he or she works.

Studies in the western countries have revealed the importance of spirituality in the wellbeing of human life. Spirituality has been found beneficial in several aspects of life. Jeff Levin's (2001) research has pointed out several health benefits of spiritual practices. For each of the three leading causes of death in the United States – heart disease, cancer and hypertension – people who report a religious affiliation have lower rates of illness. People who regularly attend religious services have lower rates of illness and death than do infrequent or non-attendees. Older adults who participate in private or congregational religious activities were found to have fewer symptoms, less disability, and lower rates of depression, chronic anxiety and dementia. Religious participation has been found a significant variable of psychological well-being among the African Americans. Religiously and spiritually active people live longer than the non religious. This holds true even controlling for the fact that religious folks tend to avoid such behaviours as smoking and drinking that increase the risk of disease and death (Jeff Levin, 2001). From the aforesaid discussion, we can understand that spirituality is a significant variable in the wellbeing of humans and this variable has to be taken seriously by the social workers. It opens up the scope for spiritually sensitive social work. Spirituality has the scope to improve the physical, mental, social and interpersonal functioning of human life.

In the practice of integrated or holistic social work, spirituality plays prominent role. In order to have a meaningful intervention, the social workers have to consider all that are significant to the clients. In professional social work practice spiritual aspects of the human condition cannot be overlooked. To the extent, spirituality is important to the client, it is to be considered by the practitioner. While analyzing the history of social work profession, it can be observed that spirituality was not given the due respect in the past by the professional social workers. Canda reminds us that by the 1970's social work had become separated from the religious connections in which it was rooted and there was much professional skepticism about the integration of spirituality and social work. However, through the 1980's and 1990's there was an increased call for the profession to reconnect with its roots in spiritual perspectives (Canda, 2002: 2). *During the developmental stages of the profession, the spiritual considerations had once been sidelined. While moving closer into mainstream social work, many researchers, students and practitioners continue to worry that their interest in spirituality has been ignored, marginalized and at times actively discouraged* (Coates and Graham, 2003). Several reasons have been cited for this marginalization. *Some helping professionals are concerned with blurring professional and personal boundaries with clients. A lack of clarity surrounding definitions of spirituality and religion creates confusion and can lead to fears of proselytizing. The lack of empirical knowledge in this emergent field and the reality that it is a new area of practice discourages professionals from integrating a spiritual dimension in their work. Finally the abstract and experiential nature of spirituality makes it difficult to study spiritually influenced processes from the dominant positivist research paradigm* (John Graham, Diana Coholic and John Coats, 2006: 36). This was the situation of mainstream social work profession. This legacy is still prevalent in India. While the interest in spirituality has been revived in the US and Canada, it is yet to find followers in India. Before, exploring the scope of spiritually sensitive social work in India, let us understand various dimensions of spiritually sensitive social work as it is practised in the west.

The emergence of spiritually sensitive social work is largely the contribution of Prof. Edward R. Canda of the University of Kansas, USA (Canda and Furman, 2010). According to Canda (2011), spirituality in the context of social work practice can be understood from *three perspectives*-spirituality as an aspect of the whole person, spirituality as centre of the person, and spirituality as the wholeness of the person in relation with all.

(i) *Spirituality as an aspect of the whole person* refers to 'bio-psycho-social-spiritual perspective' (Canda, 2011). It recognizes that spiritual factors are as important as biological, psychological and social factors that contribute to human development. Neglecting spiritual aspect of human personality results with a partial treatment of humans. We need to understand what are the spiritual aspects of the people with whom we work with, what are their ultimate beliefs, what gives meaning to their life, what spiritual factors affect their decisions in life and what are the spiritual factors available for facilitating the helping process. Spiritually sensitive professional social work is about discovering and engaging the clients' and communities' spiritual strengths and resources in the helping process. It is essentially recognizing that spirituality is the essential aspect of holistic social work.

(ii) *Spirituality as the centre of the person* refers to the deepest concern of the people which includes the search for a sense of meaning, purpose and morality. People who are engaged in spiritual practice (whether religious or non-religious) come to a deep sense of who they really are in their centre. At this centre point (referred by some religious traditions as 'True Self' or the

'Devine Within') we experience a sense of peace and clarity, and a connectedness with all. Then we tend to become less ego-centric and more altruistic, more connected, more empathetic, and more able to flow in the helping process with spontaneity. In this process we might truly hear our clients, with compassionate sensitivity and engage in an empowering helping process that is appropriate to the situation (Canda, 2011). All the spiritual exercises in every religious context is an attempt to explore into the inner space, where the humans feel peaceful, joyful, calm and above all acquire a transcendent consciousness that we are part of something larger and substantially part of the cosmic reality. In Sanskrit, it is sometimes called as the experience of '*Satchitananda'* ('Sat' means truth, 'Chit' means awareness, knowledge or wisdom and 'Ananda' means joy and happiness). Such an awareness is very beneficial for the individual as it enhances to his or her self-management skills. Spiritually sensitive social work is exploring the spiritual orientation of the people and to understand the basic unity of the mankind and unity of humans with everything in this universe.

(iii) *Spirituality as the wholeness of the person in relation with all* refers to an expansive consciousness, a quality of mind beyond divisions and dichotomies, transcending all our particular individual and cultural and religious aspects and diversities. When social workers experience this mode of consciousness, they can attend to the diverse needs of people without discriminating or oppressing anyone and encourage everyone to live in harmony with this wonderful yet endangered planet earth (Canda, 2011). Spirituality helps the humans to experience a collective consciousness. It helps us to experience a sense of oneness beyond the ethnical, cultural, linguistic, regional and religious differences among us. Spiritually sensitive social work gives a great emphasis on non-discriminating attitude on the part of the social workers. It also gives us a solid basis for eco-social work, sensitising us about the need for checking environmental degradation. It also inspires us to empathise with the downtrodden and work selflessly for social justice. It fosters an attitude among the social workers towards working for a just, equitable and inclusive society.

Religion and spirituality have intrinsic connection. When we analyse the history of world religions, we can understand that religion was inseparable from science and philosophy. Religion could be termed as the first branch of science (social science) that humans discovered. Human life was closely connected with religion. The most important resource of religion was spirituality. The spiritual expression of religion was manifested in the propagation of different philanthropic values that gave solid basis for humans to organise their own life. Compassion and charity were the social values found in most of the world religions. In the context of our diverse nation, social work practice has several challenges and the solutions lie with spiritually sensitive social work. In spite of strong emphasis for love, compassion and charity in all the world religions, the miseries of the mankind have not been lessened. Poverty, inequality, discrimination, oppression, aggression, war, human rights violence, gender violence, communal violence, crimes and many other social problems are widespread. Social workers across the world have similar challenges and crises to solve. It seems that mankind has just forgotten the spiritual and religious traditions that have been guiding us for past centuries. It is right time to revisit our rich spiritual traditions and establish the lost connection of our profession to spirituality.

If everyone rediscovers from whatever religion they believe the values of charity, compassion, spiritual union of the humanity, non violence, peaceful coexistence, tolerance, love and justice, the world would have been a better place to live. Analysing the foundations of every religion, it can be seen that there is unity in the emphasis on charity and humanitarian service, which is a solid basis for social work. This is the spiritual resource available in the religious traditions, which have to be effectively mobilised by professional social workers for rendering effective services to their client groups.

Application of Spiritually Sensitive Social Work

Spiritually sensitive social work is basically recognising the role of spirituality in the helping process. In this context, we need to rise from the realm of reason to the realm of faith and hope for a meaningful intervention. With progressive appreciation for the spiritual dimension, we move from working *on* the client to working *with* the client to facilitating the spiritual energies or expressions of grace for each other (Gerald May, 1992: 8). Work of spirituality is sometimes considered as an intuitive work of the spirit in contrast with the rational application of mind. We sometimes just wonder at the work of the spirit, because we find little rational explanation for it, especially, in the events of healings from several incurables and disabilities or miraculous healing.

Spirituality helps cultivation of self management skills and also group building skills. Social workers can learn the techniques of several spiritual traditions that encourage individuals to become self supporting and help others self supportive. *When social workers facilitate community celebrations, or support couples to ritualise their time together, they are drawing upon wisdom from our spiritual traditions. Myth and ritual, properly understood, cultivate reverence and connection that combats loneliness and nihilism* (Michael McKernan, 2005: 103-104). There are cultural and social work values in spiritual and religious practices. Concerted group actions in the spiritual context compensate with the loneliness and meaninglessness felt by individuals living alone. Such ritualism renders a sense of belongingness to the participants.

Prayers are believed to have healing force. They clear our intentions in the sense that we develop a positive attitude towards a person or an action for whom or which we pray. We also tend to approach towards the object of our prayer with a positive and creative attitude. This will add to our healing forces within us. Most of the spiritual or prayer services are accompanied by reading or Holy Scriptures. Spiritual readings have inspirational role in the lives of the people who listen to them. *The lives of holy persons, saints, avatars, shaman, revered leaders and great teachers from all traditions have much to teach and inspire in our works. More than mere devotion, attention to the stories of great leaders brings light to the struggles, achievements, and the acts of courage implicit in inspired lives. The encouraging examples of these leaders demonstrate the great potential available to human beings* (Michael McKernan, 2005: 105-106). Therefore, spiritual readings have positive role to play in the context of spiritually sensitive social work. The people around the world look for role models who have shown successful ways of dealing with problems of life. Spiritual leaders and great teachers have shown the examples of effective and fruitful life on this planet. Social workers can take the inspiration and guidance for themselves from the readings of such success stories. They can also guide the service users accordingly. Spiritually sensitive social work has significant implications with regard to the major social work methods – social case work especially in the clinical context, social group work and community organisation. Spirituality has also significant implications in various applied fields of social work.

A. Spirituality and Clinical Social Work (Case Work) Practice: Studies have been reported about the effectiveness of spiritually based case work practice. Case work is working with individuals enhancing to the problem solving skills of the clients. Case work is more relevant in clinical set up and it is often known as clinical social work while the service user is addressed as client. In clinical social work, the medical and psychiatric social workers address the issues of maladjustment in psychological context. All the people in the world, whether religious or non-religious, have a system of beliefs and values that draw the basic framework of life. In other terms, we can say that all are spiritual in the sense that we can analyse everyone to find a set of beliefs, attitudes and values that have a deeper and more intuitive foundation than mere rationality. Social workers can spend time with the client exploring these deeper spiritual values and engage them meaningfully to take help these values to reorganise their life. Working on these values would definitely help them to solve their problems of everyday living, coping with or recovering from traumas. Researchers have pointed out the importance of spirituality in working with individuals. *Spirituality is the most powerful source of strength because everyone who chooses to go on in this world operates on some form of faith. A spiritual value or belief can be a powerful resource in a client's life that can be used in problem solving, coping and recovering from trauma* (Baskin, 2002: 194). *The spiritual component can be a significant variable for people in terms of re-awakening to meaning in their lives, particularly in* *the context of difficult times* (Wanda Wagler-Martin, 2005: 135). In the helping process, if we neglect spirituality we, the social workers, will miss out an important aspect which has the healing power in the lives of the clients. When we understand and recognise the spiritual strength of the clients, our social work approach becomes more holistic and there is greater scope for an effective healing process.

Wanda Wagler-Martin (2005) who is a practitioner of spiritually sensitive social work has identified some probing questions that are relevant for professional social workers in the field of spiritually sensitive social work. *(1) Are there any spiritual beliefs that give your life meaning? If so, could you tell about them? (2) Are there any specific practices or rituals that are important to you? (3) What has contributed to your beliefs? (4) How do you find ways to honour these beliefs in your life? (5) What gets in the way? (6) What do you think might be different for you if you honoured these beliefs more fully?* (Wanda Wagler-Martin, 2005: 141). All these questions may not be relevant in our context. However, an adaptation of these questions will be a useful tool for spiritually sensitive social workers in India.

B. Spiritually Based Group Work Model: There is scope for the application of spiritually sensitive social work in the context of social group work. Diana Coholic (2005) reported an investigation on the helpfulness of spiritually influenced group work with eight adult women who shared a history of substance abuse. Purpose of the group was to develop their self-awareness and self esteem. The group was organised around six experiential exercises – meditation, mindfulness practice, dream work, stream of consciousness writing, the shadow self and other arts based processes like clay modelling. Grounded theory analysis identified different aspects of the group as spiritual, making meaning (there is a reason for me to be here and be part of this exercise) was one practice that was consistently described as a spiritually sensitive process (Diana Coholic, 2005: 111).

In the context of social group work, the social workers can find some group building value in the recitation of group prayers. Group prayers are the characteristics of the world religions—Christianity, Islam, Hinduism, Sikhism, Buddhism, Jainism and Baha'ism. Group prayers facilitate creation of a sense of equality, fraternity, friendliness and selflessness among the congregation gathered in prayer. Alean Al-Krenawi and John Graham (2000) have reported their observations concerning social work implications of group prayers in Islam. Group prayers facilitate breaking down barriers in mutual exchange of social support. Group prayers create a platform for social support outside the mosque, such as family or marital advice, assistance with building a home or extension to a home, or assistance to the sick and the bereaved. The feast seasons provide the context of visiting sick friends or relatives and settling instances of marital and family discord with the assistance of all the concerned family members, neighbours and friends. Even the enemies among the Muslims are compelled to the cordial to each other during the festival seasons. In Islam, group prayers have both social and spiritual values. The group prayers unite the believers for mutual aid as well as remind them their spiritual union with the entire Muslim believers across the world including the people who are dead. *On the level of person-to-group, the practice catapults the praying individual into a worldwide body of believers, both dead and alive, thus reinforcing a sense of the integrity and strength of the religion* (Alean Al-Krenawi and John R Graham, 2000: 330).

C. Spiritually Sensitive Community Organisation Practice: Faith based organisations are many in the field of community organisation. Bosco Gramin Vikas Kendra (BGVK), Social Centre, World Vision, CASA, Salesians of Don Bosco (SDB), Missionaries of Charity, YMCA and YWCA are some of the faith based organisations active in the field of community organisation. Spiritual motivation is the major factor behind all these enterprises. Spirituality has contributed to the emergence of voluntary agencies in the field of urban and rural development agencies in India as well as abroad. Such agencies have been instrumental towards promotion of self help and mutual aid. Spiritually organised community has a sense of social security and a sense of belongingness to the community. Studies (David Este, 2004) have shown the effectiveness of spiritually based community organisation among the Black communities of Canada. Rejected by the dominant community in their efforts to integrate into Canadian society, black Canadians turned inward and formed their own institutions which provided them with a certain degree of protection from a racist and oppressive society. In a short period of time, the black church became the most important institution in African-Canadian communities and was instrumental in providing a sense of stability for community members. *For the black pioneers and for generations of their descendants, the core of the community was the church. Church membership defined community, provided opportunities to participate in community affairs and created networks for cooperative endeavours* (David Este, 2004: 302). In collaboration with the church, the various church and auxiliary organisations contributed to the development of the community. These organisations, through a series of social and spiritual activities, facilitated community members to socialise with each other. The youth in the communities received a considerable amount of attention from elders in the community who regarded them as the future leaders. The church also provided opportunities for community members to develop or display their leadership abilities (David Este, 2004: 317-318).

Attitude of Professional Social Work Trainees to Spiritually Sensitive Social Work

In the context of the international conference on spirituality and social work held at Ahmednagar, I conducted a study on a national sample of 106 post graduate level social work students regarding their attitude towards spiritually sensitive social work. A checklist of 16 items concerning the attitude of the students towards the spiritually sensitive social work was administered to the respondents. The statements in the attitude scale had five point response scale ranging from 'Strongly Agree' to 'Strongly Disagree'. The agreement of the respondents to the checklist is presented in Table 10.1.

Table 10.1: Attitude of professional social work trainees towards Spiritually Sensitive Social Work

Sl. No.	*Percentage of Respondents agreeing upon the following statements*	*% Men (N= 65)*	*% Women (N= 41)*	*Difference*	*Test Statistic*
1.	Most of the people in the world are religious.	93.85	73.17	20.68	2.87
2.	I am a religious person	80.00	87.80	(7.80)	(1.09)
3.	Religion is very useful institution.	80.00	85.37	(5.37)	(0.73)
4.	Religion offers relief to human suffering.	67.69	73.17	(5.48)	(0.62)
5.	Most of the people in the world are spiritual.	69.23	58.54	10.69	1.15
6.	I am a spiritual person	73.85	80.49	(6.64)	(0.81)
7.	Religion and spirituality are two sides of the same coin.	67.69	75.61	(7.92)	(0.90)
8.	Spirituality offers relief to human suffering.	72.31	87.80	(15.50)	(2.00)
9.	Spirituality is an essential aspect of human being.	86.15	73.17	12.98	1.66
10.	Spiritual development is important aspect of human development.	81.54	82.93	(1.39)	(0.19)
11.	Spiritual person finds fundamental unity of mankind in terms of substance, destiny and survival.	70.77	80.49	(9.72)	(1.17)
12.	Spiritual person can easily transcend the socio economic and cultural (linguistic, religious, ethnic, educational, occupational, regional and communal) divides among the mankind.	66.15	58.54	7.62	0.81
13.	The spiritual need becomes crucial when social work clients experience crisis, trauma, oppression, grief, and loss.	81.54	82.93	(1.39)	(0.19)
14.	It is a useful strategy for social workers to engage the clients' spiritual strengths in the helping process.	75.38	75.61	(0.23)	(0.03)
15.	Spiritually sensitive social work is the need of the time.	81.54	82.93	(1.39)	(0.19)
16.	I will practise spiritually sensitive social work in future.	73.85	80.49	(6.64)	(0.81)

The study has assumed that spirituality is closely related to religiosity. It is popularly noticed that spirituality is often discussed in religious context.

Therefore, the investigator emphasised spirituality in the context of religious behaviour and started the investigation by enquiring about the religiosity of the respondents before exploring their spiritual inclination. Most of the professional social work trainees have been found believers of some religions. Majority of the professional social work trainees have agreed upon all the items in the checklist. However, there is some variance in the magnitude of agreement and also some differences of opinion between men and women with regard to several items of the checklist.

The study has brought out interesting observations. It has been found that there is some gender difference with regard to the religiosity of the professional social work trainees. While more men believed that most people in the world are religious, the proportion of men who admitted that 'they themselves were religious' was less than women. Comparatively fewer women believed that most of the people in the world are religious. On the other hand, the proportion of women who admitted that 'they were religious' was more than men. It can be noted here that more religious people found other people less religious, while less religious people believed that most of the people in the world are religious.

The test statistics has proved a significant gender difference with regard to their belief in the religiosity of others. T-Table value for 106 respondents at five per cent level and 1 per cent level are 1.66 and 2.62 respectively. The derived test statistic, 2.87 is more than the table values. Therefore, the observed difference between the proportions (20.68) is significant at one per cent per cent. Such difference is rare in normal population (could be found only in one per cent of the total population). Therefore, we may assume that there is real difference between the sample populations (men and women professional social work trainees) with regard to their opinion about the religiosity of others. However, the observed difference between the religiosity of men and women has been found insignificant in the test statistic. The derived value of 1.09 is less than the table values of 1.66 (5% level) and 2.62 (1% level). Therefore, we may conclude that there is no real difference between men and women social work trainees as far as their religious attitudes are concerned.

With regard to the usefulness of religion as an institution, there is high degree of agreement by professional social work trainees (80% men and 85.37% women). Comparatively there is less agreement with regard to the religious services that offer relief to human suffering (67.69% and 73.17% respectively). Though women are found more convinced of the usefulness of religious institution as well as their role in mitigating human suffering, test statistic has nullified the observed marginal gender difference in this regard. The observed difference is by chance and insignificant.

Coming to the query on the spirituality of people, majority of professional social work trainees agreed upon the statement that 'most of the people in the world are spiritual' (69.23% men and 58.54% women). It is interesting to find that more professional social work trainees believe that they are more spiritual than others out in the world (73.85% men and 80.49% women). There is also gender difference in this regard. Comparatively fewer women believe that other people are spiritual while a greater number of women consider themselves as spiritual. We can find that this observation has some concurrence with regard to their opinion regarding religiosity of the people. However, we have to admit that all these differences are insignificant as far as test statistic is concerned.

With regard to the connection between religion and spirituality ('Religion and spirituality are two sides of the same coin') there is a high degree of agreement among professional social work trainees (67.69% men and 75.61% women). Even if women social work trainees have expressed greater degree of agreement, the observed difference is found statistically insignificant. There is no real difference between men and women in this regard.

There is a high degree of agreement among professional social work trainees upon the statement that 'Spirituality offers relief to human suffering' (72.31% men and 87.80% women). Comparing this observation with that of utility of religion in relieving human suffering, we find a break. It is spirituality that offers better service in the relief of human suffering than religion. It necessitates a study of spirituality apart from religion. We may assume that spirituality is sometimes contaminated by undesirable religious elements (it might be the organisational, ritual, legal or dogmatic part of the religion). Religion is sometimes found ineffective in mitigating human suffering, while spirituality has a better scope. There is also found a significant gender difference in the opinion about the utility of spirituality in the relief of human suffering. Women are more convinced of the effectiveness of spirituality in humanitarian service. The difference is significant at five per cent level but insignificant at one per cent level (the derived value is 2.00 which is higher than the table value of 1.66 at 5% level, but less than 2.62 at 1% level).

Concerning the importance of spirituality in human life (statements of 'Spirituality is an essential aspect of human being' and 'Spiritual development is important aspect of human development') there is a high degree of agreement among the professional social work trainees. It is interesting to find that comparatively fewer men admitted that they are spiritual (73.85%) while a large number of them (86.15%) considered that spirituality is essential for human being. The observation for women in this regard is just the reverse. While 80.49 per cent women admitted that they were spiritual, only 73.17 per cent of them considered that it is essential aspect of human life. The gender difference in this regard is just significant at five per cent level (derived value is 1.66 which is equal to the T-table value of 1.66 at 5% level of significance) and insignificant at one per cent level. There is similar opinion among men and women with regard to the importance of spiritual development as essential aspect of human being.

There is high degree of agreement among professional social work trainees with regard to the qualities of a spiritual person (statements 11 and 12). These attributes are based on the findings of Edward Canda (2011). Majority of the professional social work trainees agreed upon the statement 'Spiritual person finds fundamental unity of mankind in terms of substance, destiny and survival' (70.77% men and 80.49% women). Comparatively fewer social work trainees agreed upon the statement that 'Spiritual person can easily transcend the socio economic and cultural (linguistic, religious, ethnic, educational, occupational, regional and communal) divides among the mankind' (66.15% men and 58.54% women). The observed gender differences in this regard are statistically insignificant.

With regard to social work significance of spirituality (statements of 13-16) there is proportionately very high agreement among the professional social work trainees. It has been noticed that women social work trainees are more convinced of spiritually sensitive social work than men. However, the observed differences are statistically insignificant. While many professional social work trainees are convinced that the spiritual need becomes crucial when social work clients experience crisis, trauma, oppression, grief, and loss (81.54% men and 82.93% women), comparatively fewer professional social work trainees agree that it is a useful strategy for social work trainees to engage the clients' spiritual strengths in the helping process (75.38% men and 75.61% women). Similarly, a vast majority of the professional social work trainees opine that spiritually sensitive social work is the need of the time (81.54% men and 82.93% women) comparatively fewer professional social work trainees willing to practice spiritually sensitive social work in future (73.85% men and 80.49% women).

Conclusion

While a detailed review of literature on different aspects of spiritually sensitive social work has been presented in the first part of the paper, the attitude of professional social work trainees has been discussed with the help of first hand data in the second part. The study has revealed the extent of religious and spiritual base of professional social work trainees. It has found out that majority of the professional social work trainees are religious as well as spiritual. The study has explored into the beliefs, attitudes and value system of the professional social work trainees with regard to spiritual need and spiritual development of human beings. Majority of the professional social work trainees have right beliefs, values and attitudes concerning spiritual need and spiritual development of people. The study has also explored into the attitude of professional social work trainees in the application of spiritually sensitive social work in their professional practice and it has been found that most of the professional social work trainees would practice spiritually sensitive social work.

Both the literature review and the field investigation have pointed out the need for incorporating spiritually sensitive social work in the curriculum and practice of social work in India. The curriculum of social work education in India could include an elective if not a concentration (specialisation) on spiritually sensitive social work. The paper may include the topics like: (1) Concept, meaning and scope of spirituality, (2) Spirituality and World Religions: Contribution of world religions towards and spirituality and social work, (3) Role of Spirituality in Social Case Work and Clinical Social Work, (4) Role of Spirituality in Social Group Work, (5) Role of Spirituality in Social Action and Community Organisation, (6) Spirituality in Eco-Social Work, (7) Spirituality and the Process of Healing, (8) Spirituality and Critical Social Work, (9) Spirituality in Rural and Tribal Social Work, (10) Spirituality and Working with the Marginalised, the Women, the Differently Abled, the HIV/AIDS Affected, the Elderly, the Youth, the Juvenile Delinquents, the Migrants, the Persons in Conflict with Law.

There is also much scope for research in this area of social work practice. Undoubtedly spiritually sensitive social work is an emerging model of social work practice and very much in tune with the Indian ethos.

11

Signature Pedagogy in Social Work and Psychological Well-Being of Social Work Trainees

An Evidenced-Based Evaluatory Process

J. Harini Christopher

Social work is a profession that has two very broad and overlapping dimensions. It is a helping profession and aims at social change, (Murthy 1970). As an international profession, it embraces both academic and practical components, making it a practice-based learning (Chandrashekar, 2001), and aims toward social action, designed to remedy the roots of social malaise (Dasgupta, 1967; Gunjal, Bhushan, Molankar, 2000). Well-structured field work seminars provide opportunities for the integration of social work knowledge, skills and values (Bohanan, 2007). However, social work is not an easy profession; it requires disciplined delivery of services, set within a conceptual framework based on scientifically tested theories, which could have repercussions on the emotional and psychological well-being of the trainees.

A basic precept of the social work education powerfully intertwines two core forces, i.e., field work practice and classroom learning. Field education is systematically designed, supervised, coordinated and evaluated on the basis of criteria by which students demonstrate the achievement of programme objectives (Moorthy and Rao, 1970; CSWE, 2008). Fieldwork, also known as field instruction, field placement, field education, practicum or internship, is referred to as the "signature pedagogy" of the profession (CSWE, 2008; Maidment, 2011). It is a dynamic process of observing, amassing and implementing creative and innovative ideas (Subhedar, 2001). It is an integral part of the training for professional social workers and the onus of responsibility lies with the student, the school and the agency, to provide such learning opportunities, which will have a carry-over effect in professional development (Nagendra, 2005).

Assessment is crucial in determining what, why and how students learn (Brown *et al.*, 1997). Its role in higher education has three functions: diagnosing student's learning, offering feedback and future learning needs. Self-assessment has recently emerged as an important feature for enhancing learning in professional education [Social Work Education, 1999, vol. 18 (2)]. Some proponents opine that the evidence to its effectiveness is scant or non-existent (Desai, 2000; Marotta *et al.*, 2000) and does not, critically or reliably, discriminate between students who have met the grade and those who have not (Visvesvaran, 2000).

Emotional Distress

In India, the numbers of students in university education have been increasing; more so, in the Masters Degree in Social Work (MSW) (Ramana. 2012). Academic success is highly valued in our society and it plays an integral role in the level of achievement, motivation and mental health, (Vasuki and Charumathy, 2004). The social environment of higher educational institutions is unique in this age group (18 -25) who are at a high-risk period for onset of psychiatric illnesses (Kessler *et al.*, 2005). This often disrupts the completion of developmental and educational tasks of young adults, resulting in underachievement and unemployment (Council Report CR112, 2006; Tajularipin Sulaiman *et al*, 2009).

While youth in industrialized countries have greater opportunities for higher education, the largest proportion of university students is drawn from backgrounds with historically low rates of participation in higher education (TOK, 2004). The high-risk period for onset of stress or distress, depression, schizophrenia and bipolar disorder is in late adolescence and early adulthood which coincides entering higher education. Thus, the neglect of mental health results in serious consequences on the students and their future career (Nanda, 2001) and "urgent action" is needed to improve detection and early treatment in this group, (Blanco *et al*, 2008).

Much debate surrounding social work education questions the appropriateness and relevance of training. Many studies have examined social work student's retrospective opinions of their training courses (Shaw and Walton, 1978; Gibbs and Cigno, 1986). The review of available literature indicates the need for more emphasis on self-assessment in field work practicum and psychological and emotional distress of social work trainees as no empirical studies have addressed this. Hence, this study is an attempt to examine the broad areas of the 4th semester MSW trainees' rating on overall learning experiences of their faculty and agency supervisors and agency across four semesters and its implications on their psychological wellbeing and its relation to academic achievement.

Materials and Methods

Study Criteria

The subjects for the study were recruited from 5 of the 10 departments affiliated to the Bangalore University (BU) offering the Masters Degree in Social Work (MSW), based on the permission granted by their respective HODs. These

Departments follow an extremely well put together, common structured syllabus for theory and field work practicum and have a uniform grading system as compared to four other departments belonging to colleges that have autonomous status. Both male and female trainees, who have completed four semesters of field work training, irrespective of their specializations, who were present on the day stipulated for data collection and consented to participate, were included in the study. Trainees from autonomous colleges, which prescribe to their own syllabus and not affiliated to the BU and questionnaires with missing data, were excluded from the study. The period of data collection was from May 2012 to June 2012.

Procedure

The nature and purpose of the research study was explained to the Principals of the five Departments of Social Work. On the dates specified, the researcher met with the trainees at their respective colleges and explained the rationale for the study and how to rate the self-administered scales and clarified doubts. Trainees were assured of strict confidentiality and the importance for feedback regarding their field work practicum and gave informed verbal consent. However, at two of the colleges, the researcher had to leave the questionnaires for the trainees to complete and despite repeated requests, was not returned.

Fifty-two trainees were selected through multiphase, purposive random sampling with differences in mean and 95 per cent Confidence Interval of the difference, from a population of 145 students (Fig. 11.1). However, a number of trainees (n = 69) had to be excluded as: two of the Departments of Social Work failed to return the questionnaires; 15 questionnaires had missing data and 9 trainees were absent. The sample was restricted by the time frame available for the study.

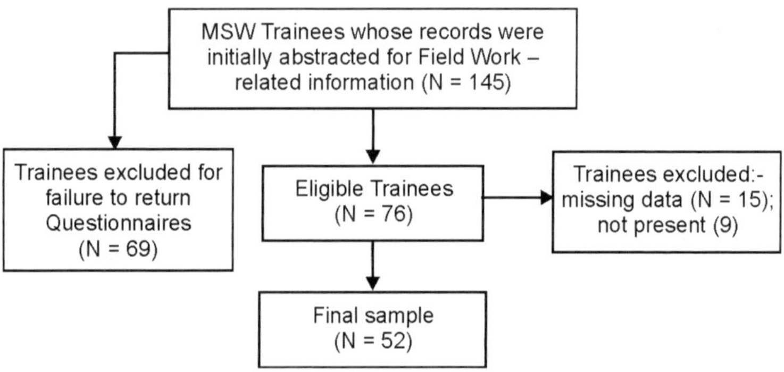

Fig. 11.1: MSW Trainees whose records were initially abstracted for Field work information and final sample screened

Measures

For the collection of quantitative data, a structured interview schedule which consisted of three parts was used. Part I intended to measure the: i) socio-demographic characteristics of the trainees (age, gender, marital status, education at under graduate level, percentage and class, languages known, previous work experience, religion and place of residence), and ii) information pertaining to thc MWS course (percentage of marks scored in the first three semesters, specialization, overall rating of the course, hobbies and awards received, if any). Part II was designed to measure trainees rating of their fieldwork practice using scales developed in the Field Practicum Manual, (Salem State College of Massachusetts, University of Maryland, Boston College and University of Nevada—Reno, 2010-2011). They are short, easy to complete, self-administered questionnaires designed to measure: i) faculty supervision, ii) Agency, and iii) Agency Supervision. The scale for the faculty supervisor has 14 questions, which assess the faculty's supervision on attitude, knowledge and skills, regularity and receptivity to trainees needs. The agency was evaluated on its competency for training and conduciveness for learning and has 11 questions. The agency supervisors were assessed on a 15 point scale covering areas on being a professional role model, competency for supervision and training and leaning needs of trainees. Each item is scored on a 4-point rating scale – (1) Poor (2) Satisfactory, (3) Good, and (4) Excellent. These scales were intended to be used for a single semester; however, the researcher modified it so that trainees could describe their experiences across the four fieldwork agencies on the same parameters.

Part III was intended to measure the degree of emotional and psychological well-being of the trainees. The General Health Questionnaire-12 (GHQ-12; Goldberg and Hiller, 1972) is a symptom and well-being, self-rating, screening of severity of symptoms compared to the habitual state of the person, on a 4-point rating scale. It has sensitivity and specificity of 80-90 per cent in relation to interview-based diagnosis. Scoring is based on four possible answers for each item, on a Likert scale (0-1-2-3) with scores ranging from 0 to 36. Scores of 0–10 indicated good mental health, 11-14 were typical, 15-19 was evidence of distress and >20 was suggestive of severe problems and psychological distress.

Statistical Analysis

Data was coded for computer analysis, using SPSS version 16. Descriptive statistics such as mean, SD, percentages and Chi-square tests were used to compare male and female trainees at baseline on socio-demographic variables (i.e. personal and educational profiles). Two-Way ANOVA was used for assessing the relationship among the variables. Repeated Measures of ANOVA (RMANOVA) analysis was used for assessing the self rating of faculty supervision, agency and agency supervision over four semesters. All analyses were two-tailed and the probability level of $p<0.05$ indicated statistical significance.

Results

Fifty-two trainees (males 53.8% and females 46.2%) participated in the study. The majority (84.6%) were in the age group of 20-25 years and mean age was 24.04±5.20 years and single (96.2%), hailing from semi-urban (50%) and rural (28.8%) areas and were from Karnataka State (80.8%). Undergraduate education profile showed that most had opted for B.A. (90.4%), had scored 1st class (57.7%), one-fourth had won awards/distinctions (25%), had previous work experience (25%) and were bi-lingual (36.5%). Less than one-half (48.1%) were satisfied with the MSW course. The main specializations offered were MPSW (28.8%), Community Development (30.8%) and HRM (40.4%) and had scored a 1st class in all three semesters.

The self rating scores across the four semester, of their faculty supervision (Table 11.1) was significant ($p<0.05$) on 'holding of individual and group supervision'. Though not significant, trainees gave higher ratings to their agencies in the 1st years placements (Table 11.2) and significant difference on 'compatibility with the student' ($p<0.05$) (Table 11.3). On the emotional and psychological wellbeing scores, significant differences between male and female trainees on ability to face problems ($p<0.01$) and feeling reasonably

Table 11.1: Self-Rating Evaluation of Faculty Supervisors over Four Semesters

Sl. No	*Variables*	*Range*	*1st sem. M±SD*	*2nd sem. M±SD*	*3rd sem. M±SD*	*4th sem. M±SD*	*Sig.*
1.	Source of instruction	1-4	2.59±.72	2.76±.78`	2.76±.80	2.78±.93	.45
2.	Held Individual and Group supervision	1-4	2.63±.86	3.00±.81	2.86±.81	2.86±.90	.041***
3.	Provided support	1-4	2.82±.80	2.82±.87	2.94±.87	2.84±.93	.73
4.	Interest in professional development	1-4	3.03±.81	3.00±.79	2.96±.81	3.03±.98	.88
5.	Receptive of ideas and opinions	1-4	2.75±.86	2.86±.86	2.61±.95	2.82±.92	.26
6.	Provided guidance	1-4	2.75±.90	2.71±.95	2.94±.95	3.27±2.82	.23
7.	Provided feedback	1-4	2.76±.78	2.84±.77	2.84±.80	2.82±.80	.83
8.	Application of learning	1-4	2.94±.72	2.92±.72	2.78±.72	2.94±.80	.51
9.	Knowledge and skills	1-4	2.88±.75	2.86±.84	2.94±.89	2.92±.91	.93
10.	Worked effectively	1-4	2.84±.84	2.96±.90	2.94±.84	2.78±.93	.60
11.	Role model	1-4	2.84±.87	3.03±.88	2.82±.92	2.86±.95	.47
12.	Overall rating	1-4	3.05±.80	2.86±.84	3.09±.84	3.03±.86	.20

Sig. ***$p<0.05$; I. Time – 1, 2, 3 and 4th semesters; M = Mean, SD – Standard deviation. Repeated Measures Analysis (RMANOVA) was used.

happy (p <0.01). Male trainees had higher mean scores and 9.6 per cent were considered to be at risk for psychological problems, while both male and female trainees (11.5%) had indications of severe emotional distress.

Table 11.2: Self-Rating Evaluation of Agencies over Four Semesters

Sl. No.	*Variables*	*Range*	*1st sem. M±SD*	*2nd sem M±SD*	*3rd sem M±SD*	*4th sem M±SD*	*P Value*
1.	Conducive to learning	1-4	2.78±.89	2.78±.77	2.98±.80	3.07±.68	.13
2.	Trainees needs	1-4	2.78±.77	2.90±.74	2.78±.77	2.86±.76	.76
3.	Variety of experiences	1-4	2.90±.77	2.86±.74	2.96±.79	2.92±.65	.89
4.	Learning needs	1-4	3.46±.39	3.01±.67	2.78±.84	2.94±.77	.36
5.	Resources available	1-4	3.55±.09	2.92±.78	3.03±.81	2.96±.81	.34
6.	Innovative Service	1-4	3.07±2.92	2.96±.81	2.86±.81	2.84±.87	.70
7.	Learning experience	1-4	2.84±.91	3.13±.76	3.03±.79	3.05±.82	.23
8.	Satisfied with placement	1-4	2.90±.74	3.01±.77	2.90±.79	2.96±.81	.82
9.	Competent for training	1-4	2.78±.74	2.84±.80	2.98±.82	2.88±.83	.54

Time – 1, 2, 3 and 4th semesters; M = Mean, SD – Standard deviation, RMANOVA was used, not significant.

Table 11.3: Self- rating Evaluation of Agency Supervisors over Four Semesters

Sl. No	*Variables*	*Range*	*1st sem. M±SD*	*2nd sem M±SD*	*3rd sem M±SD*	*4th sem M±SD*	*P Value*
1.	Role model	1-4	2.63±.90	2.67±.80	2.90±.84	3.03±.73	.40
2.	Ease with supervision	1-4	2.78±.87	2.65±.81	2.84±.80	3.48±4.25	.40
3.	Useful feedback	1-4	2.75±.90	2.73±.74	2.80±.79	2.96±.86	.34
4.	Advocates	1-4	2.73±.88	2.86±.79	2.84±.84	3.32±2.74	.21
5.	Role expectations	1-4	2.80±.90	2.86±.79	2.65±.88	2.86±.81	.42
6.	Learning experiences	1-4	2.71±.84	2.63±.68	2.80±.86	2.94±.77	.42
7.	Compatibility	1-4	2.76±.78	2.88±.78	2.96±.83	3.15±.69	.05***
8.	Constructive learning	1-4	3.19±2.90	2.71±.74	2.92±.83	2.88±.87	.39
9.	Helps develop skills	1-4	2.71±.89	2.84±.80	2.75±.83	2.82±.83	.79
10.	Focuses on learning	1-4	2.90±.84	2.61±.82	2.82±.85	2.92±.76	.12
11.	Professional development	1-4	3.42±4.12	3.46±5.80	2.90±.93	2.92±.65	.66
12.	Supervision and Training	1-4	2.94±.82	2.78±.69	2.67±.85	2.94±.80	.16
13.	Encourages evaluation	1-4	2.65±.83	2.76±.75	2.86±.90	2.88±.83	.32
14.	Allows questions and concerns	1-4	2.82±.83	2.86±.86	2.80±.92	3.00±.90	.53

Sig. ***p <0.05; Time – 1, 2, 3 and 4th semesters; M = Mean, SD – Standard deviation. Repeated Measures Analysis was used.

Table 11.4: Self-rating Evaluation of Trainees Emotional and Psychological Well-Being

Sl. No.	*GHQ -12 DOMAINS*	*Range*	*Male (28)*			*Female (24)*		
			Mean	*SD*	*Sig.*	*Mean*	*SD*	*Sig.*
1.	Able to concentrate	0-3	.60	.73	.21	.87	.79	.21
2.	Lost sleep over worry	0-3	1.21	.99	.89	1.25	.98	.89
3.	Playing a useful part	0-3	.92	.81	.52	1.08	.92	.52
4.	Capable of making decisions	0-3	1.14	.97	.29	.87	.85	.29
5.	Felt constantly under strain	0-3	1.14	.89	.33	.89	.82	.33
6.	Couldn't overcome difficulties	0-3	1.17	.90	.77	1.25	.89	.77
7.	Enjoy normal daily activities	0-3	1.14	1.04	.82	1.08	.88	.82
8.	Able to face your problems	0-3	1.28	1.15	.04**	.75	.60	.03**
9.	Feeling unhappy or depressed	0-3	1.03	1.03	.51	1.20	.83	.50
10.	Been losing confidence	0-3	.75	.92	.74	.83	.91	.74
11.	Thinking you are a worthless person	0-3	1.07	1.11	.31	.79	.83	.30
12.	Feeling reasonably happy	0-3	1.25	1.07	.09**	.79	.83	.09**
Total		0-3	12.75	7.22	.75	12.16	6.11	.75

Sig. ** $p<0.01$; GHQ-12= General Health Questionnaire, M= Mean, SD – Standard deviation. Chi-square test was used

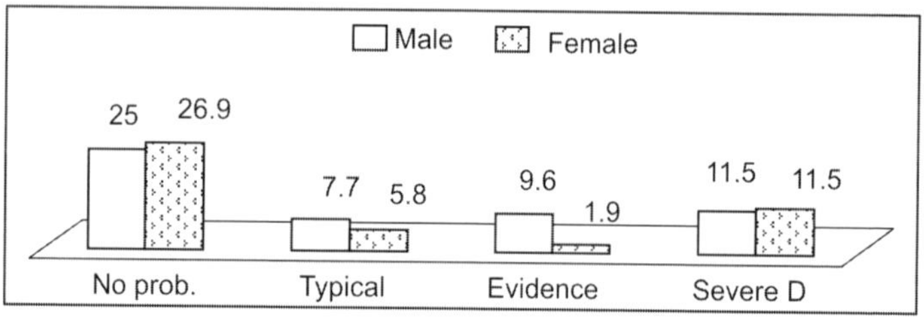

Fig. 11.2: Comparision of Psychological Distress in Male and Female Trainees

Discussion

Mean age of 4th semester trainees was 24.48 (4.23) years ($p<0.05$), range 21-47 years. Trainees (85%) were between 20-25 years. Similar results by Desai (1994) showed that most first year participants (70%) were between 22 to 23 years. Studies from the West (Neil and Sellick, 2001) showed that American and European MSW students were much older and ranged from 24 to 50 years. The sex ratio of the trainees showed more males (53.8%) than female (46.2%) trainees. A study by Desai (1994) showed similar results, which had more male (61%) than female (38%) trainees. However, among most schools of social work in the country, female trainees were clearly larger in numbers.

The study showed that there are significant ($p<0.01$) differences in choice of specializations, with more males (50%) opting for Labour Welfare/personnel management, while female trainees (50%) choose medical and psychiatric social work, which were comparable to Desai's study (1994). An analysis of the marital status reveals that all with the exception of two students were single (96.2%). Related findings by Desai (1994) revealed that a majority (91%) were unmarried. However, Western studies (Neil and Sellick, 2001), report contrary findings where almost half of the trainees were or had been married and more than one half had children.

The educational background of the trainees in this study shows that a majority (90.4%) were from an Arts stream and only 7.7 per cent had a BSW education, as compared to 13% in Desai's study (1994). This could be attributed to the larger numbers of students from the BSW stream, who are required to have a minimum one years' work experience to qualify for the MSW course. One-half reported their overall rating of the MSW course to be satisfactory (53.8%). Desai's (1994) study also reported similar findings, with 53 per cent were satisfied with having selected social work as a career. Although trainees had scored an overall 1st class, there was only a marginal improvement across the three semesters. They had fared better in their undergraduate courses.

A good supervisor has been described as being a good teacher and practitioner with the ability to tap the trainee's unique personality, natural ability and capacity to learn, (Desai, 2001). The Trainees self rating scores of their faculty supervision (Table 11.1) shows inconsistent ratings across the four semesters, with the exception of 'held individual and group supervision', which was statistically significant (p <0.05). The first year supervision was rated as being better than the second year and across semesters most trainees lacked continuous supervision and guidance in the 3rd' and 4th semester which relate to their specialization year and requiring more inputs. The lowest rating given over four semesters was in the domain 'was a source of instruction' and 'faculty's interest in their professional development'.

There is an "unhealthy reliance on the field to provide all practicum learning, (Maidment, 2003) while trainees are not equipped with adequate skills, (Ejaz, 1991). This makes is difficult to foster the integration of empirical and practice-based knowledge to promote the development of professional competence, (CSWE, 2008). Table 11.2 contains the ratings of the Agencies over four semesters which are conducive to their objectives. Though not statistically significant, trainees in the first year gave higher ratings to their agencies as 'meeting learning needs', ironically the same parameter was rated lowest in their specialization year. Trainees were less satisfied with their agency placements in the second year as compared to the 1st year.

Educators of social work are in a dilemma as to how to link theory to practice (Patil, 2001; Sheafor, Horejsi, C.R. and Horejsi, G.A., 2000). However, the success of field work does not depend entirely on their opportunity to work in any one field or agency, but in the ability of trainees to learn to use the social work principles and techniques in any agency, (Nagendra,

2005). Higher ratings of agency supervision were seen in the 4th semester (Table 11.3) in all domains except in the 'impact of supervision in their professional development'. There is a statistically significant difference across the four semester on 'Compatibility with the student' ($p < 0.05$), indicating supervisors attributes in their learning experiences.

Ramana (2012) highlights the trends in social work education in South India which ultimately impacts the trainees: sub-standard quality of education (academically and administratively), skewed teacher-student ratios, commercialisation of social work education, expensive fee structures, concept of paid seats and capitation fees and absence or weak supervision of fieldwork training. Among the administrative problems were: lack of adequate faculty, inadequate infrastructure, lack of specialised libraries and smart classrooms. Other factors were: lack of good libraries, production of high quality literature, teaching methodologies, teaching materials and teacher competence. All these, collectively or individually contribute to emotional well-being of the trainees— It is well documented that the mental health problems among today's university cohorts in the industrialized countries are more frequent. Guthrie et al (1998) in a 5-year prospective longitudinal cohort study found that a small group of students repeatedly experienced psychological distress during their medical training. In Pakistan a cross-sectional descriptive study on all interns and residents at the Aga Khan University Hospital found that more than 46 per cent of the trainees scored over the threshold of more than four for morbid stress (Kasi, 2007).

Male and female trainees (Table 11.4) were comparable on their self-rated emotional and psychological wellbeing scores. There was significant differences between the two groups on 'ability to face problems' ($p < 0.01$) and 'feeling reasonably happy' ($p < 0.01$), with female trainees having lower mean scores on these domains. Though not significant, male trainees scored higher on 'ability to make decisions', were 'under constant strain', had 'difficulty facing problems' and had 'feelings of low self worth'. While female trainees had marginally higher scores on 'lost sleep over worry', 'were not playing a useful part in things', 'felt they were unable to overcome their difficulties' and 'been feeling unhappy or depressed'.

In this study, 'evidence of distresses' was more in male trainees (9.6%). However, contrary results from Western (Ross, Cleland, Macleod, 2006) and Eastern countries (Profile of Turkey, 2004) on gender and psychiatric morbidity showed no gender difference among adolescents with respect to mental health problems. On the other hand, 'severe distress' was reported by an equal number of both male and female trainees (23%). Similar results were reported in USA by Becker, Martin, Wajeeh (2002), wherein 37 per cent of the young adults, who were mostly college students, had a diagnosable mental disorder. In British universities the counselling services reported an increase in the proportion of seriously disturbed students (Phippen, 1993).

Socio-demographic factors are among the strong predictors of depression and anxiety (Harrison 1999). In our study, the higher percentage of male students (53.8%) might be indicative of a gender imbalance among population, who were also found to be at higher risk for mental health problems. Our findings of lower GHQ scores among female students are similar to other Indian studies (Nanda, 2001; Chawla, 2012). In our study, females in the age group of 26-30 years and those in the MPSW specialization had poorer emotional health. Research has shown that women in this age group are more prone to emotional distress. This shows that there is a lot of pressure in academic circles, parental and society to be achievers. The study also found that both male and female trainees from Bachelor of Arts stream had scored lower grades over the three semesters and had higher levels of emotional distress. Female trainees, who had scored distinction in the undergraduate courses, had higher levels of emotional distress as compared to their male counterparts.

An interesting finding is that male trainees, who rated the four semesters of the MSW course, as 'poor' and female trainees, who rated it as 'excellent', had comparably higher levels of emotional and psychological distress. There is increased pressure on males in our culture to get a job, support aging parents and take over parental responsibilities and to be the breadwinner, while also thinking of career prospects. Whereas females usually get married and are not under much pressure to pursue employment or make ends meet. Also most of the curricula are being influenced heavily by the market, availability of jobs and is highly competitive, (Meenai, 2012). Trainees from semi-urban (50%) and rural (28.8%) areas had higher rates of emotional distress. This could be due to the fact that two departments of Social work from established institutions, catering mainly to the urban population, failed to return the self-rating proformas. Similar results were reported in other Indian studies (Sharma and Singh, 2001; Chawla, 2012) where students from urban areas reported better mental health.

The New Educational Policy (1986) has encouraged equal educational options for its citizens and with government quotas, reservations and financial incentives, has resulted in an increase of students from rural and other backward communities of the country in the educational stream. Many of them are first generation in colleges of higher learning, resulting in migration from rural to urban areas. Significantly higher rates of mental illness have been reported among these migrants (Gavin *et al*, 2001) leading to the creation of a "fringe population" who live from hand to mouth (Trivedi, Sareen and Dhyani, 2008). Most migrants endure years of isolation, lack of technological connectivity, deprivation, poor health, poverty, unemployment and inadequate housing. Most schools of social work are located in urban areas where the medium of instruction is English, (Meenai, 2012) and not much indigenous literature is available in local languages, for students to comprehend the concepts, feel socially disconnected, adding to their stress levels and depression.

Social work education in India has been in existence for more than 65 and in the last few decades has emerged as one of the most demanding professions, yet has been unable to establish an identity amongst the professions (Singh, 2012). There is a dearth of scientific exploration and inability to come to the forefront of nation building processes, (Jamia Millia Islamia, 2012). Over the years, the profession has been surveyed periodically (Dadlani, 1961; IJSW 1967; Pathak, 1987); reviewed officially (UGC, 1965, 1980) and discussed on occasions (Desai and Narayan, 1998; Nair, 1981). Problems and issues concerning social work education have also been identified and debated by some authors (Desai, 1991; Gore, 1981; Pathak, 1971, 1987, Siddiqui, 1989; Thomas, 1967). While social work educators have grown numerically over the past six decades and their economic condition has steadily improved, their performance as academicians and scholars has been disappointing (Pathak, 2000). But the ironical fact is that the quality of social work education has been neglected (Ramesh, 2010).

Therefore, this study adds to the body of literature showing that the present difficulties/lacunae in supervision of faculty, agencies and agency supervisors leads to increased emotional and psychological distress in Social Work trainees, over their two year course curriculum.

Based on findings, it is suggested that the Foundation course should cover theoretical inputs like History and Philosophy of Social Work and core subjects, orientation visits to agencies, enhancement of language (medium of instruction and local) computer skills, and sports as well as games. This has scope for self and faculty assessment which would be included in the internal marks and monitoring of their emotional and psychological health.

The study has following limitations:

(i) Selection of Departments of social work could not be done randomly, but based on the permission accorded by the HODs, (ii) Deletion of trainees from autonomous colleges, due to lack of uniformity in course curriculum,(iii) Lack of availability of indigenous tools for self assessment, and (iv) Cross-sectional design did not allow to study other cause-and-effect relationship of emotional and psychological well-being. Therefore, a prospective study is necessary to study the association of psychological morbidity with demographic variables, sources of stress and Quality of Life.

Conclusion

It is important to take into consideration the self assessment of trainees of their faculty and agency supervisors and the type of agency. There is need for transparency, as this is important for the overall learning and practice of the trainees. Evidence in literature indicates that students in university education are at a higher risk of emotional and psychological distress, but no studies to date have been conducted to assess the psychological morbidity of social work trainees who are in the economically productive age group. The study endorses these findings in the Indian context. In addition, this is a group at risk and preventive strategies in the form of mandatory supervision and constant multi-level monitoring of emotional distress in trainees is required. The findings of the study cannot be generalized for all university students; however, the study variables can guide other researchers in their studies on the mental health status of social work students.

12

NADA Protocol for Protection, Treatment and Recovery

A Social Worker's Perspective

Suneel Vatsyayan, Ajay Vats and *V. Vindhya*

The National Acupuncture Detoxification Association (NADA) is a not-for-profit training and advocacy organization which encourages community wellness through the use of a standardized auricular acupuncture protocol for behavioural health, including addictions, mental health, and disaster and emotional trauma. NADA works to improve access and effectiveness of care through promoting policies and practices which integrate NADA-style treatment with other western behavioural health modalities. It will be appropriate to mention that some expressions such as substance abuse/drug abuse, patient/client, abuse/harmful use and addiction/dependence are interchangeably used throughout this article.

It is estimated that there are about 62.5 million alcohol users, 8.7 million cannabis users and about 2 million opiate users in our country. There are an estimated 250 million tobacco users of age 10 and above. Serious public health problems result from alcohol and other drug consumption. Drug abuse and its impact among women is now becoming more evident in India. Licit substances like tobacco and alcohol are widely prevalent, while abuse of illicit substances like cannabis, heroin, other opiates including opium and propoxyphene is recognized throughout the country.

Table 12.1: Common Drugs of Abuse in India (Males)

Drug Type	*Current Prevalence*
Tobacco	55.8%
Alcohol	21.4%
Cannabis	3.0%
Heroin	0.2%
Opium	0.5%
Other Opiates	0.1%
(National Household Survey 2002)	

Interventions for Substance Abuse

Interventions for substance abuse in India are largely limited to Ministry of

Social Justicc and Empowerment funded 400 de-addiction centres, 110 hospital based psychiatry departments limited to tertiary intervention for those with established late stage problems. Now there is fast growing in numbers of peer led de-addiction centres across the country to fill the gap in the demand and available services. According to National Institute on Drug Abuse (NIDA) (1999) guiding principles for effective intervention no single treatment is effective for all individuals. The treatment should be culture and gender specific, and geared towards addressing individualized needs of the patient. Counseling and other behaviour treatment are critical components of substance use disorder treatment. The treatment which focuses on motivation, relapse, life style change and problem solving ability yields better outcome results.

A gap between the streets or 'natural settings' associated with drug use or the outreach worker and the threshold of the drug treatment programme where the drug user is expected to arrive committed, ready or interested in quitting drugs. Drug treatment that is limited to abstinence and acceptance of the addict identity has excluded the majority of drug users who are not ready or interested in quitting drugs or takingon this identity or disease (c). Much of the therapeutic nihilism (the belief that nothing works) associated with substance use is related to the delays in help seeking and help providing. Help is rarely offered early in the substance abuse phase, it is often delayed until end-stage addiction develops. At this stage, the recurrent, relapsing nature of the problem makes treatment more difficult. However, it must not be forgotten that addiction, much like hypertension or diabetes is a chronic, relapsing condition and life style related new learning and requires long-term intervention and monitoring with objective of helping him to help himself (3).

Nobody can undermine the role of psychosocial interventions in the management in all the phases of substance abuse. There are inherent challenges in the effective delivery of these interventions.

1. Poor treatment retention: It is the patient and not the therapist who invariably controls the duration and intensity of treatment because the patient is usually free to drop out at any time or fail to comply with the expectations of their therapists
2. "I have a problem" or 'I think I should quit' or 'I have to do something about this'...Each time he carries a feeling of failure and a burden of guilt not to be successful in each desire and attempt. Society never provides a person a right to fail. Person becomes more and more vulnerable and continues to live with mixed feeling of ambivalence and not ready to forgive himself and carry the burden of past deeds and thoughts.
3. Many of treatments methods and processes create barriers and have no way to deal with these vulnerabilities of a traumatized person with addiction problem.

4. Neither patient nor the therapist is ready to lose the control and start blaming themselves for being failed in their attempts to help.
5. Personal characteristics of therapist affect the outcome: There are indications that the therapist is a significant factor in determining treatment outcome for psycho-social interventions.

Resistance in Psychosocial Intervention

Occasionally, despite a counselor's best efforts, some clients fail to act in their best interests and negatively respond to all counseling interventions. These clients are often called oppositional, reactionary, noncompliant, intractable, and unmotivated (3). The behaviours displayed by these difficult clients are often collectively referred to as resistance. In clinical terms, resistance is defined as "a process of avoiding or diminishing the self-disclosing communication requested by the interviewer because of its capacity to make the interviewee uncomfortable or anxious" (6). It is an active process that has the potential to become a fundamental obstacle to positive counseling outcomes. Resistance interferes with the counselor's perceived efficacy, impedes client motivation, and undermines the change process (5).

The Bio-Psycho-Social Perspective of Drug Abuse

The WHO definition of health as a state of complete physical, mental and social well-being and not merely the absence of disease and infirmity reflects the holistic view of health most widely accepted today. Even drug abuse can be considered within this model, as it is a bio-psycho-social problem (1).

Manifestations of Drug Addiction

- Irresistible urge for drug
- Lack of self -control
- Change in daily routine of activities—neglect of personal appearance and hygiene
- Moody—often subject to extreme of temper
- Guilt feeling
- Lack of self-confidence and self-image.
- Inability to take decisions.

Treatment Components: The following components are involved in treatment of drug abuser.

- Detoxification
  - Treat Withdrawal
  - Prevent Complications
  - Correct/Treat Damage Done

Usually done in hospitals/specialized setting and using medicines.

- **Psychotherapy** and **Counselling**
  - Individual Therapy
  - Family Therapy
  - Group Therapy with recovering addicts. As in AA, NA
  - Craving Control Techniques
  - Behavioural Therapies
  - Relaxation and Leisure Timc
- **Rehabilitation**
  - Whole person recovery
  - Commitment to a drug free life
  - Acceptance of higher value
  - Adaptation to work and responsibilities
  - Social re-integration
  - 'De-addiction'–usually done in a specialised facility.

Addiction is a bio-psycho and social problem in nature, so treatment approach needs to be equally broad and inclusive. As drug addiction is one of the major emerging areas of social work practices, one of the authors is a social work practitioner realised while working with addicts how other disciplines NADA (National Acupuncture Detoxification Association) acupuncture can be used as an adjunct treatment. He was trained as an apprentice at Lincoln Recovery and Acupuncture Centre, New York, in the year 2001. Then he introduced it at Navjyoti Delhi Police Foundation drug treatment Centre as a value added service. He observed that use of such techniques can also be applied for the healthy rapport building and developing trust with the clientele.

Social Work and Acupuncture Works on Similar Dimension

The internationally accepted definition of professional social work is very well received. The social work profession promotes social change, problem solving in human relationships and the empowerment and liberation of people to enhance well-being. Utilising theories of human behaviour and social systems, social work intervenes at the points where people interact with their environments. Principles of human rights and social justice are fundamental to social work. Acupuncture and all Qi (Chi)-flow therapies "Help the body help itself." So is the goal of the social work.

NADA Protocol

At three designated ear points in each auricle (outer ear), clinicians trained through NADA apply fine gauge, sterilized, one-time use stainless steel needles just under the skin, where they remain for up to an hour while the client (in most circumstances) relaxes quietly in a comfortable chair. Ordinarily, groups of clients sit together while undergoing the treatment.

The procedure functions as an adjunct to a comprehensive treatment programme offering the basic therapeutic elements of counseling, education, family involvement, mutual support group involvement, supportive health care of general nature. Clients in all types of treatment settings including inpatient, outpatient, incarcerated, shelters, harm reduction and street outreach can utilize this treatment. Among the benefits reported by clients and clinicians are improved programme retention, a more optimistic and cooperative attitude toward the process of recovery, as well as reductions in cravings, anxiety, sleep disturbance and need for pharmaceuticals.

The NADA protocol is also known commonly referred to as: acu detox, acupuncture detoxification, three point ear acupuncture protocol. Beyond the actual needling treatment, a key element of the protocol specifies qualities of behaviour and attitude on the part of the clinician, consistent with what is known as the Spirit of NADA. There are no diagnostic procedures as part of NADA Protocol. The ear points provide a balancing effect: some may fall asleep; some feel relief of depression; some seem to be meditating. These balancing effects continue from one to several days even though the patient may be exposed to contrasting emergencies during that time. It is a coping and preventive effect (7, 8).

The Spirit of NADA

Since the NADA Protocol works by mobilizing the existing internal resources of the patient, every aspect of a clinician's interaction with persons in need is to help them help themselves. Opening access to the treatment itself comes first. This occurs through eliminating unnecessary bureaucratic, socio-economic and environmental barriers to starting a programme of recovery. The next task is to create a zone of peace within which patients can begin to experience their own inner strengths. Finally, and in respect to the other aspects, keep it simple. As a social work practitioner, these are the following challenges:

- Can we treat a client before assessment and diagnosis are completed so that the client can be calm and cooperative enough for a useful diagnosis to be made.
- Confronting about drug use is necessary?
- Can we help a client even while they are in denial about the need for treatment.
- Can we make a client relax without him losing control.
- Is the treatment to which client may return at any time, especially following a relapse and still find all the benefits.

By introducing NADA Protocol, one can learn that Acudetox is Non-verbal…non-threatening. Acupuncture is usually non-threatening because it is non-verbal—the person does not have to explain or justify himself and it does not have to be associated with labeling or diagnosis, or an expectation that the person be interested in abstinence, much less drug or alcohol free at the time they are treated.

(i) *Acupuncture is useful because it doesn't revolve around the drug:* The acupuncture allows greater flexibility in treatment approaches because social worker can step out of the expert role because the approach itself models a more horizontal relationship: 'Did you swab your ears and are you ready for a treatment?'

(ii) *Acupuncture does not confront the person:* Michael Smith has noted that a verbal exchange is not required, nor is a readiness to talk with counselors or a willingness to complete an assessment or fill out a form. NADA Acupuncture has many characteristics in common with counseling. It uses group process in a tolerant, supportive and present-time oriented manner. Participation is independent of diagnosis and level of recovery. Both approaches are simple, reinforcing, nurturing, and conveniently available. The emphasis on 'self-responsibility' is common to both systems. In practice, acupuncture provides an excellent foundation for counseling process. Smith says, *"Acudetox counseling teaches the person to relax from the inside out." This increased sense of calm and the quieting of symptoms that occurs as a result of the acupuncture treatment stimulate patients' own "Qi" (one's inner energy) and bring them back into a more balanced state.* As person become calmer inside, they become much more aware of themselves and others. From this quieter, inner place the person can then make more careful choices in their reactions to life situations. Interpersonal relations and unresolved feelings can be a source of stress. The past and current traumatic events can leave a person with addiction problem chronically stressed. The bodily energy is balanced with NADA Ear acupuncture, peace of mind is restored so is life balance can be partially restored and works as foundation for growth and recovery.

The 21st century has brought a remarkable expansion in the use of the NADA protocol. It is used in 130 prisons in England. Correction officers provide all the treatments under a five year training contract by Smart-UK. The jail programme was expanded because of an 80 per cent reduction in violent incidents. Post-trauma treatments have been given to community members after 9/11 and Katrina. Treatments for firemen have been permanently institutionalized in both cities. Ear acupuncture for stress has been used by hundreds of para-military (Border Security Force) personnel and prisoners in Gujarat and Delhi through Nada-India.

NADA acupuncture has changed the face of psychiatric hospital care in Northern Europe. Around 3,000 nurses have been trained in 100 different government facilities. Refugee services in war-torn areas have been particularly impressive. The DARE programme in Thailand has provided ear acupuncture for many years with a dozen different Burmese tribes in border camps. NADA was introduced during a 2-week training sponsored by Real Medicine Foundation in refugee camps in East Africa in May 2008. By the end of the year, 18,000 treatments were provided by the refugee trainees. Support was provided for survivors of a violent land dispute. (7,8). NADA Protocol has become part of the one month and three month training courses organized by National Intuition Social Defence (Ministry of Social Justice and Empowerment) for addiction counselors and social workers.(4)

In summary, NADA Ear acupuncture helps social work practitioner to encourage patients to participate in individual and group counseling sessions at Stress Reduction service or drug treatment service more effectively. It is a nonverbal, non-threatening, "first step" intervention, that has an immediate calming effect on people. Initial participation with Ear acupuncture has been found to improve patients' overall treatment retention and to facilitate their subsequent involvement in bringing back work life balance. NADA acupuncture adds a valuable component to the behavioural health fields. Acudetox in the addiction treatment field and its worldwide acceptance validates and strengthens the entire acupuncture and social work profession as well.

13

Recovery Oriented Services (ROSES) for Persons with Psychiatric Disability

NIMHANS Experience

Faseela Jaleel, B. P. Nirmala and *Jagadisha Thirthalli*

Mental Health problems lead to an invisible disability which challenges an individual from performing his/her basic daily activities to skills that are needed for an independent living. Impairment in social and occupational functioning along with cognitive deficits is commonly found in persons with severe mental disorders like Schizophrenia, Bipolar Affective Disorder (BPAD), Obsessive Compulsive Disorder (OCD) etc. Recovery from Psychiatric disability is now seen as a realistic goal and has become a guiding vision for the improvement of mental health services (Ralph, 2000). It is at this stage, Psychiatric Rehabilitation is necessary for the individuals suffering from problems in personal and social life due to the illness. The rehabilitation professionals had changed their primary focus from clinical outcomes to the social and occupational functioning of the individuals and reintegration in community. At the same time, the symptoms should not be too severe that it will affect the independence of the person. Hence, enabling persons with persistent and serious mental illness to live a normal life in the community made a shift away from focus on an illness model towards a recovery model. The recovery model emphasizes hope and feasibility of full recovery, and states that recovery is not only achievable, but it should also provide the basic overarching framework for our mental health systems (Anthony, 1993).

The concept of recovery in functional criteria is operationally explained as: (a) symptoms low enough in severity and frequency so as not to impede everyday functioning; (b) work in a competitive, market job or attending a normal school at least half time; (c) reasonably cordial family relationships, recognizing that occasional family discord is normal; (d) social relationships with at least one friend with whom one engages in social and recreational activities in normative community environments at least once every two weeks; (e) independent living as defined by money management, illness management, self care, personal hygiene within normal standards (Liberman, 2012).

Vocational rehabilitation is considered as a major therapeutic intervention to achieve functional recovery and in reintegrating the persons with mental illness to the community. Training in vocations has many targets including symptom reduction, reduction of Expressed Emotions as they go away from family, social skill development, improvement in cognitive functions, etc., but the most important goal is to have a financially viable occupation. Vocational rehabilitation is based on the assumption that work not only improves activity, social contacts etc., but may also promote gains in related areas such as self-esteem and quality of life, as work and employment are a step away from dependency and a step to integration into society (Rossler, 2006). Vocational rehabilitation significantly improves social functioning, cognitive functioning and psychopathology (Kumar, 2008). Hence, the ultimate goal of all rehabilitation interventions is to help the client in achieving financial independence and thereby re-integrate the client to the community.

In a recent review article by Chandrashekar et al (2010), it was pointed out that although there is a stress for culture specific rehabilitative measures in India, the models followed by various rehabilitation service providers and clinical benefits of such attempts are not published for the benefits of psychiatric community. This paper is an attempt to showcase the recent experience of NIMHANS in providing Recovery Oriented SErviceS (ROSES) to persons with psychiatric disability.

Setting and Methods

National Institute of Mental Health and Neurosciences (NIMHANS), Bangalore (now Bangaluru) is one of the earliest Government institutions in India to start Psychiatric Rehabilitation Services including a day care centre for the mentally ill. Vocational activity in productive areas was part of the Mysore lunatic asylum since the time of inception in 1838. The patients were engaged in agricultural activities. In 1930s, thrust was given for occupational therapy which continued to be an important component of treatment. In the year 1971, a separate building was constructed for rehabilitation of mentally ill which houses the day care centre and sections for activity therapy. The day care centre is the largest facility for rehabilitation of the mentally ill in India where Recovery Oriented Services (ROSES) are provided for the individuals through a multidisciplinary approach. Around 80 clients attend the day care centre on a regular basis with an expected duration of stay for a period of six months to one year.

The present paper is a case series of the vocational rehabilitation efforts made by the Psychiatric Rehabilitation unit of NIMHANS during the period from June 2011 to November 2012 in providing Recovery Oriented Services to its consumers. Five candidates with similar clinical diagnosis (Schizophrenia or its subtypes with any co-morbidity) who were attending the day care services during the period and are successfully rehabilitated were selected for the case series which includes four males and one female. Their age ranged from

29 years to 64 years. The duration of illness ranged from 7 years to 33 years. All the candidates were assessed using SERWICE (Services for Enhanced Recovery With Intensive and Comprehensive Engagement) proforma which is a semi structured open ended questionnaire to elicit information on socio demographic details, current symptomatic status, co-morbidity and side effects, understanding about illness, drug treatment and adherence, Basic Activities of Daily Living, Independent Activities of Daily Living, Social and Occupational functioning, Cognitive functioning, Expressed Emotion, client's and family's perceived need for intervention, short term and long term goals of client and family, potential barriers for rehabilitation etc. Each item in the questionnaire is elaborated in detail so as to get a subjective understanding about the perception of client and care giver about the item. Based on assessment, intervention plans were planned for each candidate by a multi disciplinary team and the same was implemented.

Case 1

Ms. S, 29 year old single female studied up to 12th standard and completed ITI course in COPA belonging to Middle Socio Economic Status of Bangalore was presented to the Psychiatric rehabilitation unit in 2006 with a diagnosis of Mild Mental Retardation with Undifferentiated Schizophrenia in remission with co-morbidity of hypothyroidism, obesity and Poly Cystic Ovarian Disease (PCOD). The history revealed family history of epilepsy and mental retardation in maternal uncle, hypertension and diabetes mellitus in father and cardiac problems in paternal uncle; personal history of forceps delivery, delayed milestones and irregular menstrual cycle and past history of thyroid problems and exam anxiety which is associated with vomiting.

In SERWICE assessment, symptoms of occasional depressed mood, loss of interest in daily activities secondary to stressors related to job placement were found. The client had high expectations about job in spite of having good understanding about the illness. The client was independent in Activities of Daily Living whereas Instrumental Activities of Daily Living were impaired and client was dependent on parents for the same. The social functioning of the client was not adequate as she had deficits in social skills such as over talkativeness, not maintaining interpersonal distance, not behaving according to social situations etc. Expressed Emotion i.e., Over involvement from the parents were noted during the assessment where the client was always being protected by them and parents were not willing to make the client independent.

Based on the assessment, an intervention plan was made which included behavioural intervention, skill training in instrumental activities of daily living, social skills training, vocational counseling and job placement, and family intervention to reduce expressed emotion and to explore future care giving options. The client was initially posted to the craft section in the day care services of NIMHANS and then to the administrative office and Medical Record Department of the hospital for developing work habits and vocational training. During the process three attempts were made by the Psychiatric Social Worker to place the client in suitable job with the active involvement of the family which was not successful. The treating team then collaborated with an NGO which assists the disabled in job placement. The client was placed in a BPO as a Front Office Executive and then trained by the NGO according to the job profile. The treating team continues to visit the client in her workplace and provides workplace solutions to both employer and the client as part of supported employment. The process of making her independent in transportation, money management, cooking and shopping are ongoing. The client has also improved in her social skills for which behavioural interventions are implemented.

Case 2

Mr. A, 50 year old single male studied B.Sc Physics and Post Graduate Diploma in Computer and Electronics from Middle Socio Economic Status of Tamil Nadu currently staying in Bangalore with sister was presented to the Psychosocial Rehabilitation Services of NIMHANS in 2011 with a 30 year history of Paranoid Schizophrenia and Nicotine Dependence Syndrome. The history reveals family history of ADS and NDS in first and second degree relatives, personal history of multiple substance use, Anti social personality disorder and involvement with the law, Head injury and organic personality change.

SERWICE assessment revealed the symptoms of suspiciousness, irritability, low mood, poor self confidence and Nicotine use. The client had poor insight about the illness and the social functioning was poor. The client was less interactive and used to avoid social functions. Occupational status was the most challenging problem for the client where he had a history of multiple job changes. The cognitive deficits in terms of memory, attention and concentration, and cognitive errors such as negative automatic thoughts were challenging the client from taking up a new job. The primary social support for the client was his sister with whom he was staying in Bangalore and the other two siblings were also involved in the rehabilitation process even though they were living in other places. Criticality and over involvement were observed as expressed emotions from the family members.

The priority according to the client being job placement, he was referred to the computer section of the day care centre of NIMHANS for vocational training. Simultaneously, medication management, individual therapy using Cognitive Behaviour Therapy principles, neuropsychological assessment and cognitive remediation, intervention for substance abuse and job placement were planned and implemented. During his training period in the computer section, monetary reinforcement was given to the client for improving his self confidence. Multiple attempts were made by the Psychiatric Social Work team for the placement and finally the team collaborated with an NGO which assists the disabled in job placement. The client was placed in a BPO as a Front Office Executive and then trained by the NGO according to the job profile. The treating team continues to visit the client in the workplace and provides workplace solutions to both employer and the client as part of supported employment. The client has difficulties in work due to his cognitive deficits but the agency understands him and accommodates to his challenges due to which the client is able to be more confident and make progress. The individual therapy and treatment follow up is going on regularly.

Case 3

Mr. S is a 41 year old single male studied up to 11th standard hailing from Middle Socio Economic Status of Bangalore, Karnataka diagnosed with Paranoid Schizophrenia since 16 years of age. He was brought to the Psychosocial Rehabilitation Services of NIMHANS in 1998. The client had a family history of postpartum psychosis and Congestive Cardiac failure in mother, deafness in father and paranoid schizophrenia, substance use and epilepsy in brother.

On admission, the client had prominently negative symptoms including profound disability in social role functioning such as inadequate social interaction, lack of interest in activities, poor self care and mild disability in speed of performance. The client lives with his brother who is diagnosed to have paranoid schizophrenia and was financially supported by the other siblings.

The client was initially placed in the printing section of the day care services of NIMHANS for developing a healthy work habit and vocational training. Interventions were also initiated in improving his Self Care and Activities of Daily Living (ADL), social skills etc. and vocational counseling and guidance were given. When he made progress in work, he was shifted to the Medical Records Department printing section. The client has recovered and was performing well in the section but the attempts for placing him in a competitive job was not successful as he was not confident enough to leave the protected environment of the hospital. Six such attempts were made but client had not joined or continued the work. Considering his performance, the team approached the private agency which supplies man power (contract staff) to the hospital when there was a vacancy for helper in one of the departments. The application of the client was processed and he was recruited. The client is continuing the job and there is positive feedback from his supervisor about his performance.

Case 4

Mr. G., 37 year old single male educated up to 10th standard belonging to Middle Socio Economic Status of Bangalore was presented to Rehabilitation Services in 2009 with a 19 year history of Schizophrenia Not Otherwise Specified with co-morbidity of Mild Mental Retardation, Symptomatic Seizure Disorder (GTCS – Global Tonic Clonic Seizure) and vericose vein. The client's family history revealed Diabetes Mellitus in mother, Alcohol Dependence Syndrome in elder brother who committed suicide in 2011 and personal history was nil significant.

During admission in Rehabilitation Services, the client had symptoms of hallucinatory behaviour, poor self care, muttering to self, smiling to self, increased anger and irritability. Deficits were noted in social and occupational functioning as the symptoms were interfering his daily functioning. Disability assessment using IDEAS (Indian Disability Evaluation and Assessment Scale) showed 60% disability. The client also has Peri Oral Tardive Dyskinesia due to the side effect of treatment.

Along with medication management, the client was referred to the Medical Record Section for vocational training. He was involved in the group work activities as part of social skills training and neurology review was also carried out periodically. The job placement was a priority for the client and family members and they were ready to accept any kind of job. Hence the client was provided training in hospital attender job by attaching with the attenders working in the rehabilitation services. The multi disciplinary team reviewed his progress regularly and when the client was able to do the work independently, the client and family was given guidance for submitting application in the private agency which supplies man power to hospital as contract staff. The client has gone through the process of recruitment and was selected as a hospital attender. He is regular and punctual in work but still have symptoms which do not interfere with his functioning. The client is on regular follow up with the treating team.

Case 5

Mr. J is a 64 year old married male studied up to 10th standard belonging to Lower Socio Economic Status of Bangalore. He was brought to Psychiatric Rehabilitation services in 1993 with a 14 year history of Undifferentiated Schizophrenia. Co-morbidities include Tardive Dyskinesia and Cholestrol. The client has a family history of psychiatric illness in elder sister and suicidal death in son.

On SERWICE assessment, the client had the symptoms of hallucinatory behaviour like muttering to self, stereotypic behaviour like praying to wall and making sound, touching head with the tools and table stand etc. The social and occupational functioning of the client was inadequate. Cognitive deficits such as poor attention, concentration and memory were also noticed. It was also observed that the family consists of the patient and wife and there is less social support from the relatives. Client's wife who is working as a housemaid was the earning member of the family. They were facing financial difficulties due to the expenses of medication and treatment for both Husband and wife.

The intervention was initiated with medication optimization and he was posted to the tailoring section of Day Care Services initially for developing work habits. The client's occupational functioning was poor and he was then shifted to candle making section. It was found that the client can do supervised work even if symptoms are persistent. Based on the perceived need for economic security by the wife who is the primary care giver, she was also trained in candle making so that they can start a unit in their home. The client and care giver had completed the training under supervision of a qualified instructor. The client was not able to acquire all the skills but can help the wife in preparing candles if monitored properly. The family was helped in starting the unit with supervision by the therapist and they were also helped in getting market. The Psychiatric Social Work team had collaborated with the General Post Office and linked them with the client and care giver for a regular market for the candles.

Discussion

Generally, Psychiatric Rehabilitation focuses on vocational rehabilitation wherein different models such as Sheltered Employment, Placement, Supported Employment, Individual Placement and Support (IPS), Integrated Supported Employment (ISE), Home based rehabilitation etc. In a developing country like India, adaptation and implementation of a single vocational rehabilitation model is not practical considering the limited resources and man power. Therefore, in the Psychiatric Rehabilitation Services unit of NIMHANS, we try to look into the strengths of each client and uses different approaches for different clients with the active involvement of the client and the family/care giver. Vocational rehabilitation being the final outcome, the client and family is seen as a unit and provided interventions in addressing issues related to illness and its management, social and occupational functioning, cognitive remediation, behaviour modification, skills training in Activities of Daily Living (ADL) and Instrumental Activities of Daily Living (IADL), family intervention and so on. There is no specific model followed in this case series but based on the resources available, different models were tried for different clients.

Individual Placement and Support (IPS) model was followed for case 1 and case 2 and the outcome was successful where the clients were able to obtain employment. Various studies in the area of vocational rehabilitation for people with severe mental illness found that individual placement and support (IPS) was more effective than other approaches in helping individuals to gain and retain competitive open employment (Crowther *et al.*, 2001) (Bond *et al.*, 2007). Individual Placement and Support (IPS) is a variant of supported employment developed by Drake & Becker with the primary goal of not changing the individual, but to find a natural match between the individual's strengths and experiences and a job in the community. IPS is based on the eight key principles of Supported Employment (Bond, 2004) and all the eight points were taken care during the rehabilitation of case 1 and case 2 which includes: (i) a single-minded focus on competitive employment; (ii) eligibility for services based solely on client choice, with no exclusion on the basis of work readiness, substance use problems, lack of motivation, treatment non-compliance and so on; (iii) rapid job search upon programme admission using the 'place then train' approach; (iv) attention to client preferences in the job search, rather than dependence on job availability; (v) close integration between the employment services and the mental health treatment team; (vi) ongoing, individualized support and job training after clients obtain employment; (vii) systematic benefits counselling; and (viii) consultation with employer or job supervisor including advocacy accommodations. The process was made successful through the involvement of the NGO which is working for the placement of Persons with Disability. By collaborating with them, the Psychiatric Rehabilitation team of NIMHANS could identify jobs according to clients' preferences and follow 'place and train approach. There is continuous and close integration between the employment service provider and the psychiatric social work team where the team members make frequent visits to the work place and provide individualized support to the clients. The team members also meet the job supervisor and discuss workplace solutions to make accommodations in the work.

For case 3 and case 4, traditional vocational rehabilitation model was followed which uses a step-wise 'train and place' approach to vocational rehabilitation. In this model, comprehensive vocational assessment is carried out initially and then pre-vocational services are provided in generic work skills and personal development such as self-esteem, assertiveness, and stress management. Participants must learn pre-vocational and work readiness skills before they are considered ready to be placed in competitive work settings. However, placements are often sheltered through being owned by the hospital or rehabilitation agency (Corrigan *et al* 2007). The clients were provided pre-vocational services and training in specific job skills in the day care centre of NIMHANS so as to make them ready for the job in one of the departments of the hospital. The hospital as a system responds to the needs of the individual and sets example by providing job to the consumers.

Even though there are no specific examples stating the effectiveness of home based rehabilitation, Pillai *et al* (2010) reported that educating patients and their care givers about simple home based rehabilitation practices that can be carried out in homes is effective. In this process learning the basic principles of work- behavioural management, identifying and giving various activities in home and supportive handholding given to the patient and caregivers by professionals, paraprofessionals or trained volunteers can help the patient very well in rehabilitation. For case 5, home based rehabilitation was found to be the best suitable option considering the age of the client and family background. The client could not be placed in an open or sheltered job because of the interference of symptoms to his functioning. Constant supervision was required keep the client engaged in any activity. Therefore, the client and the caregiver was provided training in candle making and was provided assistance in initiating the production at home along with networking the family with potential market.

In all the cases, family involvement was a supportive factor without which the efforts made by the multidisciplinary team would not have produced the fruitful results. The extent of family support for persons with psychiatric disabilities in rehabilitation process has often been cited as a major factor. According to Wig (2000), "Family support, which is so easily available in developing countries, is the anchor of treatment and rehabilitation of the mentally ill in the outpatient management." Unlike developed countries, mental health services in India not only encourage family involvement, but also often make it a pre-requisite of care (Stanhope, 2002).

In addition to family support, family environment is also seen as a protective factor in recovery. The interventions carried out in NIMHANS always addresses the issues of family so that the attitude and response of the family members can be changed and used as a facilitating agent in the rehabilitation process. Usually, the Expressed Emotions like criticality, hostility and over involvement from the family restrict the client from achieving functional recovery. The modification of family environment through interventions like psycho education, communication skills, problem solving techniques, improving interaction etc. are practiced in NIMHANS for better rehabilitation outcomes. Studies show that higher level of Expressed Emotions (EE) among families of those with psychiatric disabilities lead to higher rates of relapse (Vaughn & Leff, 1976). It is also observed that EE rates are considerably lower among families in developing countries (Lefley, 1999) but in the present case series, there were two families with high EE which was addressed.

The major challenge in implementing the vocational rehabilitation was the lack of man power. Even though the psychiatric social workers along with the team members were able to make success in identifying vocational opportunities and placing the clients, the number of such attempts are very less when compared with the consumer needs. Placement officers or employment specialists are required in rehabilitation settings considering the growing need of vocational rehabilitation among persons with psychiatric disability.

Conclusion

Focus on recovery in the delivery of mental health services has been advocated by many for system improvement. There are also examples of states adopting language consistent with the psychiatric recovery model in official documents and using such concepts in policy and planning decisions (Ralph, 2000). India being a developing country, it is very difficult for us to follow the conventional models of rehabilitation. The stigma attached with mental illness is still present in the society and it comes as a major barrier for employment of persons with mental illness. As a first priority, the mental health professionals can work towards identifying job/income generation activities for the clients in the hospital premises itself or provide home based rehabilitation options that are feasible and affordable for the clients. The various mental hospitals can follow this example of engaging patients in work force of the hospital, and thereby help in holistic rehabilitation of the individual and family—both financial independence and treatment of the clients. Since the man power in the area of mental health and rehabilitation are not matching with the current needs of the society, identifying job markets and influencing the policies of employment providers through an employment specialist or placement officer can be kept as second priority. This way of helping the clients will boost the morale and can lead to better functional recovery among the persons with psychiatric disability.

14

Globalization and NGO Response to HIV/AIDS

Concerns for Social Work Practice

Tarun Bikash Sukai

The Acquired Immunodeficiency Syndrome (AIDS) is the fourth leading infectious cause of adult deaths in the world. At the end of 2007, UNAIDS estimated 33.2 million (30.6-36.1 million) people living with HIV/AIDS worldwide. While 30.8 million (28.2-33.6 million) of these were adults, 15.4 million (13.9-16.6 million) were women and 2.1 million (1.9-2.4 million) were children under the age of 15 years. More than 25 million already died since the beginning of the epidemic, bringing the number of infected more than 65 million worldwide (UNAIDS 2007). AIDS is now considered not only as a health problem, but also as a developmental and security threat. Although the epidemic began in USA more than 30 years ago, over 96 per cent of new infections now occur in low and middle income countries, which are unfortunately least equipped to respond effectively to the challenge (UNAIDS 2007). It is now well recognized that AIDS is affecting developed and developing countries differently. In developed countries, AIDS is now a chronic disease and a manageable health problem largely due to the availability of anti-retroviral medication. However, in developing countries, AIDS is now destroying societies, nations and communities. The antiretroviral treatments (ART) that have increased the longevity of patients in the industrialized countries are unfortunately beyond the reach of those in the developing world. Therefore, the disease is widening the gap between the 'haves' and 'have-nots'; between rich and poor nations; and thereby presenting a new ethical and human rights dilemma (Narain 2004).

Globalization is midwife both to the spread of AIDS, as modern travel facilitates rapid dissemination of HIV infection across national borders, and through concerted global action, triumphant conqueror over its devastating impact and expansion. Globalization has affected all facets of life. In recent years, we have witnessed an unprecedented debate on Globalization. The term "globalization" has been given a number of meanings. The definition of globalization can be quite elastic, going beyond economic integration of the world to encompass political and cultural integration as well (Osmani, 2005). In general, globalization is the term used to characterize the processes of growing interconnection and interdependence in today's world, generated to a large degree by growing international economic, cultural and political cooperation and links, as well as by the need to respond together to global problems which can be solved only on a planetary scale (Dommen, 2001). Attentions have been focused on the origin and main features of Globalization and its potential impact on world economic, political and social order. This policy debate is quite understandable, as the pace and consequences of globalization have implications for every individual, community or nation. It is changing the lives of people in developed as well as in developing countries. There are both positive and negative impacts of globalization. The optimistic view sees the increased interdependence attendant upon globalization resulting in an increased willingness of nations to work together in pursuit of improved health because this would serve their rational self-interest. On the other hand, the pessimistic view sees globalization as a phenomenon, which has reduced government's capacity to provide basic health services in the developing countries. As the epidemic of HIV/AIDS continues to expand to all corners of the globe, it is clear that every sector of the society must respond. Among the organizations responding to the crisis, non-governmental organizations (NGOs) are emerging as a powerful force in the effort to contain the AIDS epidemic. In India, National AIDS Control Organization (NACO) also recognizes NGOs as its primary allies and critical partners in undertaking targeted interventions among high risk groups, disseminating information, delivering counseling services and in providing care and outreach services for people living with HIV/AIDS (PLWHA). Several statements and judgements are made by different distinguished personalities on the impact of globalization, but the debate is still far from over. Some of the common questions asked by the people are: What would be the impact of globalization on NGOs engaged in combating AIDS? Will globalization increase fund flow? Will it help NGOs to provide better services through international networking? Will NGOs be able to deal with increasing numbers of people living with HIV/AIDS? In order to get some insights on these aspects, a study was conducted among the NGOs engaged in HIV/AIDS prevention and care in West Bengal. This paper has tried to analyze the impact of globalization on the NGOs engaged in combating AIDS in general with the help of secondary data and perceptions of NGO-functionaries in West Bengal about the future trends in particular.

Methodology

West Bengal State AIDS Prevention and Control Society regularly consults NGOs and implementing different programmes of NACO through them in the state. To know about the impact of Globalization on the NGOs working in HIV/AIDS field, questionnaires were mailed to all implementing NGOs of West Bengal. Out of 60 NGOs, responses received from the 27 (45%) NGOs.

Globalization and Health

The impact of Globalization as it becomes evident in economic sphere has not left social and political sphere untouched. In the economic sphere as there is greater emphasis on privatisation and opening of economy for foreign capital. The debt situation of the third world countries—itself a product of first world's lending policies in the past—became the vehicle for neo-colonial onslaught. Future loans from IMF and World Bank are linked with broad package of macroeconomic policies in the form of 'Structural Adjustment Programme (SAP)'. SAPs forced the privatization of many government assets, sharp public sector budget cuts especially on health and education, scaling back of labour protections, the elimination of price controls and subsidies on food, and the imposition of "user fees" for health services and education. The quality and provision of basic services in many countries are either decreased or privatized. A decrease in the availability of public services can result in adverse affects on the rights to education, to health, to an adequate standard of living, and on women's rights. The right of everyone to social security may not be ensured by arrangements that rely entirely on private arrangements and on private schemes. In theory, SAPs were intended to stimulate growth and help reduce the burden of poverty; but in practice, the austerity measures often exacerbated poverty (Schoepf *et al* 1992).

The optimistic view sees the health benefits of globalization to poor countries and to poor communities in rich countries. It argues that increased pace of cross-national exchanges should facilitate diffusion of technological innovations such as new and effective contraceptive methods, techniques for enabling access to clean water, inexpensive refrigeration, efficient transport and communication technologies, and new and effective systems for prevention and treatment of infectious disease (Barnett, 2002). Globalization can also facilitate the realization of human rights such as the rights to information and to education, which in turn are important for the realization of the right to health.

On the other hand, the pessimistic view sees globalization as a phenomenon, which causes the increasing loss of sovereignty by nation. Increased movements of people seeking employment, changes in behaviour, and increased movement of goods across the world, for instance, have contributed to the more rapid spread of diseases such as malaria, AIDS and tuberculosis. The adverse health effects associated with this are aggravated by reductions in basic services as limited resources in developing countries constrain the governments' capacity. In addition to the fact that multinational pharmaceutical companies have fought to keep prices of important drugs high, making it harder for governments to protect and fulfill the right to health. These companies also tend to invest more into research into diseases that affect rich countries rather than those that affect the poorest inhabitants of the low-income countries. That's why the pursuit of an HIV/AIDS vaccine has been of less interest to big pharmaceutical companies as they get more profit from development of treatments than vaccines. These concerns have been particularly evident in the some pharmaceutical companies' efforts to ensure strong patent protection for their products, and their obstruction of production of cheaper, generic versions of important medicines. Pharmaceutical companies have brought cases against countries like South Africa and Philippines for their initiatives to make drugs available at lower cost through compulsory licensing or parallel imports. The US government has brought legal challenges against Thailand, Brazil and other countries' initiatives to allow compulsory licensing for production of inexpensive generic versions of expensive drugs to treat HIV/AIDS.

In this context, role of the international agencies are also needed to be discussed. Although neo-liberal economic ideologies and the World Bank have not always been identical, they have certainly been very close. The World Bank has had a profound influence on health provision in poor countries as the largest external financer of health activities in low and middle income countries. Over the past two decades, the thrust of the World Bank's strategies was to emphasize the role of the market in health care provision. Government's role was to be mainly regulatory, by supervising the marketplace, insurance legislation, ensuring "acceptable" levels of access. But, it ignores the social ethics of health care and defines health services as commodities to be delegated to the market sector of an economy; ignores the provision of public goods such as immunization and public sewage; and generally seeks to shift the larger burden of curative services to the private sector, which makes it available to foreign investment. The WHO, whose work in this area is underpinned by human rights concerns because of its focus on equity of access to drugs, has taken a number of initiatives to this end. WHO says that patents should protect the interest of the patent-holder while safeguarding public health, and supports measures, which improve access to essential drugs (WHO 2000; WTO 2001). But World Trade Organization (WTO) did not agree to change Trade Related aspects of Intellectual Property Rights (TRIPS).

In addition to all these, brain drain is another problem. Data from international migration-tracking organizations show that health professionals from poor countries worldwide are increasingly abandoning their homes to take up jobs in wealthy countries. As the populations of the developed countries are aging and require even more medical attention, they lure away local health talent from developing countries. As per the Journal of the American Medical Association (JAMA), already one out of five practicing physicians in the United States is foreign-trained. The poor countries could be pushed even further into trouble, unless the brain drain from the developing world can be stopped.

The years ahead could witness remarkable improvements in the health of billions of people, or they could see poor societies pushed into even deeper trouble. The emerging outcome will depend on whether it is possible to expand the developing world's local talent pool of health workers, restore and improve crumbling national health infrastructures of developing countries, and devise effective local and international systems for disease prevention and treatment.

Globalization, NGOs and HIV/AIDS

Globalization forces have reduced state controls over the economy at the national level, increase pressure for democratic accountability, or raise questions about state sovereignty. These developments have created political space for civil society organizations as alternative sources of services once provided by the state, as watchdogs over and advocates for government policy formulation and implementation, as policy entrepreneurs or implementers with state partners, and as social innovators to guide improved services. When globalization expands political space, civil society actors may emerge to respond to the concerns of impoverished and marginalized groups that would remain voiceless under prior regimes (Brown *et al* 2000). The emergence of international NGOs, networks, coalitions, and social movement organizations as potentially important political actors at both national and international levels has been stimulated by the need to create collective responses to threatening circumstances created by globalization. International NGOs and NGO alliances are emerging as increasingly influential players in international decision-making. The focus of NGOs on official UN deliberations on the international policy agenda was evident at a number of major UN conferences and their preparatory meetings. There has been a dramatic increase in their importance in many arenas over the last two decades. This change has been characterized as a "global associational revolution" (Salamon, 1994). NGOs formed coalitions and played a significant role in the accords to ban landmines, to establish International Criminal Court, to introduce code of conduct for baby food sales, to include women's reproductive health rights and on many more issues.

Thus, the role of NGOs in society can't be ignored. This is true also in the field of prevention and treatment of HIV/AIDS. Two years after its first appearance in 1981, the AIDS virus had spread to 60 countries and it rapidly became a global pandemic. Its distribution is unequal: spatially, in terms of countries and parts of countries; socially, in terms of social and cultural groups; and economically, in terms of income and wealth classes (Barnett & Whiteside, 2000). The potential impact of AIDS makes it a challenge in economic, political, social and religious spheres as well. Amongst the organizations responding to the crisis, NGOs are emerging as a powerful force in the effort to contain the epidemic. In 1980s, when AIDS started gaining public attention, close friends, family members and people living with HIV/AIDS (PLWHA) were amongst the first to provide care and support. Despite reluctance and slow actions from many governments, these NGOs, particularly AIDS Service Organizations (ASOs) came forward to provide critical care and support to HIV affected people mainly because of their closeness and trust of the people on the ground. Diverse groups at risk of HIV infection have been reached by NGOs in a wide variety of innovative programmes (Mercer *et al.* 1991). In the developing world, the NGO response to HIV/AIDS emerged somewhat more slowly. However, as the epidemic progressed, NGOs have mobilized impressive efforts for training, education and other supportive services while official declarations denied the existence of the problem (Morna and PANOS 1991; Haslegrave 1988; Mercer *et al* 1991). The importance of NGOs in the NACP of developing countries has also evolved overtime.

Until the late 1990s, the governments of the majority of acutely threatened African States were silent about AIDS – the epidemic that ravaging their countries. The UN was of little help either. As the epidemic of HIV/AIDS continues to expand to all corners of globe, it is clear that every sector of the society must respond. It was not until 1987, six years into the pandemic that the WHO responded to the reality that millions of people had been infected with HIV in all continents. The WHO established the Global Programme on AIDS (GPA) in 1987 under the leadership of late Dr. Jonathan Mann. GPA successfully mobilized national responses, but it soon was plagued by conflict with other bodies of UN system. These rivalries, as well as an increasing preference by the wealthy nations for bilateral programmes in the face of declining foreign aid budgets and for UN reform after the cold war – led to calls for a more multi-sectoral response (Merson, 2005). Accordingly, the decision was made in1996 to disband GPA and replace it with a Joint UN Programme on AIDS (UNAIDS), to coordinate AIDS targeted programmes. UNAIDS has been working along with its eight co-sponsors–UNICEF, UNDP, UNFPA, UNESCO, UNDCP, ILO, WHO, and World Bank (WB).

UNAIDS is actively engaged with leading global advocacy efforts, establishing baseline global facts on the pandemic, and coordinating accordingly the efforts of its eight co-sponsoring agencies, all of which maintains their own substantial HIV/AIDS programmes. Later on, United Nations High Commissioner for Refugees (UNHCR) and the World Food Programme (WFP) are also included in UNAIDS as co-sponsors. The Figure-A shows the spending of UN Agencies on HIV/AIDS during 1996-2005. During 1990s, all countries established National AIDS Control Programme and adopted strategies and intervention to prevent the spread of HIV/AIDS. Lessons learnt from the experiences of last two decades clearly indicate that national responses should not wait for AIDS cases to soar. Instead they should

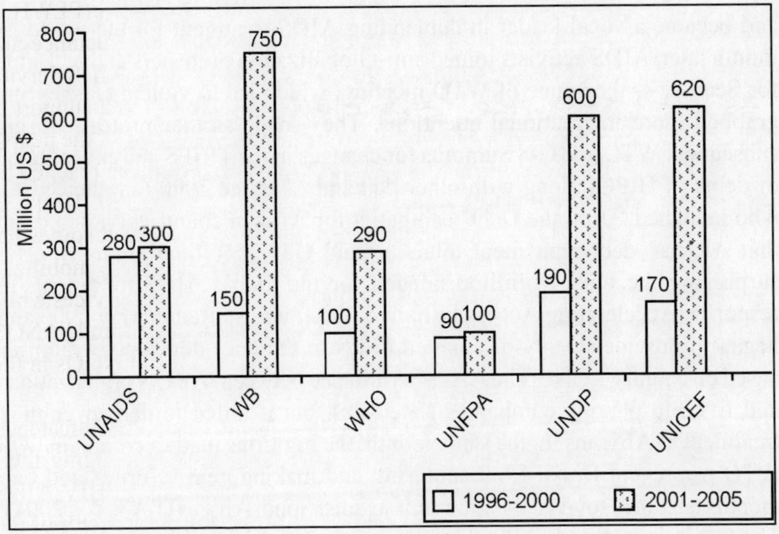

Source: UNAIDS, 2007.

Fig. 14.1: UN Agency Spending on HIV/AIDS

focus on responding quickly, mobilizing all sectors and recognizing and collaborating with NGOs and the private sector.

In 1996, the same year when UNAIDS was established, researchers announced a new therapy to prolong the lives of people with AIDS. This highly active antiretroviral therapy (HAART) promptly saved millions of lives in developed countries. The HAART costs over US $10,000 per patient per year—a price affordable to few in developing countries. Wealthy nations increasingly disenchanted with the UN system and facing less in the way of AIDS mortality seemed more and more disengaged from the pandemic, despite its increasing devastating impact on the resource-poor countries. A recent Oxfam study pointed out that the one-third of total PLWHAs live in countries classified by World Bank and IMF as heavily indebted poor countries (HIPC). Throughout the late 1990s and into the present decade, activist organizations like AIDS Coalition to Unleash Power (ACT UP), Health Global Access Project (Health GAP), South Africa's Treatment Action Plan (TAC) and others have carried on sustained campaign targeting large multinational pharmaceutical firms to introduce different pricing system for the developing countries that would open the possibility for government and NGOs to purchase ARVs at discounted rates (Irwin *et al* 2003). Activists' direct actions were complemented by the policy and advocacy work of US watchdog Consumer Project Technology (CPT), Health Action International and Medecins Sans Frontieres (MSF). In October 1999, MSF was awarded the Nobel Peace Prize and became a vocal leader in demanding AIDS treatment for the world. A month later, AIDS activists joined anti-Globalization protesters at the "Battle for Seattle"— the venue of WTO meeting, which led to violent clashes and grabbed more international attentions. They made similar protests during subsequent WTO and G-8 Summits for changes in the TRIPS and cancellation of debts of HIPCs along with other demands. Jubilee 2000 (another NGO, who launched 'Drop the Debt' campaign for African countries) pointed out that Africas' debt repayment totals around US$ 15 billion annually – far surpassing the US$ 10 billion needed for the global AIDS treatment. In response, Accelerating Access Initiative (AAI) was started in May 2000 and began to provide steeply discounted drugs to the least developed countries based on country's GNP. The AAI is an alliance between five UN organizations and five big pharma companies (later six), but it failed to deliver enough treatment to Africans. In the same month, the big firms made a complain with WTO to prevent Brazil from acquiring and making generic drugs and two months later they revived their lawsuits against South Africa (D'Adesky, 2004). The turning point in the global battle was the pioneering decision by Cipla – a leading Indian generic drug manufacturer to offer ARV medicines to the frontline groups of African countries like MSF for $360 a year (i.e. less than $ 1 a day per patient) or for $ 600 if purchased by the governments. Responding to the pressure of public opinion and market competition from the generic drug companies, major research based pharma companies announced initiatives to lower their own prices on AIDS medications in poorer regions. Later on, they also settled the matter with Brazil and withdrew the lawsuit against South Africa (D'Adesky, 2004).

However, NGOs' roles are not just restricted to the role of advocacy and implementing agencies in the HIV/AIDS field. It is also actively participating in the decision making process at the local, national, regional and international level. Since UNAIDS was set up in 1996, civil society or NGO has been a key partner. UNAIDS was the first United Nations programme to have formal civil society representation on its governing body. The UNAIDS model helped inform the governing structures of the GFATM. Civil society members hold three seats on the GFATM Board, namely the Developed Country NGO, the Developing Country NGO and the Communities Affected by the Diseases (referred to as the "Communities Delegation"). Each of these constituencies has full voting rights. Country Coordinating Mechanism (CCM) is central to the Global Fund's commitment to local ownershipand participatory decision making. Thesecountry-level partnerships develop and submit grant proposals to the Global Fund based on priority needs at the national level. After grant approval, they oversee progress during implementation. NGOs are also represented in other UN bodies and similar international organizations. They are also engaged in training, research, documentation, networking and consultancy work. In 1992, the Global Network of People Living with HIV/AIDS (GNP+) was officially launched, which had a huge impact at the regional and national level. For example, Asia Pacific Network of People Living with HIV/AIDS (APN+) and Indian Network for PLWHAs (INP+) were formed respectively at the regional and national level. Another organization – International Council for AIDS Service Organisation (ICASO) similarly influenced and maintains a strong network with other such organizations at the regional and national level. For example, there are regional level organizations like Latin America and Caribbean Council of AIDS Service Organisation, Asia Pacific Council of AIDS Service Organisation (APCASO), etc. ICASO played a significant role in the development of a consortium of NGOs in 2005 to support civil society-led monitoring, advocacy and reporting around the implementation of the UNGASS Declaration of Commitment. The International AIDS Alliance produced a toolkit to help NGOs evaluate and build their capacity to respond to the epidemic. In December 2004, NGOs from around the world came together and created the HIV/AIDS Code of Practice for NGOs. It provides a set of principles of good practice for advocacy and AIDS programming, to which NGOs can commit themselves and be held accountable. Thanks to the combined efforts of organizations and networks, the basic principle of ensuring meaningful involvement of civil society, and particularly of people living with HIV, is now being written into the policies and strategies of many organizations, institutions and AIDS programmes.

Around the turn of the millennium, several key changes made these same rich nations to be receptive again to UNAIDS advocacy. As a result of all these changes, millions of persons saw the impact of the pandemic, when the XIII International AIDS Conference was held in 2000 for the first time in a developing country (Durban, South Africa). All these have resulted in increasing partnerships, greater involvements and enhanced political commitments to scale up effective interventions to fight this global adversary (GFTAM 2002; WHO 2001). For example, United Nations Millennium Development Declaration adopted unanimously in 2000 by all members, encompasses eight Millennium Development Goals (MDGs), three of which are health related: reducing child mortality, improving maternal health and to have halted and begun to reverse the spread of TB, AIDS and malaria by 2015. In June 2001, the ground–breaking UN General Assembly Special Session on HIV/AIDS (UNGASS) mobilized political and financial commitments from both the developed and developing countries. In Doha Summit (November 2001), WTO issued a ruling allowing the poorest countries to use compulsory licensing and other trade mechanisms to access generic drugs in case of public health emergencies such as AIDS, TB and malaria. But, it put a condition that generic drugs could only be produced for domestic consumption, not for export. This ruling affected many poor countries; those who don't have the capacity to produce the generic drugs. In January 2002, the Global Fund to Fight AIDS, TB and Malaria (GFTAM) was established. The Global Fund is a unique global public-private partnership between governments, civil society, the private sector and affected communities represents a new approach to international health financing. The Global Fund provides more than 20 per cent of international funding to fight AIDS, as well as two-thirds of international funding to fight malaria and tuberculosis. Since its creation in 2002, the Global Fund has become the dominant financer with approved funding of US$ 8.6 billion for 450 programmes in 136 countries (GFATM, 2007). Besides these, many international organizations have been set up to assist in funding and implementing HIV prevention and care programme and related health initiatives worldwide. These include the President's Emergency Plan For AIDS Relief (PEPFAR) set up by George W. Bush, the Global Alliance for Vaccines and Immunization (GAVI), the Global Health Council, the Bill and Melinda Gates Foundation, the Rockefeller Foundation, the World Bank's Multi-country AIDS Programme (MAP), the William J. Clinton Presidential Foundation, etc. In 2003, PEPFAR pledges US $ 15 billion for a period of five years to fund AIDS programme in 12 African nations, Haiti and Guyana. But most of the money would be spent through USAID (i.e. through bilateral arrangement) and only US $ 2.0 billion was channeled to GFATM. Despite global progress in expanding HIV treatment access, including in some of the world's most resource-limited countries, more than 70 per cent of individuals who were medically eligible for antiretrovirals lacked access to these drugs in 2006. As HIV disease progresses among HIV-infected people who are not yet on therapy, the number of people needing therapy will grow much larger in the future. In 2005 (14-16 September), UN General Assembly World Summit adopted a resolution towards the universal access to HIV prevention, treatment, care and support by 2010. The African Union and the G-8 countries have also endorsed this move.

However, despite marked increases in financing for the HIV response during this decade, the Figure-C shows the gap between resources available and the amounts needed during 2005-2007. This gap would be wider over the next several years if current funding trends continue. Substantial progress has been achieved in bringing essential HIV services to those in need in the low and middle-income countries, where 95 per cent of PLWHA reside. The number of people receiving antiretroviral drugs in these countries increased five-fold between 2003 and 2006, and declines in HIV prevalence have been reported in several countries following the implementation of strong HIV prevention measures. If the scale-up of HIV services continues at the same pace as in the recent past, the necessary funding is projected to reach US$ 15.4 billion in 2010 (US$13.4 – US$ 17.6) and US$ 22.5 billion in 2015 (US$ 18.8 – US$ 26.9). Yet the current pace of scale-up could not achieve universal access by the agreed target date of 2010, endangering the world's ability to halt and begin to reverse the HIV epidemic by 2015, as provided in the Millennium Development Goals (MDGs). By 2015, an estimated 8.0 million people would be on ART, instead of 21.85 million as estimated by UNAIDS if resources expanded to achieve universal access in 132 low and middle-income countries.

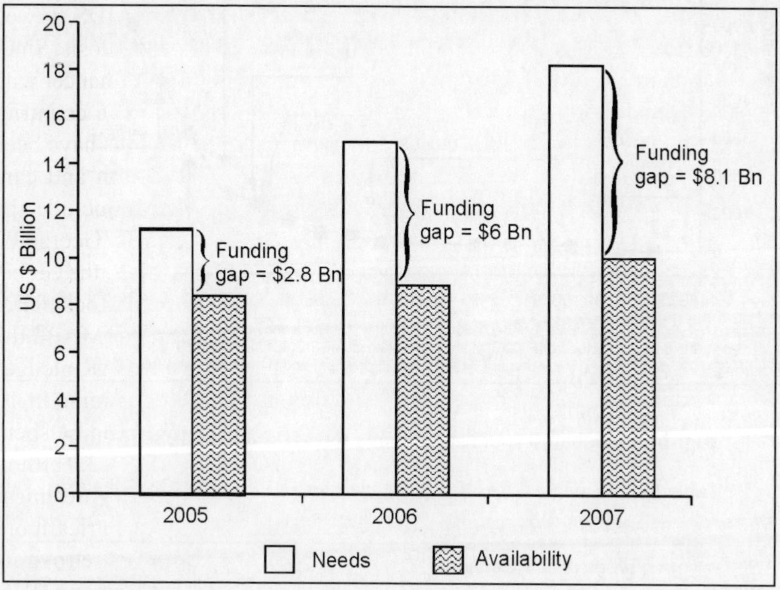

Source: UNAIDS, 2007.

Fig. 14.2: Funding Gap between Resource, Needs and Resource Availability (2005-07)

The Figure 14.2 indicates the global mobilization of resources from 1986 that is unprecedented with respect to the management of chronic illness in low-income and middle-income countries–generating an estimated US$ 10 billion in financing in 2007.

Table 14.1 shows that to meet the goal of global universal access by 2010, available financial resources for HIV must be more than quadruple by 2010 compared to 2007 – up to US$ 42.2 billion (US$ 31.9 – US$ 51.4) – and continue to rise to US$ 54.0 billion by 2015 (US$ 44.6 – US$ 63.3). This would demand an urgent worldwide mobilization of technical resources over the next three years to overcome the many impediments that have to date slowed programme implementation and scale-up, such as weak procurement and supply management systems and overburdened health delivery systems.

UNAIDS also calculated the financial resources needed to achieve universal access by the countries in terms of the income category. Table 14.2

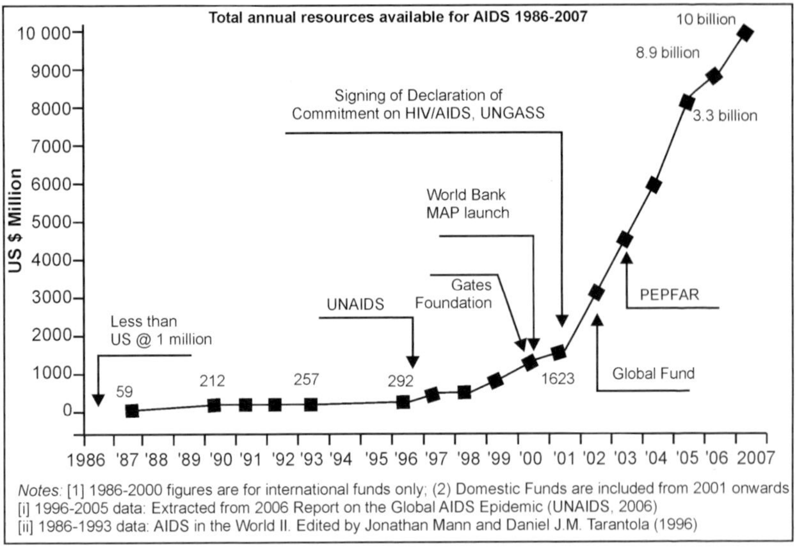

Source: UNAIDS, 2007.

Fig. 14.3: Global Resources Available for AIDS during 1986 to 2007.

Table 14.1: Financial Resources Needed for HIV Services by Scenario

(US$ Billion)

Sl No	*Types of HIV Services*	*2009*	*2010*	*2015*
1.	Prevention	11.4	15.0	15.4
2.	Treatment and Care (including palliative care	10.8	15.4	22.7
3.	Orphan and Vulnerable Children	2.4	4.4	4.5
4.	Programme Costs	5.0	6.1	10.1
5.	Prevention of violence against women	0.6	1.3	1.3
	Total	**30.2**	**42.2**	**54.0**
	Range	(24.7-36.1)	(31.9-51.4)	(44.6-63.3)

Source: UNAIDS, 2007.

shows the breakdown of resource needs by income level of country. As in the past, upper-middle income countries will continue to finance almost the totality of their responses to HIV, particularly in Latin America, Eastern Europe and Asia. Thus, it is anticipated that domestic public sources will supply roughly one-third of the global amounts needed to close the looming resource gap. External sources will be required to cover roughly two-thirds of the global amounts needed to achieve universal access, with the majority of such assistance focused on low-income countries, especially in sub-Saharan Africa.

Table 14.2: Financial Resources Needed Categorized by Income Category

(US$ Million)

Sl.. No.	*Countries*	*2008*	*2009*	*2010*
1.	Low income	9,117	13,916	20,286
2.	Lower-Middle income	5,814	8,944	12,511
3.	Upper–Middle income	5,276	7,308	9,448
	Total	**20,207**	**30,168**	**42,245**

Source: UNAIDS, 2007.

Although the level of resources needed for HIV is higher than comparable estimates for other MDGs, it is important to note that nearly one quarter of total resources required for HIV will support health systems strengthening, which in turn will substantially buttress efforts to achieve other health-related MDGs. Table 14.3 indicates the UNAIDS estimated financial resources needed to achieve universal access in terms of activity area. These investments in the health sector include those with both direct and indirect impact on the epidemic. Overall, approximately one-third of these HIV resource needs estimates are for selected activities addressing the social drivers of the epidemic, for social mitigation and other services that are termed non-health activities. Cross-cutting activities include: civil society strengthening, global advocacy and coordination, policy, human rights and stigma. UNAIDS has calculated the financial requirements by computing the number of people in need, the target coverage and the unit cost of the intervention, with amounts expressed as funds needed for each year as cash flows.

Table 14.3: Financial Resources Needed Categorized by Activity Area

(US$ Million)

Sl. No.	*Activity Area*	*2008*	*2009*	*2010*
1.	HIV specific health services	10,060	15,068	20,807
2.	Health system strengthening and Cross-cutting activities	4,938	6,019	7,227
3.	Non-Health services	5,209	9,081	14,211
	Total	**20,207**	**30,168**	**42,245**

Source: UNAIDS, 2007.

The high levels of funding that will be needed to move towards universal access in the coming years reflect the world's failure to respond to the epidemic before it achieved crisis dimensions. This same principle holds true today – we cannot afford the costs of inaction. A comprehensive scaled-up HIV prevention response would avert more than half of all new infections that are projected to occur between 2005 and 2015 (Stover *et al*, 2006). Unless we can prevent new infections, future treatment costs will continue to mount.

While these obstacles are significant, the global community stands a better chance of overcoming them than ever before. Never before has this level of funding been achieved. Never before have major world leaders focused so intensively on a global health problem. The challenge now is for all players – including recipient nations – to continuously surmount the national obstacles to a unified AIDS response (Merson 2005).

Perception of NGOs about the Impact of Globalization

So far India is concerned, NGOs like other countries were first to respond especially in the initial years when response to HIV/AIDS from the government was slow. In response to international as well as national pressure created by the NGOs, the government of India started a medium term plan in 1989 for three years in collaboration with WHO. Since its establishment in 1992, National AIDS Control Organization (NACO) also recognizes NGOs as its primary allies and critical partners in undertaking targeted interventions among high risk groups, disseminating information, delivering counseling services and in providing care and outreach services for people living with HIV/AIDS (PLWHA). NACO recognized the importance of NGOs and involved them in NACP-I (1992-1999), NACP-II (1999-May 2007) and NACP-III (2007-2012). NGOs have been putting pressure on government to provide ART at free of cost, to improve health infrastructure, to ensure protection of human rights of PLWHAs, etc. The government introduced free ART from April 2004. At the national level, Indian Network of PLWHAs (INP+) along with its different state branches established strong network with regional level organizations like APCASO, APN+, etc. as well as with GNP+, ICASO, etc. at the international level. They have also tied up with different International NGOs and implementing different projects. With this strong networking, Indian NGOs have been putting more pressure on the government by demanding introduction of second line ART, amendment of Immoral Traffic Prevention Act, abolition of Indian Penal Code (IPC) Section 377 that treats MSM behaviour as a crime, recognition of sex workers as workers and provision of social security through labour laws, etc. Because of their efforts, NACP-III has incorporated several provisions like supply of second line ART, introduction of 'Smart Card' for PLWHAs receiving ART, establishment of PLWHAs' Network and Civil Society Forum at the district level, promotion and active involvement of CBOs more in future, etc. But, within the country, there is no networking between NGOs engaged in HIV/AIDS care and NGOs working in other fields. Even there is no federation of NGOs working in HIV/AIDS field at the national and state level. However, Indian NGOs are represented in different international forums like UNAIDS, GFATM and many others.

In West Bengal, the situation is no way exceptional from the national scenario. West Bengal State AIDS Prevention and Control Society regularly consults NGOs and implementing different programmes of NACP through them in the state. There is no state level federation or networking among the NGOs in HIV/AIDS care, nor with NGOs working in the other field. It implies that may be HIV/AIDS is considered by the NGOs as an isolated phenomenon, not as a threat to the development of the country. To know about the impact of Globalization on the NGOs working in HIV/AIDS field, questionnaires were mailed to all NACP implementing NGOs of West Bengal. Out of 60 NGOs, responses received from the 27 (45%) NGOs are discussed below.

1. *Fund Fow and Role of NGOs:* It is found that 81.5 per cent of the NGOs are of the opinion that fund flow will increase due to globalization. All the NGOs feel that the role of NGOs will also be increased in the era of globalization and justified their opinion with reasons. Some of these reasons are: (A) government is not capable alone, (B) NGOs are more effective and (C) this is a global trend. Table 14.4 shows that 44.4 per cent of total NGOs under the study feel that NGOs' role will be increased due to government's inability and global trend (AC). While 37 per cent NGOs feel that the government is not capable alone and NGOs are more effective than the government (AB).

Table 14.4: Reasons Responsible for the Increasing Role of NGOs

Sl. No.	*Reasons*	*No. of NGOs (%)*
1.	A	3 (11.2%)
2.	B	1 (3.7%)
3.	AB	10 (37.0%)
4.	AC	12 (44.4%)
5.	ABC	1 (3.7%)
	Total	**27 (100%)**

Source: Responses received through mailed questionnaire.

2. *Networking:* All the NGOs under the study are of the opinion that networking with national and international NGOs will help to fight against HIV/AIDS. They have also expressed the benefits of networking in this regard. Some of these are: (A) through exchange of information, (B) through training and exposure of staff in abroad or foreign NGOs and (C) by creating pressure

Table 14.5: Benefits of Networking

Sl. No.	*Benefits of Networking*	*No. of NGOs (%)*
1.	B	1 (3.7%)
2.	AB	6 (22.2%)
3.	AC	1 (3.7%)
4.	ABC	19 (70.4%)
	Total	**27 (100%)**

Source: *Ibid.*

on the policy makers. Table 14.5 indicates that about 70 per cent NGOs under the study feel that all the above benefits will be available from networking, while 22.2 per cent NGOs think about first two benefits only.

3. *Meeting the Future Demands:* Considering the increasing future needs and demands of PLWHAs, NGOs have expressed their views on the ways through which these demands can be fulfilled. Some of the ways are: (A) unified efforts of the government, NGOs, private companies and common people, (B) multinational companies will have to lower price for ART drugs for the developing countries, (C) government will have to ensure supply of ART at free of cost and (D) international agencies like WHO, UNICEF, ILO, etc. will have to play more active role for the developing countries. Table 14.6 shows that most (88.9%) of the NGOs under the study have suggested all the above mentioned measures for meeting the future demands of PLWHAs.

Table 14.6: Ways to Meet the Future Demands of PLWHAs

Sl. No.	*Ways to Meet Future Demands*	*No. of NGOs (%)*
1.	A	1 (3.7%)
2.	D	1 (3.7%)
3.	AB	1 (3.7%)
4.	ABCD	24 (88.9%)
	Total	**27 (100%)**

Source: *Ibid.*

4. Overall Impact: With regard to the overall impact of Globalization on NGOs working in HIV/AIDS care, none of the NGOs under the study express that impact will be worst. While 66.7 per cent of them feel that impact will be good, remaining 33.7 per cent NGOs can't predict the impact just now.

Conclusion

From the above discussion, we understand that HIV/AIDS is considered as a global problem and this globality of the disease has given importance in the international development and aid policy agendas. Alongside this, certain practices for coordination, communication and implementation are established. This formulation around the HIV/AIDS pandemic is very much similar with Gordenkar and Weiss's (1996) definition of global governance: "efforts to bring more orderly and reliable response to social and political issues that go beyond capacities of the states to address individually". We also find that globalization has created enough space for the NGOs to play a more active role in all spheres including HIV/AIDS prevention, care, support and treatment. Globalization has also helped to strengthen the networking at the national, regional and international level not only among the NGOs working in HIV/AIDS field, but also with NGOs working in the other fields. It has also brought together NGOs of the North and of the South. The networking helps the NGOs in terms of sharing experiences, capacity building, training, research, etc., not just advocacy and seems to continue in future too.

We can also understand the role of NGOs within the emerging international governance of HIV/AIDS and its impact in the national and local level governance of the disease. The international policy makers believe that the existing intervention mechanisms are providing correct channels for policy interventions and have recognized that lack of adequate funding as one of the most important challenges in scaling up HIV/AIDS. As a part of the existing intervention mechanisms, civil society organizations or NGOs have been at the centre for HIV/AIDS pandemic in the world. So far, NGOs were successfully able to bring more funds by their advocacy efforts especially from the reluctant industrialized countries. In September 2007, Donors meeting held at Berlin and pledges US$9.7 billion over three years to GFATM. The pledges constitute the largest single financing exercise for health ever, and it will allow the Global Fund to move towards annual commitments of US$6 - 8 billion by 2010 (GFATM, 2007). Therefore, it is expected that financial sustainability will be continued in future too.

However, considering the large number of NGOs, it is difficult to conclude whether the interventions of these NGOs are coherent or sustainable and whether they will have a societal impact in the long run. The external resource dependency of NGOs is one of the reasons for this situation. In the governance of HIV/AIDS, most NGOs choose the intervention mechanism as prescribed by the donors or policymakers (e.g. NACO in India). Otherwise their participation would be questioned leading to their exclusion from the system. Due to the same reason, local NGOs and networks of PLWHAs are not raising their voices about the problems and issues associated with the intervention programmes. Because, it is considered to be controversial and may influence the support and funding arrangements that resemble a competitive market whereby donors/policymakers are choosing those NGOs who are willing to accept and implement their policies and priorities. Besides it, their activities like condom distribution, STI management, VCT counseling, training workshops, etc. are evaluated on the basis of exact numbers distributed, treated, tested and trained. This reflects the interests of donors/policymakers in concrete measurable outcomes for accountability purposes within a limited project cycle instead of an assessment of actual long-term impact of an intervention. In this way, the relationship between the donors/policymakers and the implementers once again influences the way latter function (Seckinelgin, 2005). To effect a change in the behaviour of the target group, the concern NGO requires sustaining efforts over long term to eliminate the causes of disease while at the same time dealing with immediate problems. In some ways, it is possible to agree with Fowler (1997) and suggest that NGOs are rich in potential capacities, but very much limited in their capabilities. At the same time, a new challenge that NGOs will have to face is the side effects of ART and huge number of PLWHAs. Because of the increased access to ART, the life span of PLWHAs will be increasing. As it is already known that ART has many side effects, which requires special attention and professional services. NGOs must be prepared and ready to deal with such new demands successfully in future. But, there is no doubt that innovative and effective interventions are created and implemented by NGOs.

Thus, globalization brings with it many benefits in addressing the spread of HIV throughout the world. However, these benefits can only be realized if appropriate programmes are available in areas of need. As part of the generous supply of aid aimed at addressing problems specific to HIV/AIDS, attention needs to be paid for building capacity in recipient countries, so that such funds may be effectively disseminated and the epidemic effectively curbed. In brief, governments, donors and civil society, as in the past, will remain at the forefront of efforts to move towards universal access to HIV prevention, treatment, care and support (Sukai 2010). Governments will have to increase funding for AIDS—both domestically and as development assistance.

15

Foreign Aid, Voluntary Sector and Social Work Practice in India

Subhashree Sanyal

According to World Bank—the term 'Non-Government organisation' (NGO) refers to a wide range of value-based, nonprofit organizations, independent from government, engaged in social action and development, "to relieve suffering, promote the interests of the poor, protect the environment, promote basic services or undertake community development". Popularly the term used in India was voluntary agency or voluntary organizations whose service was voluntary and they did not receive any remuneration or compensation. The global growth of NGOs or civil society as they are sometimes referred to in the collective is said to rank as one of the outstanding developments of our time.

The primary objective of NGO is to provide social justice, development and human rights. The World Bank has identified two main categories of NGOs namely operational and advocacy NGOs. The main purpose of the former is the design and implantation of development oriented projects. Operational NGO can also be classified as national organizations, community based organization etc. on the other hand, the very purpose of advocacy NGOs is to influence the policies and practices of international organization. Fifty years ago, NGOs had little place in public consciousness. There has been a sea change since. NGOs have now become major players both in the global and national arena, being called upon to play new roles both at the national level as well as international level. NGOs are much sort after by government and business. NGO has become part of business school and government training curriculum. With the expansion in the number and size, have come more visibility, power and influence, especially since collectively NGOs represent sizeable measurement of funds in development. Because of this they can impact the nature and direction of development, both nationally and internationally. Although the number of big NGOs is small they have acquired considerable clout. The recent enactment of NREGA and Right to Information Act was spearheaded by NGOs.

With more visibility comes public scrutiny, especially over sources of funds and fund utilization. The changes in the life and operation styles of top foreign funded NGO executives have not gone unnoticed either by peers or general public. NGOs worldwide finance their work through a variety of sources including self-generated funds [membership, sale of products], charitable donations and government grants. While public donations sustained Indian NGOs in the pre-independence period, and for some years thereafter, since 1960s the two major sources of funds for NGOs have come to be government grants and foreign aid. Both have increased steadily. External development Assistance began soon after independence but went largely into the government's account. Aid for NGOs became significant only in the last three decades. It includes both Official Development Assistance [ODA], a part of it goes to NGOs either through government or directly and private philanthropic assistance which is regulated by the Foreign Contributions Regulation Act.

Aid Scenario in India

Traditionally, aid has always been recognized as an important source mobilization for development countries. The critical nature aid for development, hence, need not be over-emphasized. Aid has been one of the imperatives to develop capacities and assets of the poor in the world to come out of poverty and hunger. If the millennium development Goals (MDGs) are to be achieved, aid has to play an important role. Notwithstanding this significant nature of aid, according to a UNESCO report, both the nature and quantum of bilateral aid to meet the goal of education for all has been incredulously insufficient. The estimated requirement was US$ 50 billion. However donor countries have pledged only US$ 16 billion up to 2006. Till 2001, only US$ 4 billion aid actually materialized. In the context, it is imperative to look at the issue of bilateral aid. India has been accepting bilateral aid from countries like the United States (US), the United Kingdom (UK), France, Japan and Germany. Many autonomous institutes, nongovernmental organizations (NGOs) and research also accept bilateral aid to implement development projects. However, of late of policy of the government had taken a decision not to accept bilateral aid from foreign countries. Many argued that since about 60 per cent of aid to India comes from multilateral agencies, India could refuse to accept bilateral aid. Some have also argued that one important reason for India to refuse bilateral aid is because of the conditions imposed to any grant-of-aid. The present government in September 2004 reversed this decision. Another important decision in the bilateral aid front taken by the government of India is to bring the entire regime of foreign funding from bilateral donors to NGOs under the finance ministry scanner.

The reasons why the government has taken this decision is not too far to seek. The government wants to weed out unscrupulous funding channels and unprincipled recipient organizations. There are growing apprehensions about the opaque and undemocratic methods in which some NGOs work. NGOs need to understand that as recipient of aid they have to demonstrate accountability for the money they receive by exhibiting their commitment towards the goal for which bilateral aid had come. The intention of the government may be noble. However, the methodology that the government proposes to adopt is not effective. Unscrupulous funders and unprincipled recipient organizations may not be weeded out by increasing the glare of the finance ministry and hence further rendering the process more bureaucratic. If may not cure the malaise but may, on the contrary, lead to creation of another malaise. By subjecting the procedure to more bureaucratic dealing the government will only end up slowing and complicating and the process. There have been protests against this particular policy decision. Many NGOs have said that this would unnecessary accentuate the problem of red tape and complicate the procedure for them to get approval for foreign funding from bilateral donors. In addition, many NGOs see this as an undue interference of the government in the matters pertaining to their micro management.

Aid is important for development. Bilateral aid will help people develop their capacities and hence take advantage of other modes of development such as trade. It is important that the money that is received in the form in bilateral aid is allocated and spent efficiently. The government needs to evolve less bureaucratic and innovative procedures to deal with the problem of unscrupulous funding.

Official Development Assistance

Foreign Development Assistance consists of two categories-Official Development Assistance [ODA] given directly or indirectly to NGOs and private philanthropic giving. The latter includes giving by foundations, International NGOs like OXFAM and Action Aid, wealthy families, service organizations such as Rotary International, Individuals who give either directly or through some organization, corporate giving and private venture capital. Among these the only two sources making a significant impact on the voluntary sector have been official aid and private institutional philanthropic giving. A large part of official aid flows to government departments or semi state owned institutions and only some of it goes to NGOs as part of the GO-NGO collaboration where NGOs are implementers and facilitators. A small fraction of the aid flows directly to the NGOs and since 2004 this has been captured in the FCRA figures.

Since 1990, ODA at a global level and in India has seen a number of ups and downs, declining steadily after the end of the Cold War but increasing around the Millennium kicked by the Monterrey Consensus of UN in 2002 for Financing for Development and the Tsunami. The levels have again declined due to fiscal problems in many western countries. The recent global crash of 2008 will only aggravate this trend at least in the near future. ODA in India enjoyed a peak period from 1955-60 but declined steadily thereafter, both in absolute amount as well as insignificance. As a percentage of India's Gross National Product [GNP], it is estimated to be only 0.4 per cent during the last decade and even smaller if one considers only the grant assistance; so too as a percentage of development expenditure in the country [estimated at 2%].

Bilateral Aid in particular is tipped to become less significant for the government in the coming years because in 2003-04 the government announced that in view of the fact that its economic position had improved, and that it was offering aid to smaller developing countries, it would no longer accept any aid with conditions or id below 25 million dollars from 6 bi-lateral donors. By contrast, external aid to NGOs, from both official and private sources has continuously increased in spite of the gloomy forecast of the NGO sector that aid to it from external sources would go down in consequence of diminished levels of aid after the end of the cold war, and diversion of private aid to African and east European countries. In 1990, the private philanthropic assistance received by Indian NGOs was Rs. 9457 million. By 2006-07 they had received the not inconsiderable sum of Rs. 122,896 million from private international donors [Annual Report of FCRA Division of Home Ministry 2006-07] in addition to the approximately Rs. 10,000 million from official donors-bi-lateral and multi-lateral. There are few widely accepted estimates of how important foreign funding is, either as a proportion of total funds invested in the voluntary sector or as a proportion of Individual NGOs budget. The estimates range from 7.4 per cent of the Rs. 179,220 million, said to be mobilised by the voluntary sector to 50 per cent of the annual investment in the sector. [UNICEF Report, 1985], whatever the exact proportion, the fact is that of the 1.2 million NGOs said to exist in India, only 33,937 associations have registered with the FCRA Authorities to receive foreign contributions plus 522 who received prior permission to receive funds during 2006-07. Of these 19011 NGOs filed a report about the receipt of foreign contributions which included the 522 who received prior permissions. Though in the total, the volume of aid is small compared to government budgets, if one considers the fact that many of the formally incorporated NGOs are very small, and that it is these NGOs who have become the leaders of the sector

The changes in the voluntary sector are matched by the changes in the aid architecture. There is much difference between pre-1990 and post 1990 in attitudes and practices of donors. International NGOs who played an important part in funding NGOs in the early years are themselves facing an identity and resource crisis, and reorganizing themselves to meet the new situation. Again their funding situation is likely to worsen due to global crisis of 2008. By contrast to ODA and international NGOs funds, private philanthropic players have become more numerous and the funds flowing from them to NGOs have increased over the period, due to the emergence of a second flowering of wealth. The way new philanthropy approaches, development is different from the way traditional philanthropy did. It believed that business methods can solve social problems and that these are superior to other methods in use in the public sector or civil society. The approach of the new philanthropist includes a more hands on engagement in the recipients work and therefore exercise more control over the recipient and the insistence on matrices or assurance of outcomes. The world leaders in the new [as in the old] philanthropy are the American Foundations, though Germany and other European Nations have also seen an increase in the number of foundations many of which have begun to have significant overseas interests. Other new sources of funds for Indian NGOs have begun to appear including funds from MNCs, the Indian Diaspora and Venture Philanthropists. New ways of doing business are doing the traditional grant making mode of transferring resources including online donations and social investments which offer either total freedom to NGOs to decide what to do with donated funds.

Due to all these changes, there is more debate at the National and International Levels on what constitutes effective aid with many interpreting this as efficient aid. Though aid money is small compared to public investments in development, its impact on the margins has been substantial. Speaking of effectiveness, the current debate also rolls around the principles of effectiveness and selectivity.

Aid Effectiveness and Principle of Selectivity

There is a large volume of empirical literature on aid effectiveness that has emerged in the last three decades or so [Hansen and Tarp, 2000] The earlier studies in this area were principally concerned with the impact of foreign assistance on domestic savings and investment. In recent years, the focus of the literature has shifted from the aid-savings relationship to aid-growth relationship [Morrissey, 2004]. Finally, in the last couple of years, the literature in this area has started to focus on the relationship between poverty and aid. However, this effort is at the initial stage of development. This shift in focus from economic growth to poverty reflects an emerging consensus in the international development community that poverty reduction should be the main focus of all developmental efforts. This is evident, among others, in the unanimous adoption of the MDGs by the UN millennium assembly. This is also reflected in the vision statements of the multilateral development institutions (although many of them did not have poverty reduction as part of their original mandates). For example, the World Bank now envisions—as it proudly promulgates in its website— "a world free of poverty." Similarly, the Asian Development Bank has adopted poverty reduction as its overarching development objective and its website enunciates its mission as "fighting poverty in Asia and the Pacific". This encouraged huge amount of aid being divulged to the third sector for development and poverty eradication. Hence foreign aid and its intrinsic linkage to the third sector were established. Aid Effectiveness could therefore be measured in terms of how well the Indian NGOs could use this aid for holistic development in the region. Therefore an important aspect of foreign aid lies in its effectiveness towards social welfare and development bringing in foreign funding and NGOs face to face.

Principle of Selectivity

According to this principle, aid should be allocated only to countries with good policies. The idea of selectivity, which has become the guiding principle of the World Bank aid allocation policy, has gradually emerged as the conventional wisdom and the operating principle of the international development community.

Drawing on the World Bank's extensive evaluation experience, the report provides a more careful yet critical assessment of its own experience with foreign assistance. It goes on to suggest five "policy reforms" for the donor agencies:

(i) First, financial assistance must be targeted more effectively to poorer developing countries with sound economic management.
(ii) Second, policy-based aid should be provided to nurture policy reform in credible reformers: conditionality does not work unless there is strong domestic support for reform.
(iii) Third, the mix of aid activities, between projects and programmes, should be tailored to country and sector conditions.
(iv) Fourth, projects need to focus on creating and transmitting knowledge.
(v) Fifth, aid agencies need to find alternative approaches to helping highly distorted countries, since traditional methods have failed in these cases.

Therefore, principle of selectivity sometimes becomes adverse to the poor countries that often are unable to undertake the clauses of the policy reforms suggested by the Donor Agencies.

The Aid Debate

In the early years of aid, the debate about the advisability or otherwise accepting aid related only to the government acceptance of aid. As the levels of ODA became insignificant, as a proportion of total external resource flows to the government, while the amounts going to the NGOs increased significantly, the focus of attention shifted from the Government to the NGOs. Most of NGOs like foreign aid as they see it as money to overcome the past deficits and a bridge between India and the larger world. Some of the critics object to India seeking foreign aid per say, whether to government or NGOs. Others are critical only of aid to NGOs. They do not mind if the government accepts foreign assistance or if companies raise resources abroad, but object to aid to NGOs on the ground that those NGOs who are closer to the grassroots and represent the social and cultural values of society, but are small and financially weak, can be easily manipulated than the other two sectors of society.

The critics of aid to NGOs line up a number of charges which broadly fall into following four categories:

(i) Aid leads to cultural imperialism especially domination by the west and NGOs are more susceptible to donor agendas than the government.

(ii) Extremist's activities financed with fund from abroad and NGOs are used as fronts.

(iii) There are charges that foreign money is used for religious conversions by Christian NGOs who work at the grassroots adding to religious strife between communities.

(iv) Excess and easy money from foreign aid has an adverse impact on the development agenda and values of the sector.

In relation to NGOs, specifically foreign aid is accused of distorting NGO missions and agendas, creating a deep divide in the sector between donor aided and non-donor added NGOs, increasing corruption in the society. Bunker Roy a stringent critic of aid to NGOs famously called for a ban on foreign funding on the grounds that it has destroyed the values held dear by the voluntary sector [Roy, 1988]. Against this background foreign aid has become a major source of critic for the NGOs. Meanwhile donors too have their viewpoints and dilemmas since their funds too are finite and they are accountable to their constituencies who expect to see some tangible results from their use, they want proper utilisation of their fund and therefore tend to exercise control over NGOs. The other side sometimes seize this as donors driving NGO agendas. In short the source of funds is very important not only to the viability of an NGO but also its credibility and the nature and direction of its growth.

Issues of Transparency and Accountability

With greater visibility and influence comes responsibility. In the case of NGOs this maxim could be better phrased that with a higher profile come louder calls for greater responsibility. Concerns about the role and accountability of

NGOs have been voiced from different quarters in recent years. Some donors, governments, corporations, and international agencies raise important questions about the effectiveness of NGO work and the legitimacy of their advocacy. Some NGOs have also recognized the need to ensure good practice in the wider voluntary sector. For this emerging agenda to lead to positive development outcomes, we need to ask what initiatives will improve the accountability of all institutions to the people whose lives they shape, and what initiatives could serve merely to undermine NGOs.

During the past ten years, NGO have identified public trust, legitimacy and credibility as essential elements of their capital. In turn, they have recognized the need to improve their accountability to preserve and enhance this capital. This theme has also been taken up by government organizations that have called in the sector to demonstrate the ways in which they account for their actions (although some of these state agencies themselves are not acutely accountable). However, the fundamental questions of whom NGOs are accountable to is really asked, because it is complex and has more than one answer. Systems of accountability to funders and international agencies are well established and focus on financial reporting, but there has been less emphasis on demon-starting accountability to other stakeholders (beneficiaries). This suggests a reluctance to come to terms with monitoring and evaluation, which have remained vexed issues for many in the sector. The progress that has been to date suggests that NGOs have responded to the challenges of accountability through communications systems (e.g. providing information on operations) rather than addressing it in all aspects of management. Accountability is a characteristic of institutional culture that should run through all aspects of operations and the review demonstrated the need for advice and guidance to help make this happen.

There are numerous examples of government policies that aim to regulate the sector. The principal means adopted for NGO regulation have been registration systems (administered either by the state or in same causes delegated to NGOs or a quasi-independent commission). At their best, these arrangements have drawn on a participatory process and included the views of a change of NGOs alike. At worst, they result in centralized mechanisms that place too great a bureaucratic burden on governments and ironically results in the under-regulation of NGOs when systems break down. The NGO sector has expressed a strong preference for system of self-regulation, where frameworks can be tailored to suit particular contexts and meet specific needs. However, there have been few attempts at developing this kind of regulatory framework. In some instances, codes of conduct and best practice have been initiated but little has been done to confirm whether these have been effective. Some lessons have been learned (the value of standard development by NGOs themselves; and the need for the validation of standard) and these could from the basis for the further development of self-regulatory framework. Whether regulation is implemented by governments or NGOs, there is need for participatory process that encourages dialogue and negotiation has been recognized. This process must start with common agreement on a vision for desired regulatory framework.

There is a degree of frustration expressed by some NGOs at the lack of tangible evidence that progress is being made towards achieving ideals and visions. There is a link here to the debate on accountability. The frustration reveals a need for system of monitoring and evaluation that can help measure the impacts of NGOs. This data in turn could be used in discussions with stakeholders on NGO effectiveness and form part of a strategy to strengthen accountability. NGOs are now ready to move from best practice (which could be interpreted as an ideal) however, this well requires practical advice and guidance. A mix of framework, guiding principal and cause studies would provide the basis for learning materials that help address contemporary challenges. The pace of globalization presents some opportunities for taking this agenda forward and a challenge for the Commonwealth in particular. Governments and NGOs alike are seeking ways of addressing issues such as accountability, monitoring and evaluation. The review shows that each country has a particular context and blueprints should be avoided at all costs. However, there is more scope for sharing experience than over. The Commonwealth with its ability to bring together countries with a shared common law tradition and its interface between governance and development has the potential to play a leading role in helping state and non-state actors navigate these water ways.

Aid: The New Realities

The Indian government has tried to signal a change in its status from 'aid-taker' to 'aid-giver' by announcing that it would stop taking bilateral aid from a number of small countries like Denmark, Netherlands, Norway, etc. The basic purpose of this move is political, to support India's claim to a new status in international affairs, including a permanent seat in the Security Council but it is important to pay attention to its economic motivation too. Foreign Aid to voluntary sector has assumed a primal importance in any civil society initiative today. What we can deliberate now is the role of social workers keeping in view the current civil society functioning and scenario. With aid being the centre of focus of any NGO, policies and programmes social workers and social work learning is slowly shifting to more "paper" than "field" related skills. Speaking lucidly, knowing how to make a budget and proposal for funding is considered a better skill than a grassroots community development. This can also be debatable keeping in view the idea of social work practice and its methods. The question arises is whether social workers should be more trained in group and case work than budgeting, funding and target delivery keeping in mind the funding interests of the agencies where they work.

Voluntary sector is changing with the changing pace of society. The big funding agencies and NGOs are targeting specialised programmes catering to the need of donors more than of its recipients. What can be reflected upon is how helpful are these overseas aid and are they really delivering the benefits that they intend to in the long run. Somewhere the real ethos of social work practice in India is slowly becoming questionable. The Global Fund and other important initiatives, such as PEPFAR, are fully funded. Therefore, efforts must be made to develop new funding sources and mechanisms (such as the recent Airline Tax for AIDS, TB and Malaria) should be scaled up. The philanthropic foundations will have to play an increasingly prominent role as core funders especially domestic aid and business community must rapidly accelerate action on this aspect. Civil society sector will have to continue and fulfill their vital functions and has to perform their role in advocating just policies, advising better programmes and actively engage with government to take call of development agenda.

16

Management and Service Delivery of Civil Society Organisations: A Study

Jitendra Kumar Misra

A Civil Society Organization (CSO) is a legally constituted, voluntary association of individuals or groups that is neither a governmental agency nor a for-profit enterprise, although it may and often does receive both government and corporate funds. Regardless of funding source, a CSO maintains its status only to the extent that it excludes government representatives from membership or participation. Business representatives, however, may participate, either as staff or directors.

With the fiscal space acquiring enough resilience to accommodate more initiatives of the type generically bundled into what are ascribed to provide a 'human face' to India's growth story, there has been an upsurge of interest in the organizations that occupy a place between the State and the market – agencies that comprise the voluntary sector. We call these comprising the Third Sector, Non Government Organizations (NGOs), Not for Profit Organizations (NPOs), Non Profit Institutions (NPIs), Voluntary Organizations (VOs) or Civil Society Organizations (CSOs) as per our want. A recent study commissioned by the government put the number of such entities, accounted for till 2009, at 3.3 million. That is one NGO for less than 400 Indians, and many times the number of primary schools and primary health centres in India. Even this staggering number may be less than the actual number of NGOs active in the country. The estimates from within the sector suggest that NGOs, or NPIs, raise anywhere between Rs. 40,000 crore and Rs. 80,000 crore in funding annually. The government has been the biggest donor—Rs. 18,000 crore was set aside for the social sector in the XI Plan—followed by foreign contributors (according to the latest figures available, around Rs. 9,700 crore was raised in 2007-08).

CSOs are largely operating as service providers with concentration in the area of education, health, nutrition for mother and child, income generation, small loan for self employment and environmental activities. A lot of government and other donor resources are provided to CSOs to implement these projects. However, the state continues to be a major source of funding for the NGOs in India. Not only, the CSOs require to showing best practices in implementing projects and providing services to the community, but also CSOs stakeholders require transparency, accountability for resource use, good project performance and organizational learning to benefit future projects. CSOs must have sufficient administrative, human resource and financial management capability and efficiency in management and service delivery of their programmes, in order to conceive sound plan and successful implementation of the projects. CSOs are facing growing pressure from governments and the public to be more open about their funding sources, who they represent, how they make their decisions and what impact they are having. The general perceptions of the public about CSOs are that they are not managed well, they suffer from uncertain strategic focus, unclear governance structures, weak or autocratic leadership, low priority to human resource development and excessive influence of donors and political forces. Despite the huge amount of resources provided to the CSOs to implement various projects and despite the fact that these projects have impact on communities, it is not clear how effectively these projects are managed and implemented by local CSOs.

In this research paper, research aims to explore the dimensions of management and service delivery practices of Civil Society Organizations (CSOs) and develop a self assessment tool for CSOs. In order to improve the image of Civil Society Sector and effective management and service delivery of the project, there is an urgent need to study the management and service delivery of CSOs and to suggest the ways to improve the quality of service delivery to the community as well as strengthen the organizational and programme management capacities of CSOs. Since there is general perception that, the CSOs are not being managed properly, the Civil Society Organizations receiving grants from Government departments in Delhi are chosen for the study.

Objectives of the Study

The key objective of the study is to understand the Management and Service Delivery of Civil Society Organizations in relation to their role in Development. The specific objectives of the study are as follow:

(i) To assess the organizational capacities of the Civil Service Organizations in relation to their governance, administration, human resource management and financial management systems.

(ii) To study the Programme Management of Civil Society Organizations in terms of strategic planning, knowledge management, stakeholder involvement, new opportunity development, community involvement, external relationship and Leadership.

(iii) To assess the Service Delivery mechanisms in terms of implementation status, field oversight and supervision, quality assurance and standards and monitoring and evaluation.

(iv) To gather the responses of the beneficiaries about service delivery of Civil Society organizations, and

(v) To develop a self assessment tool for Civil Society Organizations to assess their management and service delivery capacities.

Research Methodology

An exploratory and descriptive research design was adopted to conduct the study. The nature of data obtained for the present study is qualitative and quantitative in nature and the study adopted a combination of survey research and participatory methodologies. The purposive sampling was used to select Civil Society Organizations implementing project with grant of Government departments in Delhi were consider for the study. A sample of 10 CSOs was drawn by using quota and convenience sampling method to ensure the representation of all sizes of CSOs in sample, has been tried for this research. Data collection tools such as Interview Schedule, Focus Group Discussion, Questionnaire and Checklist were used in the study. Document analysis of CSO, focus group discussion with staff and beneficiaries of the project of CSO and detail interview with Chief Executive of CSO was conducted.

Results

The CSOs under study were found registered under Society or Trust act. Most of them working for more than 10 years on Health, HIV/AIDS, Women and Children issues. The nature of the projects handled by CSOs were Targeted Intervention Project for High Risk Group to prevent of HIV, Gender Resource Centre for women empowerment, Health Clinic, Non Formal Education Centre, Self Help Group, Old Age Centre for senior citizen, Drug de addiction Centre, Mental Health Education Centre and Care and support centre for PLHIV.

On the basis of analysis of the organizational capacities, programme management and service delivery of the selected Civil Society Organizations (CSO) in Delhi. The level of the organization on the degree of institutionalization that characterizes the Civil Society Organization practices was analyzed. The organizational dimensions of the CSOs explore the conditions that enable the functioning of the Civil Society Organizations in Delhi. It provides an assessment of the management and service delivery of the CSOs in terms of Organizational Capacities, Programme Management and Service Delivery, which all together offer a clear picture on the degree of institutionalization that characterize Civil Society Organizations. The final Score of the level of the organization dimension is arrived at by combining three main dimensions; fifteen sub dimensions and 75 indicators dealing with:

- Organizational capacities in terms of governance, administration, human resource management and financial management.

- Programme management in terms of strategic planning, knowledge management, stakeholders' involvement, new opportunity development, community involvement, external relationship and leadership.
- Service Delivery in terms of implementation status, field oversight and supervision, quality assurance and standards, and monitoring and evaluation.

The figure 16.1 indicates the overall score 41.2 per cent, which shows average performance of the level of Management and Service Delivery of CSOs in Delhi. Organizational Capacities with governance, administration, human resource management and financial management focuses principally on the organizational internal practices of Civil Society Organizations. The score of the organizational capacities of CSOs is 44.3 per cent. This score viewed average organizational internal practices among CSOs in Delhi.

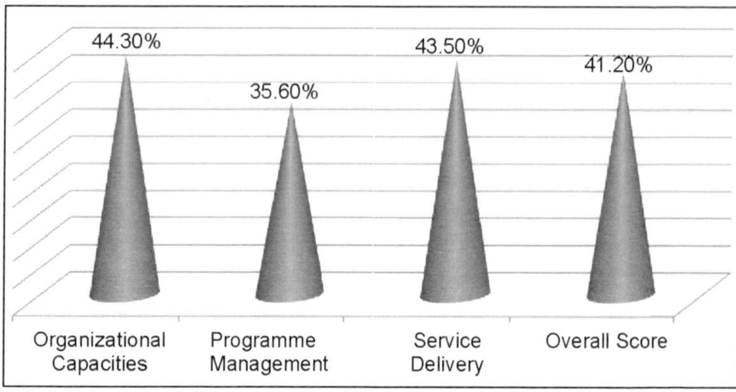

Fig. 16.1: Level of Management and Service Delivery of CSOs

Programme Management with strategic planning, knowledge management, stakeholders' involvement, new opportunity development, community involvement, external relationship and leadership focuses on programme management aspects of the Civil Society Organizations. The score of the programme management is 35.60 per cent. This score indicates the below average practices are followed by CSOs for management of their programmes. The aspects of programme management like knowledge management, community involvement and stakeholders' involvement has not focused by CSOs, while managing their programmes. Service Delivery provisions with implementation, field oversight, quality assurance and standards and monitoring and evaluation principally focused on performance management of the CSOs. The percentage and score of this dimension is 43.5

per cent. This score shows that, the average practices followed in service delivery. The monitoring and evaluation is the weakest area to practices by CSOs in Delhi. The aspects of field oversight and supervision were also found below average. Overall, CSOs were found good in their function of developing reports, average in developing plan, review of the programmes, following standard guidelines and weak in sharing information and stakeholders' involvement. The responses of the beneficiaries indicates that, they were not consulted and involved in planning, implementation and monitoring of the project, which were implemented for them by CSOs.

Self Assessment Tool (SAT) for CSOs

The purpose of the Self Assessment Tool (SAT) is to help Civil Society Organizations to improve their performance. It helps to find out their strong and weak points. The SAT is a learning tool on problems and questions concerning the organization's strategy, it's management processes, finances, staffing, relationships with others and it's results. It asks to identify causes of problems and helps in the decision-making to overcome them. The tool is divided in six sections namely Governance, Administration, Human Resource Management, Financial Management, Programme Management and Service Delivery. Further, each section divided in various sub sections. Like governance has sub section of Mission, organizational plan, Annual Report, Board Composition and responsibilities and Board Meetings.

Each sub-section is broken down further into four stages of organizational capacity development ranked from one, indicating weak capacity, two, indicating average capacity, three, indicating good capacity, to four, indicating strong capacity. In addition, each section will receive a compiled score and an overall organizational capacity score aggregating all sections will be calculated. This approach to scoring will help the organization to identify key strengths and priority need areas. The sample of the structure of the tool is as follows:

Annual Report		*Score*
Weak	The organization does not include the all aspects of report like vision and figures of physical and financial achievement	1
Average	The organization included the vision, growth history of the organization and activities report, but financial reports not shared	2
Good	The organization included the vision, growth of the organization and activities report, it has financial reports but list of donors not included and not shared with beneficiaries and stakeholders and not posted on website	3
Strong	The organization produce well written annual report including opening statement, vision, growth history, activities, physical and financial figures, list of donors, board members etc. It has shared within the organization and shared with beneficiaries and stakeholders and posted on website.	4

Findings of the study reveal an average performance of the level of management and service delivery of CSOs in Delhi. On a whole, Civil Society Organizations in Delhi operate under a relatively moderate developed framework of infrastructure and resources, with limited and required organizational, programme management and service delivery practices. Overall, the CSOs were found good in developing reports. However, they were found average in programme planning, review of their programmes and found very weak in developing operative manuals, sharing information in public and involvement of stakeholders in their programmes. The study is of enormous significance to CSOs as it provides guidance to adhere to the norms of internal governance; operations; accountability, transparency, disclosure of information, development of report, personnel policies and accounting procedures, programme planning, implementation, monitoring and evaluation practices. On the basis of the findings, a self assessment tool for CSOs has been designed, to know their organizational practices and enable them to improve themselves. The self assessment framework will provide stakeholders better understanding of the key stages of organization practices and performance that can enable them to translate it in to practice for improvement in the accountability and image of the Civil Society Organizations (CSOs).

17

Identity and Marginalization

A Case of Gujjar and Bakkarwal Community of Jammu and Kashmir

Iqball Majeed Bhat

Jammu and Kashmir, a contested state within the Indian union, is engulfed by the armed conflict that has ridden havoc in the state from last two decades. The regular loss of human lives, damage to property and infrastructure has been followed by the changing patterns of livelihood across various ethnic groups. One of the ethnic groups known by the name of Gujjar and Bakkarwal[1] has also been victim of this conflict. This paper particularly looks at the politics that has been played out in terms of identity and welfare for this economically and socially backward ethnic group. Having to live their lives in the upper reaches of the Himalayas, these people have to face hardship not only from nature but from the dominant structures of state. In Jammu and Kashmir Gujjars and Bakkarwals, in course of time, have evolved a socio-economic organization which operates in perfect harmony with the regional eco-system and which has enabled these communities to survive in a harsh environment. Historically Gujjar and Bakkarwals have been the pastoralists which always added to the economic production in terms of providing raw materials in the form of wool, meat, milk and the cattle at large. However because of the dominant influence of modernity in terms of technological interventions and globalization, these people are facing numerous problems. The problems are both at the level of changing livelihood patterns and the breaking down of their own socio-cultural milieu. This is not the unique case with the pastoralists in Jammu and Kashmir only, rather it is found almost in every part of the world. However there happens to be another dimension to the question of pastorals in Jammu and Kashmir. That another dimension is the presence of armed conflict, which in a turn has lead to the emergence political gambling in the state. Presence of Army and large paramilitary forces in the state along with the renegade groups and militants has lead to the complexity of problems with respect to Gujjar and Bakkarwal community. The welfare measures operated by government in terms of tribal sub plans are also not devoid of the larger political context of the state. From various studies and reports that have been undertaken, it comes out clear that most of the welfare measures have been used as a means to create a certain elite class within this community which then and thereafter controls the political context and identity of the whole community. The prominent example of this can be seen by looking at the political leadership of this community, which has been deliberately cropped out of a class lineage through hereditary leadership.

Historical Background of Gujjar and Bakkarwal Community

The Gujjars are generally held to have first entered Jammu and Kashmir from the Punjab and the North West Frontier Province (Census of India, 1941). The different waves of migration and the various phases of displacement followed by attempts at adapting to the new ecological and socio-economic contexts probably led to the emergence of several professionally specialized and preferentially endogamous subgroups in Jammu and Kashmir. There are varying versions on the origin and history of Gujjars but most historians agree on their central Asian origin (Chowdhary, 2011). While some others believe that the Gujjars are of Indian origin and inhabited the regions around Mount Abu in western Rajasthan, Malwa and Gujarat. Warikoo (2005) is of an opinion that many of the names like Gujarat, Gujranwala etc. are only after the name of the Gujjar community which predominated in these areas. Gujjar in Jammu and Kashmir are attested for long, but the first explicit documentary reference to the Bakkarwal here is dated 1899 (McDonell, 1899). The term was first used literally, that is, to designate a professional category of 'people with goats', as opposed, say, to those with cattle. It was only around 1912 that official documents turned this professional category into an 'ethnic' one, distinguishing between two types: 'locals', who had lived and migrated within the state's borders for at least one generation, and 'foreigners' who were considered undesirable new migrants (Rao, 1999).

In Jammu and Kashmir all Gujjars are muslims and except for a few hundred families, they are nomads' semi-nomads, pastoralists. "Gujjars Constitute 88 per cent of the total tribal population in J&K and their projected population for 2011 is around one million which is eight per cent of the total population of the state. In terms of ethnic, cultural and linguistic classification Gujjars are the third largest identity in the state after Kashmiri Muslims and Dogra Hindus. Their population is scattered and they move all across the state except, leh district and their largest concentration is in Poonch 40 per cent succeeded by 33.1 per cent in Rajouri" (Negi & Raha, 1982).

According to Negi & Raha (1982) Gujjar and Bakerwals of Jammu and Kashmir can be divided into the following three groups according to their mode of subsistence:

(i) The Gujjar who are now more or less settled agriculturalists.
(ii) Dudh Gujjar who are semi-agriculturalists and pastoralists. They raise the stock of cattle and buffaloes and trade in milk products.

(iii) The Bakkarwal who raise flocks of sheep and goats and lead an almost completely nomadic life.

Identity Formation of the Community

The term 'identity' refers to the attachments that people have to particular communities, ways of life, sets of beliefs, or practices that play a central role in their self-conception or self-understanding. When people claim that a practice, a place, or an activity is important to their identity, they usually mean that it reflects something important about their sense of who they are or that they cannot realize something important about themselves without access to it. From last several decades the questions regarding their identity have gained prominence not only in political circles but also in terms of the academic discourses. The question of Gujjar Bakkarwal identity has further been made a complex issue with the polarization of the state along communal lines to which is the testimony of 2008 elections in the state. The other testimony to this fact can be seen in the recent demand of giving Baba Ghulam Shah Badshah University[2] a tribal university status. The term 'identity' refers to the attachments that people have to particular communities, ways of life, sets of beliefs, or practices that play a central role in their self-conception or self-understanding. When people claim that a practice, a place, or an activity is important to their identity, they usually mean that it reflects something important about their sense of who they are or that they cannot realize something important about themselves without access to it. When they claim that an ascriptive characteristic, such as their race, gender, or ethnicity, is central to their identity, they mean that they understand themselves partly in terms of this characteristic. Even ascriptive aspects of identity, such as gender, ethnicity, or race, have important non-ascriptive dimensions in the sense that people may not identify with features of what, in any given social context, their relation to a group is typically understood by others to entail.

People often do not follow what Anthony Appiah (2005) calls the 'scripts' of the collective identities that structure possible narratives of their individual self. Or they make of these scripts what they wish and bind themselves to groups in ways that are, at the same time, of their own making and difficult to change without causing real damage to themselves. Amartya Sen (2006) makes a similar point when he argues that identities are not prior to one's capacity to reason but instead present people with choices that engage their capacity to reason (Eisenberg, 2009). The relation between identity and respect for persons arises because identity refers to the distinctive way in which individuals or groups come to understand themselves in a social context. Thus when one looks at the emergence of the strong tendency of the assertion of the Gujjar Bakkarwal identity in the state of Jammu and Kashmir, one cannot keep eyes shut to the political reality amidst the armed conflict. This is so because as argued by Charles Taylor, "Identity is the background against which our tastes and desires and opinions and aspirations make sense' (Taylor, 1994). Thus the question of identity not only gains prominence as a phenomena to be understood for national integration as any political scientist will argue but for a public health professional identity assumes different significance. One can never hesitate in making a preposition that identity ofcourse determines the accessibility and utilization of health care services in any defined geographical territory. For a public health researcher the question of identity will nevertheless be meaningful endeavour for analyzing the issue of utilization and accessibility of health services in a certain defined geographical location. It has often been seen that certain social realities like caste does act as a barrier for the utilization of health services by specific communities. Similarly, incase of Gujjars and Bakkarwals of Jammu and Kashmir the social inferiority from the dominant identities of the state does hinder them to access the health services. "Bear can be more faithful than the Gujjar," is a common adage that prevails in Kashmiri society. Therefore the discrimination on the basis of identity not only manifests interms of marginalization at the social level but it does so interms of institutional marginalization. The number of medical health professionals from the community of Gujjar and Bakkarwal is yet far from satisfactory level. Therefore the members of the community are largely at the receiving end. Thus identity does refers to the ways in which social properties become embedded in a person's self-conception (Appiah, 2005), or crucial to their personality, including their citizenship, gender, ethnicity, language, religion, life projects, and ethical commitments (Copp, 2002). Gujjars and Bakkarwals of Jammu and Kashmir are all the followers of Islam and that too Sunni sect. The question of their identity has always remained in a state of fluidity within the academic as well as social discourses. It has been found out that on one hand they being followers of Islam have Muslim identity of which they are fully aware and to which others like Kashmiri Muslims associate them as their own. On the other hand their ethnic identity of being Gujjars and Bakkarwals have also been played out well by the state as well as by many different groups. This disjuncture and identity fluidity gains further prominence because of the prevailing resistance movement in the state of Jammu and Kashmir. According to Navnita Chadha Behara (1996), 'Gujjars were first politicized in the 1970's when prime minister Indira Gandhi cultivated them and propped them up as a possible counter weight to the valley Muslims. The first step in this direction was the recognition of the Gojri language and the allocation of time on J&K radio for its programmes".

In the larger discourse of resistance movement Gujjars have been caught in a dilemma. They have not been fully accepted as nationalists by the Indian state, because their Muslim identity has always been liked with the Muslim character of the resistance movement in Kashmir. The Amarnath land row in year 2008 is a testimony to the fact that Gujjars were brutally harassed by the Hindu community of Jammu region only for fault of their belonging to the Muslim identity. Their houses and herds were torched by the Hindu mob in places like Samba and Kathua of Jammu province. Otherwise these people have been using the using the Jammu province as their winter pasture due to harsh climate in Kashmir valley in winters for decades. Besides this as argued by Sanjay Chaturvedi (2005) in his book 'Politics of Autonomy', Gujjars and Bakkarwals continue to live with poverty and deprivation, and are conveniently, but not unknowingly left out of increasingly communalized binary geographies of the Hindus and the Muslims underpinning the dominant discourses of freedom movement. Deprived of the political vision of their own, located at the border and periphery of the modern nation states, the voices of the Gujjars often problematise nationalist narratives of history and identity. Many authors who have written about Kashmir argue that they have been active followers of the jihad. "The Muslim Gujjar community of Jammu and Kashmir at present is faced by two different phenomena, Gujjar consciousness and Muslim consciousness. The Gujjar voluntary organizations are making the Gujjars conscious of their ethnic identity while the Islamic organizations and institutions are endeavouring to promote Muslim consciousness (Khatana, 1991). Allegiance to the larger Gujjar identity as often propounded by status coist political regimes in Jammu and Kashmir can be seen through the framework of resistance movement. The evident example of this is the support provided by the Gujjar community of Jammu and Kashmir to the protesting Gujjar community of Rajasthan for reservation in the jobs. Many of the Gujjar leaders of Jammu and Kashmir went to Rajasthan and addressed the protesting gatherings. There have been attempts to give rise and prominence to the consciousness of ethnic Gujjar identity so as not to make them a part of larger resistance movement. However there is also a reality of these Gujjars being socially excluded from the larger Kashmiri identity of the majority Muslims in the state.

Till this time, they are being regarded as an inferior, short tempered and out layered community within the state of Jammu and Kashmir. They have always been seen by Kashmiris only with the identity of Muslims. However one must take note of the fact that Gujjar community have been active supporters of resistance movement to which is the evidence of the formation of Gujjar liberation front in1991 (Asia Watch, 1991). The Gujjar liberation front was formed by the Gujjar and Bakkarwal community to fight the Indian occupation of Jammu and Kashmir State. Still in the larger discourses of the secessionist movements they have not been considered as an active partner in the movement. On the other hand mainstream political forces have always demonized their involvement as a kind of talibanisation.

Marginalisation of Scheduled Tribes (Gujjar and Bakkarwal Community)

Schedule tribes at large in India are the receiving end. The overall indicators show a very dismal picture of scheduled tribes in India. The table below clearly depicts the condition of scheduled tribes in India

Table 17.1: Key Health Indicators

Indicators	*ST*	*Total (India)*
Infant mortality	62.1	57
Neo-natal mortality	39.9	39
Post-natal mortality	22.3	18
Child mortality	35.8	18.4
Under five mortality	95.7	74.3
ANC checkup	70.5	77.1
% Institutional deliveries	17.7	38.7
Child vaccination (Full immunization)	31.3	43.5
% Households covered by a health scheme/Insurance	2.6	31.9
Prevalence of any anaemia (<12.0g/dl) in women	**68.5**	**55.3**

Source: National Family Health Survey (NFHS) 2005-2006.

From the data it is clear that child mortality is almost double when it comes to the schedule tribe population as compared to the national average. Similarly the percentage of institutional deliveries is half of the national average and the percentage of household insurance shows very dismal picture when compared to the national average. Children born in SC and ST families have higher risk of dying than others. "The risk is higher for children born in scheduled tribe (ST) families as compared to scheduled caste (SC). For example, a child born to an SC family has 13 per cent higher risk of dying in the neonatal period and 18 per cent higher risk of dying in the post-neonatal period, as compared to others. Similarly, a child born to an ST family has 19 per cent higher risk of dying in the neonatal period and 45 per cent risk of dying in the post-neonatal period"(NIMS, ICMR and UNICEF, 2012). Jammu and Kashmir, a contested state within the Indian union, is engulfed by the armed conflict that has ridden havoc in the state from last two decades. The regular loss of human lives, damage to property and infrastructure has been followed by changing patterns of livelihood across various ethnic groups. One of the ethnic groups known by the name of Gujjar and Bakkarwal has also been victim of this conflict. This ethnic group is one of the socially isolated and economically backward groups in the state of Jammu and Kashmir. Having to live their lives in the upper reaches of Himalayas, these people have to face hardship not only from nature but from the dominant structures of state. Historically Gujjar and Bakkarwals have been the pastoralists which always added to the economic production in terms of providing raw materials in the form of wool, meat, milk and the cattle at large. However, because of the dominant influence of modernity in terms of technology interventions and globalization, these people are facing numerous problems. The problems are both at the level of changing livelihood patterns and the breaking down of their own socio-cultural milieu.

As revealed by the review of literature this is not a unique case with the pastoralists in Jammu and Kashmir only, rather it is found almost in every part of the world. However, there happens to be another dimension to the question of pastorals in Jammu and Kashmir. The dimension is the presence of armed conflict, which in a turn has lead to the emergence of political gambling in the state. Presence of military and the large paramilitary forces in the state along with the renegade groups and militants has lead to the complexity of problems with respect to Gujjar and Bakkarwal community. Gujjars have been one of the major suffers of the conflict. The spread of militancy and the intrusion of the Indian troops into the hilly areas including pastures have put at stake the livelihood of this community. This community is at the constant struggle with militancy and Indian troops in their day to day living. The nomadic movement of this community is under the severe threat because of the security concerns that these people have to face. This ethnic community not only has the threat of their lives but also fear loss of their livestock. It has been found out that Indian troops and militants very often take away the sheep from these people without paying them. Moreover the milk products like ghee are also not left for these people. In this threat of existence, there has been a change in the livelihood patterns of these people. We must also remember that there is a class dimension to this changing pattern of livelihood. From the literature it comes out that rich Bakkarwals are now hiring the poor ones for rearing their sheep and goats and themselves have got settled in the towns and low lying plains. Aparna Rao in her paper "From Bondsmen to Middlemen, Hired Shepherds and Pastoral Politics" (Rao, 1995) has shown that most of the wealthy Gujjar and Bakkarwals take people from poor families and make them bonded shepherds. Rao argues that this change has happened only after the eruption of the armed struggle in the state of Jammu and Kashmir. This change arose out of the fear as was propagated by the Indian Army and the militants present in the upper reaches of Himalayas happen to be pastures of this community. The change of livelihood pattern among this community can also be seen in terms of the number of people engaged in other occupations. Many of the Gujjar Bakkarwal people now work as agriculture labourers and other causal workers in the cement factories. This change is a kind of enforced one due to armed conflict. The pastures at the upper reaches of Himalayas have become the abode for both militants as well as Indian forces.

In this constant danger of life this community has left going to these upper reaches along with their herd. However those people who could not find any other means for their sustenance are still using the same pastures and have complained of harassment from all the stake holders. Indian army forces these people to become informers and militants label them to be acting as informers. Thus in this dilemma these people are suffering a lot. Since this community been socially marginalized and economically backward, lots of other problems still haunt them. These people are still far from dreaming the modern education and health facilities. However government has always played politics on the name of welfare for these people. Most of the scholars argue that giving tribal status by the Indian government to this community in 1991 was a political move rather than a welfare measure. It is being argued that since the eruption of secessionist movement in 1989 and its gaining of larger indigenous support alarmed the Indian state. Thus a kind of divisive politics in the name of welfare was played out by the state and the Gujjar Bakkarwal community was provided with the tribal status. The welfare measures operated by government in terms of tribal sub plans are also not devoid of the larger political context of the state. However having said this one cannot clearly make an argument as how far has presence of armed conflict made an impact on the overall health and education indicators of the Gujjar and Bakkarwal community. There are no studies so far available which could clearly mention the extent of the impact of armed conflict on the Gujjar Bakkarwal community. There remains still the need to find out any direct linkage with respect to the key health indicators and presence of armed conflict. But one should not hesitate in stating that presence of armed conflict has lead to the plethora of sufferings for the Gujjar Bakkarwal community some of which are individual and some collective. The regular loss of life and livelihood is a pertinent reality which can be clearly ascertained from the lived experiences of the Gujjar Bakkarwal community. Some of the data which has come out from the census and many other studies do showing a dismal picture with respect to over all schedule tribe population in Jammu and Kashmir. One must remember that Gujjar and Bakkarwal together constitute around 80 per cent of the total tribal population of the country. Therefore the worsening condition of scheduled tribe population in Jammu and Kashmir is mostly of the Gujjar and Bakkarwal community. Some of the key indicators that have been compared between scheduled tribes and total population in Jammu and Kashmir also point towards the discrimination of the community as such.

The data clearly brings forth various issues with respect to the Scheduled tribes at large and Gujjar and Bakkarwal Community specifically. Though there is no segregation of the data interms of the individual scheduled tribe groups but one must remember that it is mostly Gujjar and Bakkarwal which constitute around 80 per cent of the total tribal population of Jammu and Kashmir. Some of the indicators as have been highlighted in red need special attention. Look at the below poverty line population, it is comes very clear

Table 17.2: Key Indicators of Jammu and Kashmir

Indicator	*ST*	*Total (J&K)*	*Source*
Population	1493299 (11.9%)	12541302	Census 2011
Infant mortality rate	83	45	SRS 2009
Under five mortality rate	122	55	SRS 2009
Sex ratio	910	883	Census 2011
BPL population	8.8	3.3	Planning Commission 2004-2005
Literacy rate	36.5	68.74	GIO, NSSO, 2009-10
Birth rate	N.A	18.6	SRS 2009
Prevalence of any anaemia in children	61.0	56.5	NFHS 2005
Death rate	N.A.	5.7	SRS 2009
Unmet need for family planning	22.5	N.A.	NFHS 98-99
TFR	3.6	2.2	SRS 2009
% of households having electricity	47.3	80.6	Census 2001
Vaccination (BCG) coverage	65.3	96.5	NFHS 2005-06
% of Households having latrine facilities	41.2	53.1	Census 2001
% Having pacca houses	17.7	55	Census 2001

N.A: Data not available.

that the scheduled tribes in Jammu and Kashmir are almost two and half times more in number than the total below poverty line population numbers. Similarly when one looks at the percentage coverage of immunization it is also half of the total general population. Similar kinds of trends are observed in case literacy rate and the percentage of *pacca* houses. Thus the data is a clear indication of the fact that the scheduled tribes in Jammu and Kashmir are at disadvantage. Gujjars and Bakkarwals have been part of the historic mosaic of Jammu and Kashmir for quite long. However they have always been left to the fringes by the dominant identities Dogras, Kashmiri Pundits and Muslims. While one goes through the pages of history of Jammu and Kashmir, there is always the marginalization of this group. The worst victims of the partition of 1947 have been the Gujjars and Bakkarwals of Jammu and Kashmir. Most of the members of this ethnic group are now residing in the Pakistan Administered Kashmir (POK) and parts of Gilgit and Northwest frontier. The partition has also left this group to bear the brunt of regular border disputes between two countries. The border tension has made the life of these people much more vulnerable to the human tragedies like cross firings, landmine blasts and night bombings. Soon after partition, the Indian administered Jammu and Kashmir began its journey with the slogan of building new Kashmir. However the story remained same for these people as they further became the scapegoats of political gambling's in the state of Jammu and Kashmir. With the just few elite representations in the political circles, the larger population of Gujjar and Bakkarwals continued to remain in slumber and destitution. The elite members of this group like Mian Bashir family[3] did nothing except from keeping their poverty intact so as to bargain out of that. The underdevelopment of this group interms of low levels of literacy, high poverty, high mortality rates and poor infrastructural facilities kept rising with the advent of time.

The poverty ridden Gujjars and Bakkarwals live a very miserable life because of lack of modern facilities. These people have to face both the natural tragedies as well as human induced tragedies. Due to historical marginalization, these people have had to face number of health problems along with the increased burden of poverty and changing livelihood issues. The Gujjar lung disease that has been discovered only after an extensive study of effects of impoverished housing of the Gujjar and Bakkarwal people. The entity 'Gujjar Lung'[4] came into existence in medical literature in 1991 when Dhar & Pathania from Government Medical College associated Chest Diseases Hospital Srinagar studied 46 Gujjar patients who had history of exposure to pinewood smoke inhalation since early age in the dwellings, with radiological evidence of milliary mottling and reticulo nodular shadows, who were empirically put on therapeutic trials of anti-tuberculosis treatment, but the shadows remained same or increased in density. Finally lung biopsy revealed features of anthracotic nodules, carbon-laden macrophages and fibrosis to Gujjar community" (Hassan *et al.*, 2006)

To Sum Up

Gujjars and Bakkarwals historically being marginalized and socially excluded group have always been politically meddled for the regime gains either by their own leaders or by the leadership of Indian mainstream political parties. However the fact of matter is that they have also not been absorbed within the larger Kashmiri identity by the separatist leadership or the Hurriyat[5] amalgamation. These people have always been reduced to the fringes and have been given space only at the time of religious gatherings. These people are continuously deprived from attaining the larger role within the dominant Kashmiri identity at every sphere of life. Living the life full of hardships and began the producers of the community they have not been fully provided the justice per se. one has already noticed above that this community is facing a kind of identity crisis. Neither are they accepted by the Dogras[6] as a part of their community nor have they been assimilated with the larger Kashmiri identity. Thus in the struggle for existence they have either become scapegoats of their own political elite or they have become puppets within the hands of mainstream Indian parties. It has been seen that neither has there been any great impact on the lives of these people with the granting of tribal status nor have there been efforts from the government at large. Miserable life which these people live can be verified from the fact that these people are still the victims of curable and communicable diseases like tuberculosis and are also the victims of malnourishment. Literacy level among this community is still very low and hardly have there been efforts to raise that.

Across the globe we have seen what modernity has done to the various tribal cultures. However incase of Gujjar and Bakkarwal community in Jammu and Kashmir, modernity has not touched them so strongly despite the seasonal migration of this community which brings it in contact with other cultures of the state. Some scholarship in the area of modernity argues that the aloofness of this community form others has brought them backwardness and their won happiness. Thus it can be said that this community has its own sufferings and survival mechanism based on their traditional wisdom and we have not been able to develop them to the large extent. Under the grab of this identity dilemma and clash of identities,. It was propounded that tribal states to these people will lead to the general welfare and development. The influx of money on the name of tribal sub plans was either grabbed by the leaders of this community which happen to be part of the larger political elite of the Jammu and Kashmir state. With some mere opening of Gujjar Bakkarwal hostel, the larger environment for these people remained same. However Sarva Shiksha Abhiyan had to some extent helped in providing primary education to the children of these people by opening mobile schools. The effect of these schools needs to be ascertained in the near future. The National Conference (political party in Jammu and Kashmir, which ruled state for a long period of time and are currently in power again) government has always made political gains out of the welfare politics. Since Sheikh Abdullah's wife happen to be from Gujjar community and that card has always been played out by the government (Rao, 1999).

The formation of Gujjar Bakkarwal councils and with the entrance of some of the non-governmental organizations, certain empowerment measures seems to pay fruits. Preserving of the larger culture of the community is being taken seriously by these councils and NGO's. The continuous translation of the literature from other languages into the gojri language is a major achievement that one can praise off. However at large one can argue that this community is still socially excluded not only from the political environment of the state but also from the lager social environment. Efforts must be taken to let these people thrive the fruits of development not at the cost of losing their own occupations and being subservient to the wishes of political regimes.

NOTES

1. In the literature the Word "Gujjar" is generally used to represent this whole tribal community in which Bakkarwal is one of the sub groups. Bakkarwals are unique because of their true pastoralistic characteristics. However in this paper Gujjar and Bakkarwal are used interchangeably.
2. This university is one of the state universities in Jammu and Kashmir which is located in Rajouri district, which second largest Gujjar bakkarwal population in the state of Jammu and Kashmir. This university was opened in the year 2002 only. http://www.bgsbuniversity.org/
3. This family has been in the political circles of Jammu and Kashmir since partition. Many of its members have been and are at the helm of affairs like ministers in the state government. They have been controlling the Bakkarwal community politics strongly.
4. Gujjar lung is a form of chronic lung disease as a result of indoor air pollution with pinewood smoke in Gujjar community—a social and ethnic group residing at hilly regions of the Indian sub-continent. These people live in ill-ventilated mud hoses called "Kothas" and use pinewood for heating and cooking purposes throughout the year, with daily exposure to smoke averaging 12 to 16 hours. A high oleoresin containing part of the wood called "Lash" is used for lighting purposes adding further to the indoor air pollution.
5. Hurriyat is an amalgamation of various secessionist parties which have been fighting against the Indian state in Jammu and Kashmir.
6. Dogras are the Hindu people who live in the Jammu province of the state of Jammu and Kashmir.

18

Sexual Behaviour of Urban Gay Men in Mizoram

Concerns for Risk Behaviour

Zothankimiralte and *Kalpana Sarathy*

The term *homosexuality* denotes erotic thoughts and feelings towards a person of the same sex, as well as any associated sexual behaviour (Gelder *et al*, 1996). Homosexuality is also understood as the romantic or sexual attraction or behaviour among members of the same sex, situationally or as an enduring disposition, and as a sexual orientation. Homosexuality is considered to lie within the heterosexual-homosexual continuum of human sexuality. *Homosexuals* are said to be individuals with a primary sexual preference or emotional attraction toward persons of the same sex. The term "Gay" is inclusive of persons who have sex within the confines of their own gender. 'Gay' is a more respectful term and is one that is accepted by members of this community. The term '*homosexual*' was coined by a Hungarian writer Karoly Maria Benkert, who under the pseudonym Kertbeny in 1869, published a pamphlet on the subject (Bulloug, 1979).

Homosexuality has been called among other things *a sin, an illness, a way of life, a normal variant of sexual behaviour, a behaviour disturbance, and a crime* (Bulloug, 1979). Men who profess homosexuality are said to have been "born that way", been enticed into homosexuality by an adult, turned to homosexuality by the lack of strong parent, been unable to attract a person of the opposite sex, been oversexed or sexually deficient, been at a lower level of human evolution, been rebels against a bourgeois materialist society, or been victims of various kinds of experiences. Terms such as "queer," "fag," "fairy," and "pervert" have been applied to them as individuals, and at various times in history they have been placed in asylums, imprisoned, executed, medicated, psychoanalysed, and ostracized; yet they have continued to exist. Most survived by *"remaining in the closet"* – that is, they never publicly proclaimed themselves but sought to mask their sexual preference by living and acting as did their neighbours (Bulloug, 1979). At present, though there are still many challenges faced by homosexuals, they are now in a much better place than they were before, laws have been passed for protection of their rights against discrimination and for same sex marriage. Netherlands was the first country to legalize homosexuality in 2001. Since then, many other countries followed the same where they have also legalized '*same-sex marriage*', and today, homosexuality is recognized across the globe. One of the first Gay Rights Movement was the '*Stonewall Riots*' (1969) in New York City, USA, which led to the formation of a very active gay rights organization called the Gay Liberation Front (GLF). Today, '*the Rainbow Flag*' constituting six colours: red, orange, yellow, green, blue, and purple – indicates homosexuality, representing the diversity of their community.

In India, gay people are also getting recognized and with the repeal of IPC 377 (2nd July, 2009), which 'decriminalizes' same-sex behaviour, they are gaining recognition and are 'coming out of the closet' in a more visible manner. Since then many gay activities had been carried out in the country like in April 2010 Mumbai had one of its biggest events when the first queer film festival was held in a mainstream multiplex and the Kolkata Rainbow held on 15 July 2012 which was attended by more than 1500 people and many online forums to support eradication of social discrimination faced by the Lesbian, Gay, Bisexual, Transgender (LGBT) community. One of the biggest organizations in the country which is doing tremendous work for gays in the country is SAATHI, and they are in fact the forerunner in the repeal of IPC 377.

The Mizoram Context

In Mizoram, as far as history could tell, homosexuality has never been accepted in the society. And with the advent of Christianity in the state, over a hundred years ago, the people have adopted a very rigid and conservative outlook, stigmatizing any behaviours that are prohibited in the Bible. These include the practice of homosexual behaviour which is unacceptable form of sexuality according to religious views. This discrimination and stigmatization has prompted the gay community to hide behind a mask and not to reveal their sexuality. Though gay men and lesbian women find little acceptance in the Mizo society, many *gay men* have started coming out of the closet. Since Gays are condemned by religious preachers, other groups and individuals, they face a great deal of stigmatization. The subject has either been not researched at all or had received low priority, there is lesser understanding about their needs, problems, issues, non acceptance, risk behaviours. The issues require research with open mind and sensitivity to ensure fair deal to this specific group.

Methodology

The design for the study is exploratory in nature and this is a cross-sectional study. The universe consists of all gay men residing in Aizawl.

Sampling: The only NGO in Mizoram, Francois-Xavier Bagnoud (FXB) which offers exclusive services to gays was identified and contacted and a list of all gays accessing services in these agencies were obtained. This number at the start of the study consisted of 180 gay men. *Snowballing technique* was used to contact as many gays in the networks of the attendees in the NGO list to arrive at the sample. A total of 70 gay men were accessed and questionnaires were distributed to them out of which 54 were returned making the return rate 77 per cent.

Data Collection: The study is based on the primary data collected through quantitative method. Questionnaire was employed as a tool of data collection and it sought information on socio demographic information, sexual history and present sexual behaviour. Form of sex practices by the respondents was also documented.

Data Analysis: Data obtained from the structured questionnaires was processed using Microsoft Excel, Microsoft Word and SPSS, and presented in the form of simple percentages.

Results and Discussions

Demographic Profile: Age is an important variable in any research because it is a determinant of how people perceive issues or hold opinion on statements to be answered. In this study, results indicate that over two-thirds of the respondents (68.5%) fall under the age group of 18-25 years revealing that gay men in urban Mizoram are of younger age and are generally in their youth.

Table 18.1: Demographic Profile

Sl. No	*Characteristics*	*Frequency n =54*	*Percentage*
1.	**Age**		
	Below 18 years	5	9.3
	18-25 years	37	68.5
	26-45 years	11	20.4
	46-60 years	1	1.9
2.	**Educational qualification**		
	Cl-X below	3	5.6
	Cl-X	14	25.9
	Cl-XII	23	42.6
	Graduate	13	24.1
	Post-Graduate	1	1.9
3.	**Marital status**		
	Never married	45	83.3
	Married	5	9.3
	Divorced	4	7.4

Educational Qualification is another important variable because educational level of a person contributes to how perceptions and attitudes are formed. Table 18.1 shows that, out of the 54 respondents, nearly half (42.6%)

had completed their 12th standard education and about a quarter (24.1%) had a graduate educational level. This indicates that the sample selected is educated, and Mizoram being the 2nd most literate state in the country, this finding is not surprising.

Marital status of respondents in a vital variable in this study because married people with multiple sex partners place several partners at risk. With regard to this, results show that though more than three-quarters of the respondent (83.3%) fall under the category of 'never married', almost a tenth (9.3%) are married, indicating that married men in urban Mizoram do have gay relationships. This is an unanticipated finding because Mizoram being Christian dominated state, married couples are not expected to have partners outside the confines of marriage, let alone have a relationship with the same sex. This finding is a very important data for the study because bisexuals have more opportunities for sexual activities and this may result in making them more susceptible to sexually transmitted diseases as compared to heterosexuals, placing them at high risk of HIV/AIDS.

Table 18.2: Sexual History (n = 54)

Sl. No	*Characteristics*	*Frequency*	*Percentage*
1.	**Age at first sexual experience**		
	Under 18 years	48	88.9
	18 to 25 years	3	5.6
	NA	3	5.6
2.	**First sexual experience was with**		
	Same gender	37	68.5
	Opposite gender	14	25.9
	NA	3	5.6
3.	**First sexual experience was**		
	By force	8	14.8
	By choice	43	79.6
	NA	3	5.6

Respondents were asked about their sexual history in order to understand how early had they encountered their first sexual experience, gender with whom the first sexual experience was shared with and also if this experience was a personal choice or otherwise. These variables are important in understanding if past sexual experiences and activities have any predisposition to the present conduct of sexual behaviours.

Table 18.2 shows that an overwhelming majority (88.9%) of the respondents have their first sexual experience *before attaining the age of 18 years*. The findings indicate that sexual behaviours of Urban Gay Men (UGM) in Mizoram are carried out very early in life, mostly under-aged, and this is also evident in research conducted by Trioden (1979) elsewhere, where he found that gay men had their first homosexual activity *at the mean age of 14.9 years*.

It is evident from the table that more than two-thirds (68.5%) of the respondents experience the first sexual encounter with the same gender while a quarter of them (25.9%) encounter it with the opposite sex. It is important to know this because many myths and misinformation exist and surround the studies on homosexuality. Some gay men realize their sexuality only after encountering the opposite gender in a sexual way. Further, participants were asked the nature of consent regarding their first sexual experience. To this question, results imply that more than three quarters (79.6%) encounter their first sexual experience *by choice* whereas more than a tenth (14.8%) of them were initiated *by force*. This is an important finding because there is ignorance on these issues in Mizoram and further, in many cases forced sexual encounter can cause victims to be placed at higher risk, become casual in their attitudes to sexual behaviours which can result in risky sexual behaviours like carelessness in choosing partners etc.

Table 18.3: Present Sexual Behaviour (n = 54)

Sl. No	*Statements*	*Frequency*	*Percentage*
1.	**Consider myself sexually active**		
	Strongly agree	2	3.7
	Agree	18	33.3
	Agree nor disagree	16	29.6
	Disagree	12	22.2
	Strongly disagree	6	11.1
2.	**Have sex with**		
	Men only	24	44.4
	Women only	1	1.9
	Both	24	44.4
	Neither	3	5.6
	NA	2	3.7
3.	**Have sex mainly with people of**		
	Same age	23	42.6
	Younger age	2	3.7
	Older age	15	27.8
	No specific age	11	20.4
4.	**Sexual intercourse following substance abuse**		
	No	15	27.8
	Yes	39	72.2

The present sexual behaviours were analyzed to understand the pattern of sexual activities among UGM in Mizoram and to find out if there are any risk behaviours related to it. Table 18.3 shows sexual activeness of respondents, sex and age of sexual partners and incidence of substance abuse before occurrence of sexual intercourse.

Results indicate that almost one-third (33.3%) of the respondents identify themselves as having *active* sexual life and in addition, two respondents (3.7%) consider themselves as *strongly active* in sexual activities. Findings reveal that UGM in Mizoram perceive themselves as active in activities related to sexual intercourse.

Respondents were also asked about the gender with whom they frequently have sexual intercourse with and this is an important variable because it will indicate if sexual activities are limited just to the same gender or if it is also carried out with the opposite gender as well thereby increasing risks for women as well. Results show that less than half (44.4%) of the respondents have *sex only with men* with a similar number (44.4%) stating that they have *sex with both men and women.* This finding reveals that many self-proclaimed gay men in urban Mizoram practice *bisexuality.* Mizo community is highly religious and many gay men probably have relationships with women as well in order to hide their true identity and use it as a shield from societal discrimination. A lone respondent said that currently he has sex with women only although his attraction is towards men only.

Age group of sexual partners was also examined to highlight the type of age group that respondents generally seek as partners to have sex with. From the results we can see that almost half (42.6%) of the respondents has sex mainly with the same age, whereas over a quarter (27.8%) have it with older age and a fifth (20.4%) with no specific age. This indicates that gay men in Mizoram have a social network usually of the same age but surprising they do tend to carry out sexual behaviours with older age men as well. Results showing more than one-fifth of the respondents showing liberty towards age of sexual partner show that there is no caution taken by UGM in choosing partners for sexual intercourse. This is can an indicator for reckless and risky sexual behaviour. Results also show that almost three quarters (72.2%) of the respondents pointed out that they have sexual intercourse following substance abuse.

The findings are alarming and suggest that gay men in Mizoram intoxicate themselves before sexual activities. This makes them more prone to experiment or indulge in risky behaviour and render themselves to contracting any kind of infections or/and diseases through intercourse. When a person is intoxicated and has sex under influence of substances, he is likely to lose track and indulge in risk behaviour and partake of activities he would normally not do, were he sober. Also, when a person is under the influence of drugs and alcohol, and he is about to have sexual intercourse, there is a tendency to be careless in carrying out safe sex practices. In many cases condoms are forgotten and in the height of intoxication, partners are also not chosen wisely, hence, giving an opportunity to contract different sexual infections and diseases. Similarly a study done by Colfax *et al* (2001) shows that there is a prevalence of high-risk activity during circuit party weekends where there is a lot of drug use which suggests significant potential for HIV transmission in this population. Also in a research conducted by Maria *et al*. (2003) it was found that cocaine consumption is one of the risk factor for contracting HIV among gay men.

Table 18.4: Forms of Sex

Sl. No	*Form of Sex*	*Frequency (n = 54)*				*Total*
		Always	*Mostly*	*Sometimes*	*Never*	
1.	Oral Sex	10 (18.52)	22 (40.74)	16 (29.63)	6 (11.11)	54 (100)
2.	Anal Sex	5 (9.26)	12 (22.22)	29 (53.70)	8 (14.81)	54 (100)
3.	Phone Sex	4 (7.41)	5 (9.26)	22 (40.74)	23 (42.59)	54 (100)
4.	Conventional Sex	3 (5.56)	4 (7.41)	17 (31.5)	30 (55.5)	54 (100)
5.	Cyber Sex	1 (1.85)	5 (9.26)	13 (24.07)	35 (64.81)	54 (100)

Figures in parentheses are percentages

Results from the data kept in Table 18.4 give us information about the different forms of sexual intercourse that UGM in Mizoram carry out. There are five forms under this; Oral Sex, Anal Sex, Conventional Sex, Phone Sex and Cyber Sex. Responses in relation to these five forms were rated as: (i) Always, (ii) Mostly, (iii) Sometimes, (iv) Never. Results show that majority of the respondents (88.89%) perform oral sex and also a huge majority (85.18%) do carry out anal sex. Cyber-sex is least performed with a little over one-third of the respondents stating that they indulge themselves in cyber sex which mainly reveals to involving in sexual activities through the use of internet.

Conclusion

Mizoram is a state known for organizing its activities around religion and its people are highly influenced by the teachings of Christianity. Therefore, gay men and lesbian women find little acceptance in this society because the Bible does not allow its practice. Although, Mizos are heavily influenced by modernization and westernization, the general population has negative attitudes and perceptions toward homosexuality which result in stigmatization and discrimination of people who practise it. Also the people are conservative with strong belief that discussion about sexual activities is highly inappropriate. These negative attitudes towards homosexuality and talk about sexual behaviour being a taboo do affect the social and psychological stability of gay men and lesbian women and further result in other risk behaviour. It is also likely to reduce their opportunities for development.

Mizo society resorts to stereotypy of gay men as *feminine* and the lesbian women as *masculine*, however unless they chose to be, and are *cross-dressers,* UGM are for the most part not easily identified. Though the stereotypes do exist, only an insignificant minority of UGM conform to them. This makes it difficult to identify them and in order to hide their sexual orientation, in most cases, gay men would not wear clothes of the opposite gender which is also evident in a study conducted by Herek (2009) where findings reveal that *felt stigma* by gay people motivates them to hide their sexual minority and attempt to pass as heterosexual. Very often too, it has also been found that gays marry their gender counterparts in order to hide their identity and to prevent themselves from the anxieties of being a social outcast. Majority gay men in Mizo society experience their first sexual intercourse before attaining the age of 18 years and are not very particular about choosing sexual partners. Most respondents declare to abusing substances before carrying out sexual activities and it was also found that almost half of the respondents indulge in bisexual behaviours. Further research is required to understand if the sexual behaviour which further leads to risky sexual activities is a result of fear of discrimination and stereotypy. If discrimination, stereotyping and stigmatization of gay population along with inappropriateness of discussions about sex heighten in the society, then it is likely that they will continue to hide their sexuality which in turn will make them more vulnerable to sexual risk behaviour. This study is therefore very important as it has implications for policy and programmes. Awareness at the community level is strongly indicated to dispel negative behaviour towards sexuality and to increase communication on issues that surround it. Forced sexual encounters need to be addressed and bisexual experiences are exploitative if partners have no information regarding the sexual liaisoning of their spouses/partners. The strong holds of opinions held at community level require to be understood and people need to be educated on the need for communication and awareness of risks to health and mental health.

19

Decent Work for Home-based Workers in India

Implications for Social Work

Shivani Chauhan Barooah

International Labour Organisation's (ILO) mission is to improve the situation of human beings in the world of work. The primary goal of the ILO today is to promote opportunities for women and men to obtain decent and productive work, in conditions of freedom, equity, security and human dignity (ILO 1999 cited in Zarka-Martres and Guichard-Kelly 2005). Thus, the notion of decent work emphasizes on four main elements—(i) work and employment, (ii) social protection, (iii) rights at work and (iv) social dialogue. While the first two components emphasize on the material force, other two emphasize on the social relations of workers. The concept of employment refers to work of all kinds and has both qualitative and quantitative dimensions attached to it and it is applicable not just to the workers in the formal economy but also to the workers in the informal economy (unregulated wage workers, the self-employed and the home workers). In addition to this it refers to both adequate opportunities and remuneration for work (in cash or kind). This dimension also encompasses safety at work and healthy working conditions. The concept of decent work also incorporates rights at work, thus all those who work have rights at work. Some of the basic rights relate to freedom of association, non-discrimination at work, the absence of forced labour and child labour in abusive conditions. Social protection is intended to protect against the risks of losing income and defined according to each society's capacity and level of development. The aspect of social dialogue refers to the rights of workers to engage in discussions with the employers and authorities over matters bearing on work. It is a means by which rights are defined, employment promoted and work secured (Ghai 2006).

The working conditions and conditions of work for the majority of workers are pitiable and inhumane especially for those in the informal economy. There is no denying the fact that the extent and magnitude of the informal economy has increased tremendously over the past few decades. There has been a sudden spurt of newer and different types of economic activities. Undoubtedly, globalization has given new opportunities for many workers, especially those who are well educated, with the skills demanded in the high-tech global economy but it has deepened insecurity and poverty for many others. (Heyzer 2005). The practice of sub-contracting in industry has grown markedly as a tool of production in global commodity chains over the past 30 years, the reasons for this development include: portability of multinational corporations' (MNCs) operations, consistent with economic globalization; cross-border production networks associated cost-cutting benefits for manufacturers and entrepreneurs; and the demand for flexibility in production output. Over the years sub-contracting has become a major source of employment, and that the majority of sub-contracting workers in global commodity chains are women. It has also been suggested that a larger proportion of such sub-contracting in reality extends down to home-based work. The reason for this is that on one side men have integrated more speedily and successfully into the industrializing economies of the Asian countries compared to women who have usually been relegated to the informal economy and have been targeted for the sub-contracting and home-based activities that have expanded increasingly in Asia (Wright 2004; Ghosh 2006). Thus women home-based workers face double burden in terms of household responsibilities in addition to their work responsibilities. Their work is also considered as a past-time activity as it is carried in the home and due to this invisibility surrounding their work their exploitation goes unabated and plight unnoticed. However due to the work of international and national bodies like HOMENET and Self Employed Women's Association (SEWA) these workers and their work is being increasingly recognized and the day is not far that decent work becomes a reality for these workers. And for the achievement of this goal the social work profession has an important role to play ranging from meso-level studies to macro-level policy formulation.

Defining Decent Work

After its inception and introduction in 1999 the concept of decent work has been dominant in the programmes and policies of the ILO. Decent work is the converging focus of four strategic objectives namely, work and employment, rights at work, social protection and social dialogue. It is an organizing concept for the ILO in order to provide an overall framework for action in economic and social development (ILO 2005). The concept of decent work is enshrined in the original principles and values of the Organization, namely, the promotion of social justice and humane conditions at work (Egger 2002). It contributes to the execution of the ILO's mandate in four ways: firstly it's a goal (it reflects the universal aspirations of people everywhere, and is both a personal goal for individuals and a developmental goal for countries); secondly it provides a policy framework; thirdly it is a method of organizing activities and programmes (the ILO has restructured and formulated its programmes around the four strategic objectives); and lastly it is a platform for external dialogue and partnership (Ghai 2005).

While operationalizing decent work for policy purposes three elements emerge as essential to the achievement of decent work objectives: the need for jobs, the honouring of core labour standards and the pursuit of further improvements in job quality (Fields, 2003). The first element of decent work is employment. As it goes without saying that for a person to have a decent job he/she must have a job in the first place. The need for more jobs is central to the decent work paradigm, and full employment rightfully occupies the prime position at the forefront of the decent work effort. Nonetheless the questions over quality and quantity of work are omnipresent. With an estimate of 205 million people unemployed across the globe in 2010 the employment goal is best expressed as adequate opportunities for productive and meaningful work in decent conditions—that signifies taking into account working time and work intensity, the need for a living income, the possibilities for personal development and the opportunities to use one's capabilities. It not only includes formal but also informal work in the home, in the factory or in the street. It includes men and women both, as much work by women especially in the home is undervalued and invisible (Rodgers 2001; Fields 2003).

The second essential ingredient concerns basic rights at work that is respect for core labour standards. In the last few years, thinking in the world community has coalesced around a set of core labour standards: freedom of association, freedom from discrimination, freedom from forced labour and freedom from child labour, aimed at promoting and assuring fundamental principles and rights at work. The jobs in which the core labour standards are not respected cannot be regarded as decent. In fact they can be characterized as indecent work: work in conditions so odious or harmful that it would be better for people not to work at all than to work in such damaging conditions (Rodgers 2001; Fields 2003). The ILO with its work spanning over more than nine decades has adopted 189 Conventions and 202 Recommendations covering all the issues of interest to workers and employers. Even though rights at work embodied in ILO's declarations, conventions and Recommendations are considered of universal validity and relevance. However it should be noted that the ratification of different Conventions is only a very rough index of the achievement of rights at work (Ghai 2005).

The third essential element of social protection aims to provide security against a variety of contingencies and vulnerabilities. These include ill-health, maternity needs, accidents, unemployment, destitution, extreme economic fluctuations, natural disasters and civil conflicts. The concept of social protection goes beyond the limited notion of social security for work related situations firstly, because it is broader in its coverage of protection and extends to the worker's family to embrace vulnerable and insecure persons outside paid employment. Secondly, the contingencies and vulnerabilities are wider in their scope (to include destitution, extreme economic fluctuations and natural and human catastrophes) thus moving beyond the conventional insecurities identified in the ILO Convention on Social Security. This all inclusive and more comprehensive definition of social security has the advantage of covering the full range of vulnerabilities of all members of society and not just the select section of the population who are often among the more advantaged groups in some countries. However this all inclusive notion of social protection doesn't imply that all countries are in the same position to design and implement the necessary policy and measures. As the items and levels of social protection provided to the population will naturally depend upon their past traditions, stages of development and resource mobilization (Ghai 2005).

In the context of decent work, social dialogue refers to various types of information exchange and negotiation between representatives of governments, employers and workers on issues of common interest. It is a means (just like the above mentioned dimensions) to promote opportunities for women and men to obtain decent and productive work in conditions of freedom, equality, security and human dignity (Kuruvilla 2006). The ways in which people's voices can be heard are a crucial aspect of decent work. As a matter of fact much of the literature on industrial relations focuses on the situation in economically advanced countries where the bulk of the labour force work as wage employees in the formal sector. As in the low-income countries the predominant forms of employment comprise self-employment in farming and other sectors, home-based work and wage employment in the informal economy. These workers lack autonomous and representative organizations to articulate their interests and engage in collective bargaining and consultations on matters affecting their livelihood. Consequently, alternate and new forms of organizations have emerged to cater to the specific interests of workers in the informal economy like SEWA in Ahmedabad, India.

Home-based Workers

Home-based work is a growing global phenomenon, it is estimated that over 100 million workers worldwide are working from their home. Due to the rise of complex global chains of production over the past half-century, home-based work has grown in leaps and bounds. The term 'home-based worker' refers to the general category of workers who carry out remunerative work within their homes or in the surrounding area; it does not include unpaid housework and domestic work in its ambit. Nevertheless, home-based work encompasses a wide diversity of work ranging from traditional embroidery and weaving to tele-work (WIEGO, 2012). Like the earliest form of home-working in India existed in the *jajmani* system during 1500-1750 B.C. The bulk of the rural manufacturing was produced by the artisan castes and was bound to the dominant agricultural castes by traditional client-patron relationship. However with the growth of a capitalist economy and democratic political institutions, the gradual decline of royal patronage also meant a decline in the main support base for skilled craft workers. There has also been a tradition of home-based work for own use or gifting in many parts of the region example, *phulkari*. Thus there is a tradtion of home-based work in the region. Moreover recently, now industries have outsourced to home-based workers in activities that have not been done traditionally by them. A study by UNIFEM finds a large number of home-based women assembling bicycle parts in Ludhiana, India; since 70 per cent of the women sampled had husbands who were technicians in adjoining factories or who were self-employed in technical trades, it seems that "the participation of household women in bicycle manufacturing trades can be considered as a spill-over of the technical occupations practised by their husbands" (UNIFEM 2000: 80, cited in Sudarshan and Sinha 2011).

There are two main types of home-based workers firstly the piece-rate workers (those working for an employer or intermediary) and secondly the own-account workers (those who do their own marketing). The piece-rate workers receive work from subcontractors or intermediaries, an employer, a trader or a firm and are paid a piece rate, according to the items produced. They do not have any direct contact with the markets for the goods they produce. As time and again, they have to buy the raw material from the factories or contractors and also arrange for tools. The cost of electricity, infrastructure, and raw material can really cut into their earnings. They can be engaged by international chains of production (garments, footwear, electronics, plastic footballs) or work for national or local markets (garments, bidi, agarbatti, textiles). The own-account workers are workers who are generally in direct contact with the market and buy their own raw material. They face competition from larger and more influential corporate houses and often do not have access to credit, except at huge rates of interests. And as they cannot buy large quantities of raw materials, the per unit cost of their products is higher. They live in remote rural areas, and generally rely on the agents, contractor or the middle persons to sell their goods directly in the markets. In terms of wages and working conditions, they are not much better off than piece-rate workers. It is often difficult to make a sharp division between the two types of home-based workers, as many own-account home-workers are economically dependent on outside forces. While many women do both kinds of work depending on what is available many more work in a commercial arrangement that disguise their dependence. For example, bidi workers all over India are required to 'buy' the raw material from the contractor and 'sell' the finished bidis back to the same contractor. The workers absorb the losses, if the raw material is damaged due to natural events such as rains, floods (Jhabvala 2002; Sinha 2006).

Although both men and women work from home, a large number of home-based workers are predominantly women and their numbers continues to rise today. There are several reasons for the preference of home-based work by women: like lack of necessary qualifications and formal training, absence of child care support, social and cultural constraints, absence of alternatives and extra income for household expenditure are some of the few reasons. There are positive aspects to home-based work also as it gives women the opportunity to combine work with domestic chores, flexible and sometimes better working conditions. However, the issues and problems of home-based workers are more complicated because of there being no direct master servant or employer-employee relationship. They are paid extremely low wages with no regularity of work, no bargaining power, have to face unfair trade practices, have no social protection and suffer from occupational health problems with no benefits as such from the employer (Mishra 2002; Sinha 2006).

Home-based work demonstrates the 'spillover' mechanisms through which insecurity associated with informality of work shift some elements of market risk and volatility onto the informal sector and in particular to women workers (Benería and Floro 2005). The working conditions of women workers working under sub-contracting arrangements tend to have little or no access to organized markets, to credit institutions, to formal education and training institutions, or to many public services and amenities. They are as not recognized, supported, protected or regulated by the government as they are under the ambit of the informal economy (COSATU, cited in Wright 2004). In addition, the fact that agents or sub-contractors may be employed by larger manufacturers means that an additional link in the chain is forged in the commodity chain, and the commission earned by the sub-contractor or agent is exacted from the producer at the lower end of the production scale. So the women working at piece-rate wages will be paying through additional labour, the agent's fee or sub-contractor's fee or sub-contractor's commission (Wright 2004). Thus women home-based workers face double burden in terms of household responsibilities in additions to their work responsibilities. Their work is not considered work as it is carried in the four walls of the house and thus due to this 'invisibility' surrounding their work their exploitation and plight goes unnoticed. This invisibility of women's work continues to be an obstacle in understanding their economic role in the household and in society (Bhatty 1987).

The invisibility of home-based workers is directly related to the traditional isolation of women within many societies that restricts their interactions with other women outside of their families or immediate communities. It is not surprising that many of these women, when surveyed, refer to themselves as 'not employed' or as 'housewives', even when they are spending 14-16 hours a day earning income to support their families (Jhabvala and Tate 1996).

In India home-based work has constituted an important economic activity for women for many years. The use of female labour through the putting out system for world market production has been established in number of industries, such as beedi making, food processing, and lacemaking (Rao and Husain 1987). Furthermore, India has a large and growing home-based work force in both urban and rural areas. The Self Employed Women's Association (SEWA) a trade union formed in 1972 was the first organization to draw national attention to these workers and, in fact, the term 'home-based worker' was coined by SEWA. The union struggles on behalf of its members at three levels: the exploitation they face directly from employers; their lack of influence before the law and with government bureaucracies; and their exclusion from the process of developing relevant policies and legislation (Jhabvala and Tate, 1996). In fact it was due to the relentless efforts of SEWA, and others like HomeNet and the International Confederation of Free Trade Unions (ICFTU) that under the auspices of ILO, the International Labour Conference adopted the *Home Work Convention, 1996* (*No. 177*) (Global Labour Institute 2000, cited in Wright, 2004). However trade unions should remember that the adoption of the Home Work Convention in 1996 was an achievement of the labour movement, but that such an achievement can only be of lasting significance if it is translated into ratifications and into national legislation (Gallin, 2007). As till date only seven countries (Albania, Argentina, Bosnia and Herzegovina, Bulgaria, Finland, Ireland and the Netherlands) have ratified this convention and as of now India doesn't figure in this list (ILO 2011) thus putting questions over the 'trickling down' of the positive effects of these conventions to the invisible and exploited women home-based workers in the urban and rural areas of a country as vast and diverse like India.

Decent Work for Home-based Workers

Since the new goal of the ILO, "Decent Work for All" came into existence aiming to secure decent work for men and women everywhere, the home-based workers also need to be ensured decent work. However, there are many factors which create impediments in the path for achieving decent work for home-based workers. First and foremost is the invisibility of these home-based workers, which is a major drawback in the achievement of decent work for them. Secondly for the piece-rate workers, the system of piece rate wages are extremely exploitative thus how to ensure decent work when the foundation of home-based work is piece-rate work. Thirdly, with a lot of social and cultural constraints governing women's work and movement in and outside the house the concept of decent work in a country as culturally diverse as India needs to adapt and redefine. Fourthly, the workplace for the home-based workers is their home or the surrounding area. Thus in this context where the living space is also the workplace the working and living conditions are intertwined in a complex manner. Fifthly, for the millions of home-based workers the sub-contractor/contractor is not the employer; these intermediaries—or sub-contractors—typically receive work orders and raw materials from firms or other intermediaries thus they need to be considered as semi-independent workers rather than as fully independent employers. Finally, the home-based workers work in isolation, the work and the women are often hidden within long production chains and many are so busy surviving that finding the time to devote to an organization is hard. Thus the lack of voice and collective bargaining power for the home-based workers accentuates their vulnerability and exploitation.

Implications for Social Work

One would like to re-assert the relevance of the subject for social work profession. The social work profession is multifaceted. The field of social work continues to be a mosaic with varied patterns (Pathak 1989: 1). This strongly suggests the multi directionality of areas of social work practice. In this background, this paper brings home an element of the multi-directionality of social work practice, as home-based work is found to be an area which requires social work intervention. The Education Policy and accreditation standards, Council on Social Work Education (CSWE 2001) highlighted that "Social Work practice promotes human well-being by strengthening opportunities, resources and capacities of people in their environments and by creating policies and services to correct conditions that limit human rights and the quality of life. The social work profession seeks to eliminate poverty, discrimination and oppression guided by a person-in-environment perspective and respect for human diversity, the profession works to affect social and economic justice worldwide" (Mohan, 2003: 113). The International Association of Schools of Social Work (2001) has defined Social Work as 'the social work profession that promotes social change, problem solving in human relationships and the empowerment and liberation of people to enhance well-being. Utilising theories of human behaviour and social systems, social work intervenes at the points where people interact with their environments. Principles of human rights and social justice are fundamental to social work'.

Social Work is the art of self, social work is what we bring to, whatever we have, our ability, and our skill. There is no denial that we are witnessing a second great societal transformation. As in transition from industrial society to information society, this transition has immense implications for the profession of social work. This transformation has also brought forth great disparities, inequalities, social injustices and oppression, supported by the production of knowledge and the development of skills with value implications.

This fact necessitates that as a profession we adopt a critical appraisal of the implications of this new practice tool. The practice of social work is about the interface of people with their families and their communities. Social workers are agents of social control but they also promote social welfare and social change to empower the individual, the group and the community. As a result, they regularly work with the disadvantaged, disenfranchised and oppressed population (Armitage 1996). The women home-based workers constitute a significant part of this population too. Their cycle of exploitation and self-exploitation has marred their lives with poverty, misery and vulnerability. The right to decent work for these women home-based workers thus seems a distant reality. The recognition of women's rights as human rights has been taking place on the global stage from the grassroots to the international conference levels—in the last two decades. Many specific human rights that are crucial to women's well-being need to be identified and acted on to stop clearly gender-related wrongs. This could make one quite cynical, for, even declarations explicitly aimed at women's rights-such as the Universal Declaration of Women's Rights (1967) and the Convention on the Elimination of All Forms of Discrimination Against Women (CEDAW: 1979) have been signed and even ratified by governments of countries whose laws or accepted practices are far from fulfilling the provisions of these conventions. Promoting women's human rights requires making changes in different areas of life. Many people fail to perceive what or how big the problem is, and many serious inequalities between the sexes are still regarded as invisible, insignificant, natural or culturally appropriate.

Modernization has changed gender relations as a result of women's entry into the public sphere. For some groups of women, modernization has reduced gender inequalities and enhanced educational and employment opportunities and for many others modernization has accentuated their poverty and vulnerability. The women home-based workers present a perfect example of the latter scenario as due to liberalization of the labour processes their opportunities for more and diverse work may have increased but the quality of their life and work-life is still the same. Moreover, there is still increased reliance on their husbands and fathers even though these women earn and contribute to the household income their contribution is devalued and presence invisible in the work sphere. Their socialization is in such manner that their husband, sons and other male members are the primary earners and bread-winners of the family. Their main role is to look after the family and children, especially of care-giving. And if in their free time they earn a few pennies that would not be called work. Thus there is an imperative need to look into this inequality of defining the concept of work itself with regards to men and women workers. The same home-based work when carried out by men is work and when carried out by women is pass-time. Thus a wave of change in the attitude of the society at large in terms how it perceives work by the different sexes is needed so that the women home-based workers get their due. Their visibility and recognition is very crucial in the path of decent work for these women home-home based workers. In light of these, social work profession needs to reorient its education, research, training and above all its practices towards decent work in order to create a society which respects human rights and social justice.

The term decent work came into being more than a decade ago and the ILO has been implementing various decent work country programmes and other events to popularize this concept. The ILO has also designated 7th October as the 'World Day for Decent Work'; however, has all this actually benefitted the home-based workers? Is a question to explore, discuss and debate. The non-ratification of the Home Work Convention by the Indian government till date signifies that the struggle for the rights of women home-based workers is yet to achieve its principal goal. In this struggle, the social work professionals, academicians and researchers have an important role to play.

References

Chapter 1

Austin, D.M. (1998): A report on progress in the development of research resources in social work. Washington DC Institute for the Advancement of Social Development.

Bartlett, H. (1970). *The Common Base of Social Work Practice.* Washington, D.C.: National Association of Social Workers.

Blakely, T.J. and Dziadosz, G.M. (2009). *Community treatment and rehabilitation: One agency's model of case management.* Care Management Journals. 4(3), 129-135.

Boehm, W. (1958).*The nature of social work, Social Work*, 3(2), 5-8.

Bose, A.B. (1995): Social Welfare at the cross-Roads, Hersey-Saiyaddain Memorial Lecture, Delhi. Delhi School of Social Work.

Burnham, J.B. (1986): *Family Therapy*. London: Routledge.

Cheyne Alice (1926): *Nature and Scope of Social work, American Association of Social workers,* New York.

Witmer, Helen L (1942): An Analysis of Social Institutions. New York: Farrar and Rinehart.

Clarke, Helen I. (1947): Principles and Practice of Social Work. New York: Appleton Century.

Fischer, J. (1973): Is Social Work Effective? A review. *Social Work*, 18, 5-20.

Friedlander, W.A. (1955): *Introduction to Social Welfare*. New York: Prentice Hall.

Gellner Ernst (1986): *Positivism and Relativism in Social Sciences*. Cambridge: Cambridge University Press.

Gore, M.S. (1981): 'The Scope of Social Work Practice', in T K Nair (ed.) *Social Work Education and Practice in India,* ASSWI.

Greenwood E. (1957): 'The Attributes of a Profession', *Social Work*, July.

Jacob, K.K. (1994): *Social Work Education in India.*Udipur: Himanshu Publication.

Khinduka, S. (1965): *Social Work In India*. Allahabad: Kitab Mahal

Lal Das, D.K. and Vanila Bhaskaran (2008): *Research Methods for Social Work*. Jaipur: Rawat.

Mary Richmond (1917): *Social Diagnosis*. New York: Russell Sage.

McGoldrich, M and K V Hardy (2008) *Revisioning Family Therapy: Race, Culture and Gender in Clinical Practice*. New York: Guilford Press.

Mead, G.H. (1934). *Mind, Self, and Society*. Chicago: University of Chicago Press.

Morales Armando T. and Sheafor, Bradford, W. (1995): Social Work: *A Profession of Many Faces.* Boston: Allyn and Bacon.

Nadkarni, Vimla and K.T. Desai (2012): Report of National Consultation on National Network of Schools of Social Work for Quality of Social Work Education, TISS.

Naik R.K. and H.Y. Siddiqui (ed) (1989): *Social Work and Social Development*. New Delhi: Geetanjali.

Nair, T.K. (ed) (1981): Social Work Education and Social Work Practice in India. Madras: Association of Schools of Social Work in India.

Narayan, Lata (2008): Editorial, Contextualising Social Work Practice in India, Special Issue, *Indian Journal of Social Work*, 69(2), April, p. 107

Nieuwenhuiz Van (1982): *Development Begins at Home-Problems and Prospect of the Sociology of Development.* Oxford: Pergamon Press

Pathak, S.H. (2012): *Social Work and Social Welfare*. Bangalore: Niruta Publications.

_____ (1989): Social Development and Social Work- some unresolved issues, in Naik and Siddiqui (Ed) *Social Work and Social Development*. New Delhi: Geetanjali.

Ramchandran P. (1968): Research in Social Work, in *Encyclopaedia of Social Work in India*. Vol. 2, pp. 386-394.

_____ (1975) *Review of Social Work Research in India, in Social Welfare: Legend and Legacy*. Bombay: Popular Prakashan. pp. 220-230.

Ranade, S.N. (1972) *Social Work Research in India*, Indian Council of Social Science Research. Mimeographed.

Rubin Allen (2000): *Social Work Research at the turn of the Millennium: Progress and Challenges*. Editorial, Social Work Practice Research, Vol. 10: 9.

Siddiqui, H.Y. (1984): *Social Work and Social Action*. New Delhi: Harnam Publication.

_____ (1987): 'Towards a Competency Based Education in Social Work.' *Indian Journal of Social Work*. April.

_____ (2005): *Social Development in the Indian Sub-continent*. Jaipur: Rawat.

_____ (2011): *A sociological Analysis of Distance Education*. Mimeographed.

Singh, S. and S.P. Srivastava. (2005): *Teaching and Practice of Social Work in India*. Lucknow: New Royal Book Co.

Sheldon, Brian and Geraldine Macdonald (2009): *A Text Book of Social Work*. London: Routledge.

Skidmore, Thackeray, and Farley (1988): *Introduction to Social Work*. New York: Printice Hall.

Thompson, Neil (2010): *Theorizing Social Work Practice*, UK. Palgrave Macmillan.

Thyer, Bruce A (2000): Editorial: A Decade of Research on Social Work Practice, research on Social Work Practice, January1, 2000: 5-8.

Vetere, A. and Dowling, E. (2005): Narrative *Therapies with Children and Their Families: A Practitioner's Guide to Concepts and Approaches*. Hove: Routledge.

Zimbalist, Sidney (1977): *Historic Themes and Land marks in Social Welfare Research*. New York: Harper and Row.

Chapter 2

Gore, M.S. (1973). Some Aspects of Social Development. Hong Kong: Department of Social Work, University of Hong Kong and Tata Institute of Social Sciences, Bombay.

Lister, R. (2004). *Poverty*. Cambridge: Polity Press.

Nair, T.K. (Ed). (1981). Social work Education and Social Work Practice in India. Madras: Association of Schools of Social Work in India.

Pincus, A. and Minahan, A. (1973). *Social Work Practice: Model and Method*. Ithaca, Illinois: Peacock Publisher.

Chapter 3

Alphonse, M., George, P. and Moffatt, K. (2008). 'Redefining social work standards in the context of globalization: Lessons from India', *International Social Work*, Vol. 51, No. 2, pp. 145-158.

Bhatt, Sanjai and Pathare, Suresh. 2004. Proceedings of National Seminar on Gender, HIV/AIDS and Social Work, NIPCEED, New Delhi.

Clifford, Manshardt, 1967. *Pioneering on Social Frontiers in India*, Lalvani Publishing House, Bombay.

D'souza Philomena, 1979. Proceedings of Sub-Regional Workshop for Social work educators and Trainers on The Development of Indigenous Teaching Materials for Preparing Social Welfare Personnel for Work with Rural and Urban Poor, Organised by UNSWDCAP and ASSWI, Madras, December, 12-21, 1979.

Desai, A.S. 1985. The Foundation of Social Work in India, *The Indian Journal of Social Work*, 46 (1)

Desai, A.S., 1987. Development of Social Wrok Education, *Encyclopaedia of Social Work in India*, Delhi: Ministry of Social Welfare, Government of India

Desai, A.M. and Lata Narayan, 1998. Challenges for social work profession towards people development, *The Indian Journal of Social Work*, 59 (1).

Desai, A.S., 1994. *A Study of Social Work Education in India: Student, the Educator and the Educational Process* (mimeo), Bombay: Tata Institute of Social Sciences.

Desai, M. 1990. Issues Concerning the Setting up of Social Work Specializations in India, *International Social Work*, 34 (1), 83-95.

Desai, M., 1997. Literature on Social Work Profession in India: 1936-1996: An Overview, The *Indian Journal of Social Work*, 58(2), 149-160.

Gangrade, K.D., 2002. Profession of Social Work in Search of its Identity, paper presented at the National Seminar on Social Work Education in India: Realities and Responses, Jointly organised by the DSA, Department of Social Work, Delhi University, Department of Social Work, Jamia Millia Islamia and DSA, Department of Social Work, Lucknow University in collaboration with the ASSWI, New Delhi, November 7-9, 2002.

George Palattiyil and Dina Sidhva, 2012. Guest Editorial – Social Work in India, Practice: Social Work in Action, Vol. 24 (2).

Gore M.S., 1985. *Forward to Unforgettable Memories: A Collection of Letters* by Elmina Lucke, Northern Book Centre, New Delhi.

Gore, M.S. 1981. The Scope of Social Work Practice. In T.K. Nair (Ed.), *Social Work Education and Social Work Practice In India*, Madras: Association of Schools of Social Work in India, 1-13.

Government of India, 1968. *Encyclopedia of Social Work in India* (2 volumes), Ministry of Social Welfare, published by Ministry of Information and Broadcasting, GOI, New Delhi.

Government of India1987. *Encyclopedia of Social Work in India* (Four volumes), Ministry of Social Welfare, published by Ministry of Information and Broadcasting, GOI, New Delhi.

Hartmut, Scharfe 2002. Education in Ancient India. *Brill*. p. 149.

Hasan, Saiyid Zafar 1967. "Social work education at the undergraduate level", in *Indian Journal of Social Work*, Vol. XXVIII, No. 1.

Kulkarni, P.D. (1993) 'The indigenous base of social-work profession in India', *The Indian Journal of Social Work,* Vol. 54, no. 4, pp. 555-565.

Kumar, Ajit. 2002. Social Work in India: A 'bright' future?, *Indian Journal of Social Work*, 63 (1), pp. 80-9.

Kumar, V.S.; Pathak, K.C.; Pednekar, P.; Raju, N.S.N. (2006), "Coastal Processes along the Indian Coastline" (PDF), *Current Science* 91 (4): 530-536.

Lucke, Elmina, 1985. *Unforgettable Memories,* Northern Book Centre, New Delhi.

Lucke, Elmina, 1987. *Remembering at Eighty Eight: Letters I should have written*, Athol Press, inc. Massachusetts.

Majumdar, K.S. 1994. *Indigenous Teaching Material in Social Work Education in India-Retrospect and Prospect* by K.K. Jacob, Himanshu Publications, Udaipur.

Mandal, K.S. 1989. 'American influence on social work education in India and its impact', *International Social Work*, Vol. 32, pp. 303-309.

Mehra C. Nanavatty, 1993. Innovative Integration of Human Resources Development Programme With Community Development: Social Work Intervention in the Global Programme of Development.

Mehta, B.H. 1986. Historical background of social work in India, *Indian Journal of Social Work*, Tata Institute of Social Sciences, Mumbai, Vol. 46, pp. 441-455.

Mohsini, S.R., 1994. Undergarduate Social Work Education in K.K. Jacob, *Social Work Education in India- Retrospect and Prospect.*

Murli Desai, 1991 Issues concerning the setting up of social work specializations in India? *International Social Work,* pp. 34: 83.

Nagpaul, Hans, 1970. Appraisal of Social Work Specialists, *Indian Journal of Social Work*. Vol. XXXI No. 2, July, 1970, pp. 151-152.

Nagpaul, Hans, 1993. Analysis of social work teaching material in India: the need fro indigenous foundations, *International Social Work*, Sage, Vol. 36, 207-220.

Nayak, P.B.; Goldar, B.; Agrawal, P. 2010. *India's Economy and Growth: Essays in Honour of V.K.R.V. Rao*, SAGE Publications.

Pathak, S.H. (1975) 'A quarter century of professional social work in India', in *Social Welfare—Legend and Legacy*, ed. S.D. Gokhale, Popular Prakashan, Bombay, pp. 170-192.

Pathak, S.H., 1971. Social Work Education in India: Some Basic Issues and Problems, *Social Work Forum*, 8(3-4), 7-28.

Pathak, Shankar, 1987. *Forty Years of Social Work Education in India. In Forty Years of Social Welfare in India*, Bombay: Indian Council of Social Welfare.

Pathak, Shankar, 2000. Social Work Educators as Scholars: Some Animadversions, *Indian Journal of Social Work*, 61(2).

Pawar, M, (1999), Professional social work in India: Some issues and strategies *Indian Journal of Social Work*, 60 (4), pp. 566-586

Peters, John, 1976. Crydignity, World Neighbors, Inc., Oklahoma city.

Ramachandran, P. and Padmanabha, A., 1969. *Professional Social Workers in India*, Bombay: United India Publications.

Ramchandran P. 1986.Perspectgive for Social Work Training: 2000 A.D, Tata Institute of Social Sciences, Bombay.

Ramchandran P., 1963. Proceedings of seminar on Social Work Research: A resume, *Indian Journal of Social Work*, 24 (3), 210-115.

Ramchandran, G. 1957. Education for Social Work in India, *Kurukshetra*, 11/1957, Volume 6, Issue 2, pp. 246-248

Ramesha Chandrappa and Ravi, D.R. 2009. *Environmental Issues, Law and Technology – An Indian Perspective*, Research India Publication, Delhi.

Singh, Shweta, Gumz, Edward J. and Crawley, Brenda C., 2010. Predicting India's Future: Does it justify the exportation of US Social Work Education?, *Social Work Education*. Vol. 30, No. 7, pp. 861-873.

Singh, Surendra, 2002. Review Article—Social Work Revisited by Brij Mohan, *Contemporary Social Work*, Vol. xix,

Singh, Surendra, 2002. Social Work Education in India—Major Issues and Concerns and Required Strategies and Approaches, paper presented at the National Seminar on Social Work Education in India: Realities and Responses, Jointly organised by the DSA, Department of Social Work, Delhi University, Department of Social Work, Jamia Millia Islamia and DSA, Department of Social Work, Lucknow University in collaboration with the ASSWI, New Delhi, November 7-9, 2002.

Singh, Y.K.; Nath, R. 2007. *History of Indian Education System*. APH Publishing Corporation. pp. 172-175, New Delhi.

Srivastava, S.P. and Singh, R.K., 2003. Social Work Today: Present Realities and Future prospects, Contemporary Social Work, XX, 71-89

The Indian Journal of Social Work, 1967. Thirty Years of Social Work Education in India, Special Issue, 28 (1).

The Indian Journal of Social Work 1993. Social Work Profession in Asia, Special Issue, 54 (4).

Trattner, W. 1989. *From Poor Law to Welfare State: A History of Social Welfare in America* 4th Ed. New York: the Free Press.

University Grants Commission (UGC Panel, Social Work Education) (2000) National Curriculum Report for Educational Programmes of Social Work Profession, New Delhi, India [online]. Available at: http: //www.ugc.ac.in/policy/ug_pg/appendix.pdf

University Grants Commission, 1965. Social work Education in Indian Universities, New Delhi.

Wadia, A.R., 1968. History of Social Work from 1818 to 1947, *Encyclopedia of Social Work in India*, Delhi: Planning Commission.

Wright, Rita P. (2010). The Ancient Indus: Urbanism, Economy, and Society, Cambridge University Press.

Chapter 4

Avril, Osborne (1985), Distance Learning in Social Work Education, London: Central Council for Social Work Education and Training in Social Work

Bhatt, Sanjai (2012), Field work Practicum in Social Work: Emerging Concerns and Challenges, in Verma, R.B.S. (Ed: 2012), *Field Work Practicum in Social Work: Emerging Concerns, Challenges and Opportunities*, Lucknow: Rapid Book Service.

Clark, F.W., Farquarson, A., and Baskett, K.K. (1982), Developing Outreach and Competency Based Methods in Social Work Education. Big Sky II Conference Papers, Canada: University of Calgary.

Desai, Armaity (1994), A Study of Social Work Education in India: Student, Educator and the Educational Process (mimeo), Bombay: Tata Institute of Social Sciences.

_____ (2000), Social Work Education and its Application to General University Education: An Interview with Prof. Armaity S. Desai. *The Indian Journal of Social Work*, Volume 61, Issue 2, April 2000. Bombay: TISS.

National Accreditation and Assessment Council (2005), Manual for Self Study of Social Work Institutions, Bangalore: NAAC.

Pawar, Manohar (2000), Social Work Education through Distance Mode in India: A Proposal. *The Indian Journal of Social Work*, Volume 61, Issue 2, April 2000, Bombay: TISS.

Thomas, Gracious (Ed: 2009), Social Work Practicum: The Practitioner's Guide. New Delhi: IGNOU.

Vinton, L., and Neil, Abell (2010), Social Work Education through Distance Learning, in Thomas Gracious (Ed.), *Origin and Development of Social Work* (pp. 167-176). New Delhi: IGNOU.

Wilson, S. (1999). Invited Commentary: Distance Education and Accreditation. *Journal of Social Work Education*, 35, 326-330.

Chapter 5

Boyer, T., 2006: the art of teaching social work: reflections on my journey in higher education, paper presented at National Convention by North American Association of Christians in Social Work in Philadelphia, USA

Chui, E.W.T., Wong, D.K.P., Wong, Y.C., Chan, C.L.W., Law, C.K. and Tam, V. 1997: Critical reflection in community work education: A social work curriculum addressing social deprivation and poverty in D. Kember, B.H. Lam, L. Yan, J.C.K. Yum and S.B. Liu (Eds.) Case Studies of Improving Teaching and Learning from the Action Learning Project (pp. 49-56). Hong Kong: Action Learning Project.

Congress E.P., (no date): Teaching social work values, ethics and human rights.

Institute for Advancement of Social Work Research, 2007: Partnerships to integrate evidence based mental health practices into social work education, Washington, USA.

Rutgers University Centre for International Social Work, Dec. 2008: Social work education and the practice environment in Europe and Eurasia, a report of United States Agency for International Development (USAID)

Wilson G. and Kelly B., 2010: Evaluating the Effectiveness of Social Work Education: Preparing Students for Practice Learning, *British Journal of Social Work*; 40: 2431-2449.

Wrenn, J. and Wrenn, B., 2009: Enhancing learning by integrating theory and practice,

International Journal of Teaching and Learning in Higher Education; Vol. 21, Number 2, pp. 258-265.

Chapter 6

Andharia, J. (2007), Re-conceptualizing Community Organization in India: A Trans-disciplinary Perspective,' in A.K. Johnson Butterfield and Y. Korazim-Korosy (eds.): *Interdisciplinary Community Development: International Perspectives*. New York: Haworth Press.

Desai, A. (1973), 'Role of the Association of Schools of Social Work in the Development of the Profession of Social Work in India,' *Social Work Forum*, 11(2): 8-12.

Flexner, A. (1915), 'Is Social Work a Profession? In National Conference of Charities and Corrections,' *Proceedings of the National Conference of Charities and Corrections at the Forty-second Annual Session held in Baltimore, Maryland*. May 12–19, 1915. Chicago: Hildmann.

Gangrade, K.D. (1971), *Community Organization in India*. Bombay: Popular Prakashan.

George, K.N. (1974), 'Role of Association of School of Social Work in Social Development,' *Social Development Aspect of Social Education*. Madurai: Association of Schools of Social Work in India, pp. 58-64.

Mathew, G. (1992), *An Introduction to Social Casework*. Bombay: Tata Institute of Social Sciences.

Mohsini, S.R. (1973), 'Proposed Five Year Plan of the Indian Association of Trained Social Workers,' *Social Work Forum*, 11(2): 18–21.

Moses, D. (1961) 'Training for Social Work,' in A.R. Wadia (ed.): *History and Philosophy of Social Work in India*. Bombay: Allied Publishers.

Nagpaul, H. (1972), 'Social Work as a Profession in India: A Sociological Analysis,' *The Indian Journal of Social Work*, 32(4): 387–411.

Nanavatty, M.C. (1952), 'Development of Social Work Profession in India,' *The Indian Journal of Social Work*, 13(3): 162–167.

_____(1993) 'Problems Affecting the Indigenisation of Social Work in Asia,' *The Indian Journal of Social Work*, 54(4): 547-554.

_____(1997), 'Professional Associations of Social Work: An Analysis of Literature,' *The Indian Journal of Social Work*, 58(2): 287–300.

Siddiqui, H.Y. (1984), *Social Work and Social Action: A Developmental Perspective*. New Delhi: Harnam Publications.

——(1997) *Working with Communities: An Introduction to Community Work*, New Delhi: Hira Publications.

Yelaja, S. (1969), 'Schools of Social Work in India: Historical Development 1936-1966,' *The Indian Journal of Social Work*, 29(4): 361–378.

Chapter 7

Bose, A.B. (1992). Social Work in India: Developmental Roles for Helping Profession.In M.C. Hokenstad, S.K. Khinduka & J. Midgley (Eds.), *Profiles in International Social Work* (pp. 71-84), Washington DC: NASW Press.

Briskin, L. and Coulter, R.P. (1992). Feminist Pedagogy: Challenging the Normative. *Canadian Journal of Education*, Vol. 17, No. 3, pp. 247-263.

Brown, C.G. (2012). Anti-Oppression through a Postmodern Lens: Dismantling the Master's Conceptual Tools in Discursive Social Work Practice. *Critical Social Work 13(1)*, 34-65.

Freire, P. (2007). *Pedagogy of the Oppressed*. New York: Continuum Publishing Company.

Gandhi, A. (2004). *Mainstreaming Gender in Social Work Education: Supplementary Reading Material–I*. New Delhi: Indira Gandhi National Open University available at http: // www.egyankosh.ac.in/handle/123456789/16382.

Gorman, J. (1993). Postmodernism and the Conduct of Inquiry in Social Work.*Affilia, 8*, 247-264.

Hall, A. and Midgley, J. (2004). *Social Policy for Development*. London: Sage.
Harris, K. (1979). *Education and knowledge: The Structured Misrepresentation of Reality.* London: Routledge and Kegan Paul.
Hudson, A. (1985). Feminism and Social Work: Resistance or Dialogue? *British Journal of Social Work, I*, pp. 635-655.
International Association of School of Social Work–International Association of Social Workers (2001). *Ethics in Social Work: Statement of Principles*, Retrieved from www.ifsw.org/en/p38000223.html.
Khinduka, S.K. (1971). Social Work in the Third World. *Social Service Review,* Vol. 45, No. 1, pp. 62-73.
Ledwith, M. (2001). Community work as critical pedagogy: Re-envisioning Freire and Gramsci. *Community Development Journal, 36(3)*, 171-182.
Madan, A. (2011). Indian Higher Education and the Need for Critical Knowledges. *Contemporary Education Dialogue, 8,* 161-182.
Mandal, K.S. (1989). American Influence on Social Work Education in India and Its Impact. *Economic and Political Weekly*, Vol. 24, No. 49, pp. 2710-2712.
Morley, C. (2008). Teaching Critical Practice: Resisting Structural Domination through Critical Reflection. *Social Work Education*, 27: 4, 407-421.
Nagpaul, H. (1972). The Diffusion of American Social Work Education to India. *International Social Work, Vol. 15, No. 1*, pp 13–17.
Nagpaul, H. (1993). Analysis of Social Work Teaching Material in India: the need for indigenous foundations. *International Social Work*; *36,* 207-220.
Pathak, S. (1981a). *Social Welfare*. Delhi: Macmillan.
Pathak, S. (1981b, June 6). Radical Image, Conservative Reality. *Economic and Political Weekly.* Vol. 16, No. 23, pp. 1018-1020.
Pennell, J. and Ristock, J.L. (1999). Feminist Links, Postmodern Interruptions: Critical Pedagogy and Social Work. *Affilia, 14,* 460-481.
Raske, M. (1999).Using Feminist Classroom Rules to Model Empowerment for Social Work Students. J*ournal of Teaching in Social Work,* 19(1), 197-209.
Redmond, M. (2010). Safe Space Oddity: Revisiting Critical Pedagogy. *Journal of Teaching in Social Work*, 30: 1, 1 - 14.
Singh, S. (2004). 'Social Work Education In India: Retrospect and Introspect', available at http: //www.egyankosh.ac.in/handle/123456789/16375.
Taylor, I. (1994). Social work education: Abstracts. *British Journal of Social Work,* 24(6): 761-769. Retrieved from http: //bjsw.oxfordjournals.org/cgi/pdf_extract/24/6/761.
UGC Model Curriculum for Social Work Education (2001) available at http: //www.ugc.ac.in/policy/social_work_education.pdf.
Vinton, L. and Nelson-Gardell, D. (1993). Consciousness-Raising through Teaching about the Global Oppression of Women. *Affilia,* 8, 91-102.

Chapter 8

Brown, S.C. and Gloyne, E.R. (1966): *The Field Training of Social Workers—A Survey*, George Allen and Unwin Ltd., London, 1966, p. 3-5.
Council on Social Work Education—CSWE (2008): Educational Policy and Accreditation Standards - EPAS, Inc., USA, p. 3-7.
Doel, A. Mark and Steven, M. Shardlow (2005): *Modern Social Work Practice: Teaching and Learning in Practice Setting*, Ashgate Publishing Ltd., Hampshire, p. 273.
Farley, O. William, Smith, Larry Lorenzo and Boyle Scott W. (2003): Introduction to Social Work, Pearson Custom Publishing, Boson, p. 8-13.http: //rapid.com/writesmartobjectives
Maurya, M.R. (1962): Field Work Training in Social Work, *The Indian Journal of Social Work*, Vol. XXIII (1), April, pp. 9-14.
Singh, R.R. (1985): *Field Work in Social Work Education*, Concept Publishing Co., Delhi, p. 43.

UGC Model Curriculum on Social Work Education (2001): University Grants Commission, New Delhi, pp. 98-99, 119 and 152.

Verma, R.B.S. and Singh, Atul Pratap (2011): *Handbook of Field Work Practice Learning in Social Work*, New Royal Book Company, Lucknow, p. 1.

Chapter 9

Australia Association of Social Workers (AASW). (2008). *AASW practice standards for mental health social workers,* http://aasw.au.

Australia Association of Social Workers (AASW). (2010). *AASW Code of Ethics*, ACT: AASW.

Australia Association of Social Workers (AASW). (2013). *Practice standards*. Canberra City, ACT: AASW.

Australian Government. (2010). National standards for mental health services, retrieved from http: //www.health.gov.au/internet/main/publishing.nsf/content/
DA71C0838BA6411BCA2577A0001AAC32/$File/servst10v2.pdf

Australian Health Ministers Advisory Council's National Mental Health Education and Training Advisory Working Party. (2002). *National practice standards for the mental health workforce.* Canberra: Australian Government Publishing Service.

Bland, R., Renouf, N., and Tullgren, A. (2009). *Social work practice in mental health.*Crow's Nest: Allen & Unwin,

Bland, R., and Tullgren, A. (2014). Recovery theory and practice. In A. Francis. (Ed.), *Social work practice in mental health.* Delhi: Sage.

De Jong, P., and Miller, S. (1995). How to interview for client strengths. *Social Work*, *40*(6), 729-736.

Deegan, P.E. (1988). The lived experience of rehabilitation. *Psychosocial Rehabilitation Journal*, *11*(4), 11-19.

Early, T., and Glenmaye, L. (2000). Valuing families: Social work practice with families from a strengths perspective. *Social Work, 45*(2), 118-130.

Francis, A. (2012). 'Journey towards recovery in mental health.' In V. Pulla, L. Chenoweth, A. Francis, and S.Bakaj (Eds.), *Papers in strengths based practice* (pp. 19-33). New Delhi: Allied Publishers.

Francis, A. (2013). Indian and Australian experience of community recovery in natural disasters. *Journal of Social Work (Samaja Karyada Hejjegalu), 21*(3), 21-47.

Francis, A. (2013). 'I get up, because I know I can go to my group today': Examining the healing power of relationship in support. *International Journal of Social Work and Human Services Practice*, *1*(1), 54-63.

Francis A, Pulla, V, Clark, M., Mariscal SE and Ponnuswami, I. (Eds.), *Advancing social work in mental health through strengths based practice*. Australia: Primrose Publications.

Gottlieb, L.N. (2014). *Strengths-based nursing care: Health and healing for person and family.* New York: Springer.

IFSW. (2012). Definition of social work, retrieved from http: //ifsw.org/policies/ definition-of-social-work/

IFSW. (2014.) Proposed global definition of the social work profession, retrieved from http: / /ifsw.org/get-involved/global-definition-of-social-work/

Iveson, C. (2002). Solution-focused brief therapy. *Advances in Psychiatric Treatment, 8*, 149-157.

Healy, K. (2005). *Social work theories in context: Creating frameworks for practice.* New York: Palgrave MacMillan.

Kisthardt, W. (1997). The strengths model of case management: Purpose, principles and helping functions. In D. Saleebey (Ed.), *The* 68 *strengths perspective in social work practice* (2nd ed., pp. 236-258). New York: Longman.

Mariscal, S.E. (2014). The strengths perspective and the strengths model of case management: Enhancing the recovery of people with psychiatric disabilities. In A. Francis, V. Pulla,

M. Clark, S. Mariscal & I. Ponnuswami (Eds.), *Advancing social work in mental health through strengths based practice* (pp. 73-87). Australia: Primrose Publications.

Miley, K.K., O'melia, M., and Dubois, B. (2004). *Generalist social work practice: An empowering approach*. Boston: Allyn and Bacon.

O'Connor, I., Wilson, J., Setterlund, D., and Hughes, M. (2008). *Social work and human service practice*. French's Forest, N.S.W.: Pearson Education.

Onken, S. (2012). *Exploring relationships in mental health.* Key note presentation at 2012 ASPAC conference, Perth, Australia, June 11-13, retrieved from https: //www.rfwa.org.au/

Ponnuswami, I., Francis, A., and Udhayakumar, P. (2012). Strengths-based approach to social work practice with older persons. In A. Pulla, L. Chenoweth, A. Francis, & S. BaKaj (Eds.), *Papers in strengths-based practice* (150-161). New Delhi, India: Allied Publishers.

Pulla, V. (2012). What are strengths based practice all about? In Pulla, V., Chenoweth, L., Francis, A., & S. Bakaj (Eds.), *Papers in strengths based practice.* New Delhi: Allied Publishers.

Pulla, V., and Francis, A. (2013). A strengths approach to mental health. In A. Francis (Ed.), *Social work practice in mental health.* Sage Publications.

Pulla, V., and Francis, A. (2014). Introduction In A. Francis, V. Pulla, M. Clark, S. Mariscal & I. Ponnuswami (Eds.), *Advancing social work in mental health through strengths based practice* (pp. 27-30). Australia: Primrose Publications.

Pulla, V., Chenoweth, L., Francis, A., and Bakaj, S. (Eds.). (2012). *Papers in strengths based practice.* New Delhi: Allied Publishers.

Rapp, C.A., and Goscha, R.J. (2011). *The strengths model: A recovery-oriented approach to mental health services*. Oxford University Press.

Rapp, C., and Goscha, R. (2014). Three decades of strengths: Reflections of the past and challenges of the future. In A. Francis, V. Pulla, M. Clark, S. Mariscal & I. Ponnuswami (Eds.), *Advancing Social work in mental health through strengths based practice* (pp. 31-38). Australia: Primrose Publications.

Rapp, C.A., and Goscha, R.J. (2006). *The strengths model: Case management with people with psychiatric disabilities* (2nd ed.). New York: Oxford University Press.

Rapp, C.A., and Chamberlain, R. (1985). Case management services to the chronically mentally ill. *Social Work, 30*(5), 417-422.

Saleebey, D. (1996). The strengths perspective in social work practice: Extensions and cautions. *Social Work, 41*(3), 296-306.

Saleebey, D. (2001). Practicing the strengths perspective: Everyday tools and resources. *Families in Society, 82*(3), 221-222.

Saleebey, D. (Ed.). (2001). *The strengths perspective in social work practice* (3rd ed.). Boston: Allyn and Bacon.

Saleebey, D. (Ed.). (1997). "Introduction: Power in the people". In *The strengths perspective in social work practice* (2nd ed., pp. 3-19).New York: Longman.

Saleebey, D. (Ed.). (2009). *The strengths perspective in social work practice* (5th ed.). Boston: Allyn & Bacon.

Sheafor, B.W., Horejsi, C.R., and Horejsi, G.A. (1996). *Techniques and guidelines for social work practice.* Boston: Allyn & Bacon.

Shekhar, R., Ponnuswami, I., and Francis, A. (2014). Efficacy of strengths-based practice in engaging with children with behavioural problems: A case study from India. In A. Francis, V. Pulla, M. Clark, S. Mariscal & I. Ponnuswami (Eds.), *Advancing Social work in mental health through strengths based practice*. Australia: Primrose Publications.

Stalker, C., Levine, J., and Coady, N. (1999). Solution-focused brief therapy – One model fits all? *Families in Society, 80*(5), 468-477.

Weick, A., Rapp, C., Sullivan, W.P., and Kisthardt, W. (1998). A strengths perspective for social work practice. *Social Work.*

Chapter 10

Alean, Al-Krenawi and John R Graham (2000) *Islamic Theology and Prayer: Relevance for Social Work Practice*, International Social Work, 43(3), Sage Publications in John Coats, John R Graham, Barbara Swartzentruber with Brian Quellette (Eds.) (2007) *Spirituality and Social Work – Selected Canadian Readings*, Toronto: Canadian Scholars' Press Inc.

Baskin, C (2002) *Circles of Resistance: Spirituality in Social Work Practice, Education, and Transformative Change* in Currents: New Scholarship in Human Services 1(1) in Michele Butot (2005) *Reframing Spirituality, Reconceptualising Change: Possibilities for Critical Social Work* in John Coats, John R Graham, Barbara Swartzentruber with Brian Quellette (Eds.) (2007) *Spirituality and Social Work – Selected Canadian Readings*, Toronto: Canadian Scholars' Press Inc. p. 145.

Canda, Edward R. and Suresh Pathare (2011) *Religion, Spirituality, and Social Work: Exploring Connections*, paper presented at International Conference on Religion, Spirituality and Social Work – Exploring Connections held at CSRD Institute of Social Work and Research, Ahmednagar, Maharashtra, India, 28-30 December 2011

Canda Edward R. Canda and Furman (2010) *Spiritual Diversity in Social Work Practice, second edition,* Oxford University Press

Canda, E.R. (1988) *Spirituality, Diversity and Social Work Practice,* in Social Casework, 69(4) in Michael Kim Zapf (2005) *Profound Connections between Person and Place: Exploring Location, Spirituality and Social Work* in John Coats, John R Graham, Barbara Swartzentruber with Brian Quellette (Eds.) (2007) *Spirituality and Social Work – Selected Canadian Readings*, Toronto: Canadian Scholars' Press Inc. p. 239.

Canda, E.R. (2002) A Worldwide View on Spirituality and Social Work: Reflections from the USA Experience and Suggestions for Internalisation, Currents: New Scholarship in Human Services 1(1) in Wanda Wagler-Martin (2005) Listening to Our Stillness: Giving Voice to Our Spirituality (Spirituality and Clinical Practice) in John Coats, John R Graham, Barbara Swartzentruber with Brian Quellette (Eds.) (2007) Spirituality and Social Work – Selected Canadian Readings, Toronto: Canadian Scholars' Press Inc. p. 136. Also http: // HYPERLINK "http: //www.socwel.ku.edu/canda" www.socwel.ku.edu/canda

Coates, J. and Graham J.R. (2003) *Introduction to the Special Edition on Spirituality,* Currents: New Scholarship in the Human Services, 2(2) in John R Graham, Diana Coholic and John Coats (2006) *Spirituality as a Guiding Construct in the Development of Canadian Social Work: Past and Present Consideration* in John Coats, John R Graham, Barbara, Swartzentruber with Brian Quellette (Eds.) (2007) *Spirituality and Social Work–Selected Canadian Readings*, Toronto: Canadian Scholars' Press Inc. p. 36.

David, Este (2004) *Black Churches in Canada: Vehicles for Fostering Community Development in African-Canadian Communities – A Historical Analysis* in John Coats, John R Graham, Barbara Swartzentruber with Brian Quellette (Eds.) (2007) *Spirituality and Social Work – Selected Canadian Readings*, Toronto: Canadian Scholars' Press Inc.

Diana, Coholic (2005) *The Helpfulness of Spiritually Influenced Group Work in Developing Self-Awareness and Self-Esteem: A Preliminary Investigation* in John Coats, John R Graham, Barbara Swartzentruber with Brian Quellette (Eds.) (2007) *Spirituality and Social Work – Selected Canadian Readings*, Toronto: Canadian Scholars' Press Inc.

Gerald, May (1992) *Care of Mind, care of spirit,* New York: Harper Collins, in Michael McKernan (2005) *Exploring the Spiritual Dimension of Social Work* in John Coats, John R Graham, Barbara Swartzentruber with Brian Quellette (Eds.) (2007) *Spirituality and Social Work – Selected Canadian Readings*, Toronto: Canadian Scholars' Press Inc. p. 103.

Geri, Miller (2003) *Incorporating Spirituality in Counselling and Psychotherapy,* Hoboken, NJ: John Wiley and Sons in Wanda Wagler-Martin (2005) *Listening to Our Stillness: Giving Voice to Our Spirituality (Spirituality and Clinical Practice)* in John Coats, John

R Graham, Barbara Swartzentruber with Brian Quellette (Eds.) (2007) *Spirituality and Social Work – Selected Canadian Readings*, Toronto: Canadian Scholars' Press Inc. p. 136.

Gratton, C (1995) *The Art of Spiritual Guidance,* New York: Crossroads in Michael McKernan (2005). *Exploring the Spiritual Dimension of Social Work* in John Coats, John R Graham, Barbara Swartzentruber with Brian Quellette (Eds.) (2007) *Spirituality and Social Work – Selected Canadian Readings*, Toronto: Canadian Scholars' Press Inc. p. 93.

Jaimon, Varghese (2011) *Religion and Social Work - the Paradigm of Spirituality and Values in Family based Social Work: a Study on Professional Social Workers*, paper presented at International Conference on Religion, Spirituality and Social Work–Exploring Connections held at CSRD Institute of Social Work and Research, Ahmednagar, Maharashtra, India, 28-30 December 2011

Jeff. Levin (2001) *God, Faith and Health: Exploring Spirituality Healing Connection,* New York: John Wiley and Sons in Michael McKernan (2005) *Exploring the Spiritual Dimension of Social Work* in John Coats, John R Graham, Barbara Swartzentruber with Brian Quellette (Eds.) (2007) *Spirituality and Social Work–Selected Canadian Readings*, Toronto: Canadian Scholars' Press Inc. p. 102.

John R. Graham, Diana Coholic and John Coats (2006) *Spirituality as a Guiding Construct in the Development of Canadian Social Work: Past and Present Consideration* in John Coats, John R. Graham, Barbara Swartzentruber with Brian Quellette (Eds.) (2007) *Spirituality and Social Work – Selected Canadian Readings*, Toronto: Canadian Scholars' Press Inc. p. 36.

Michael. McKernan (2005) *Exploring the Spiritual Dimension of Social Work* in John Coats, John R Graham, Barbara Swartzentruber with Brian Quellette (Eds.) (2007) *Spirituality and Social Work – Selected Canadian Readings*, Toronto: Canadian Scholars' Press Inc.

Urwick. E.J. (1948) *Excerpts from the Values of Life* in John Coats, John R Graham, Barbara Swartzentruber with Brian Quellette (Eds.) (2007) *Spirituality and Social Work–Selected Canadian Readings*, Toronto: Canadian Scholars' Press Inc. p. 71.

Wanda, Wagler-Martin (2005) *Listening to Our Stillness: Giving Voice to Our Spirituality (Spirituality and Clinical Practice)* in John Coats, John R Graham, Barbara Swartzentruber with Brian Quellette (Eds.) (2007) *Spirituality and Social Work–Selected Canadian Readings*, Toronto: Canadian Scholars' Press Inc.

Chapter 11

Adolescents and Mental Problems, Situation Analysis, TUBAUNFPA Population and Development Strategies Sub-Programme, Reports of the Turkish Academy of Sciences, No. 4, TUBÝTAK Press, January 2004.

Baldwin, M. (200) Does self-assessment in a group help students to learn? *Social Work Education*, 24, pp. 451-462 In: Crisp, B.R., Lister, P.G. (2002) Assessment methods in social work education: a review of literature, *Social Work Education*, 21 (2), pp. 259-267.

Balinder Singh: Addressing The Future of Professional Social-work In India, 2012, *International Referred Journal*, Vol. 3, issue 37.

Becker M, Martin L, Wajeeh E, Ward J, Shern D. Students mental illnesses in university setting: faculty and student attitudes, beliefs, knowledge, and experiences. *Psychiatry Rehabilation Journal,* 2002; 25(4): 359-68.

Blanco C., Okuda M., Wright C., Hasin D.S., Grant B.F., Liu Sh *et al.*, Mental Health of college students and their non-college attending peers. *Arch Gen* Psychiatry, 2008; 65(12): 1429-1437.

Bodhi, S. (2011). Rural, Rurality, Caste and Tribes: The Dalit and Tribe Centered Social Work Rural Practicum. *Indian Journal of Social Work*, 71(1), 149-161.

Bohanon, J. (2007). The perceived advantages of varied delivery methods for field integrative seminar among social work administrators and faculty (Dissertation). The University of Southern Mississippi. ·

Boud, D. (1991) Implementing student Self-assessment (2nd ed.) Sydney, Higher education research and development society of Austrailia in: Burgess, H. Baldwin, M. Dalrymple, J., & Thomas, J. (1999) Developing self-assessment in social work education, *Social Work Education*, 18(2).

Chandrashekar, C.R. (2001). Interpersonal relations. In Khwaja, A. (2001). A handbook on life skills.Association of lay counsellors of India, Bangalore.

Crisp, B.R. (1999), Not in the classroom: teaching social work research to off-campus students, Advances in Social Work and Welfare education, 2(2). pp 34-41, 462 In: Crisp, B.R., Lister, P.G. (2002) Assessment methods in social work education: a review of literature, *Social Work Education*, 21(2), pp. 259-267.

Dasgupta S. (Ed.) (1967). *Towards a philosophy of social work in India*. New Delhi: Popular Book Services.

Desai, M. (2000). Curriculum planning for history of philosophies of social work, *The Indian Journal of Social Work*, 61, pp. 221-239, 147 In: Crisp, B.R., Lister, P.G. (2002) Assessment methods in social work education: a review of literature, *Social Work Education*, 21 (2), pp. 259-267.

Gunjal, B.S., and Ganga Bhushan, M., (2000), *Fields of Social Work Practice*, Bharaha Publication, (Bangalore) Karnataka, India

Ejaz, F.K. (1991). Social Work education in India: perceptions of social workers in Bombay. *International Social Work*. Vol. 34, 299-311.

Eraut, M. (1992). Developing a knowledge base: a process perspective on professional education, in: Baldwin, M. (200). Does self-assessment in a group help students to learn? *Social Work Education*, 24, pp. 451-461.

Gambrill, E.D. (1999). Evidence-based practice: an alternative to authority-based practice. *Families in Society*, 80(4), 341-350.

Gambrill, E.D. (2003). Evidence-based practice: sea change or the emperor's new Clothes? *Journal of Social Work Education*, 39(1), 3-23.

Global Standards for the Education and Training of the Social Work Profession. (2004). Adopted at the General Assemblies of International Association of Schools of Social Work (IASSW) and the International Federation of Social Work (IFSW) in Adelaide, Australia.

Goldberg D.P., Hillier V.F. A scaled version of the General Health Questionnaire. *Psychol Med* 1979; 9: 139-145.

Gould, N. and Taylor. I. (Eds) (1996). Reflective learning for Social Work (Aldershot, Arena) in: Baldwin, M. (2000) Does self-assessment in a group help students to learn? *Social Work Education*, 24, pp. 451-461.

Guthrie E., Black D., Bagalkote H., Shaw C., Campbell M., Creed F. Psychological stress and burnout in medical students: a five-year prospective longitudinal study. *Journal of Royal Society of Medicine*. 1998 May; 91(5): 237-243

Gutierez, L. and Alvarez, A.L. (2000) practice, Journal of Community Practice, 7, pp. 39-56. In: Crisp Education students for multicultural community In: Crisp, B.R., Lister, P.G. (2002) Assessment methods in social work education: a review of literature, *Social Work Education*, 21 (2), pp. 259-267.

Harrison J., Barrow S., Gask L., Creed F. Social determinants of GHQ score by postal survey. J Public Health Med 1999; 21(3): 283-8.

Hollister, C.D. and McGee, G. (2000). Delivering substance abuse and child welfare content through interactive television, Research in Social Work Practice, 10, pp. 417-427, In: Crisp, B.R., Lister, P.G. (2002) Assessment methods in social work education: a review of literature, *Social Work Education*, 21 (2), pp. 259-267.

Jagdish and Srivastava A.K, *Manual for Mental Health Inventory*; published by Manovaigyanik parikchhan Sansthan, Chowkaghat, Varanasi.

Kasi P.M. *et al*. studying the association between postgraduate trainees' work hours, stress and the use of maladaptive coping strategies. *Journal Ayub Medical College Abbottabad*, 2007; 19(3): 37-41

Lawani, B.T., and Subhedar, I.S., (2006), *Social Work Perspectives*, Om Publication, New Delhi, India

Maidment, J., Chilvers, D., Crichton-Hill, Y. and Meadows-Taurua, K. (2011). Promoting research literacy during the social work practicum. Aotearoa New Zealand *Social Work Review*, 23(4), 3-13.

Marotta, S.A., Peters, B.J., and Paliokas, K.L. (2000). Teaching group dynamics: an interdisciplinary approach, *Journal for Specialists Group Work*, 25, pp 16 -28 in: Crisp, B.R., Lister, P.G. (2002) Assessment methods in social work education: a review of literature, *Social Work Education*, 21 (2), pp. 259-267.

Meena Z. Presentation of Key Issues, Challenges, and Strategies Emerging from the Zonal Meetings by Convenors National Consultation on National Network of Schools of Social Work for Quality Enhancement of Social Work Education In India May 2-3, 2012

Nair, T.K. (Ed.) (1981) Social Work Education and Social Work Practice in India, Madras: Association of School of Social Work in India, in: Desai, M. (2000). *The Indian Journal of Social Work*, 61 (2), pp. 212-220.

Nanda, A.K. (2001), in Mental Health of High School Students: A Comparative Study; *Indian Psychological Review*, Vol. 56, No. 1, page 2-7.

Neil, E. and Sellick, C. (2001) A description and evaluation of a social work training programme in Moldova, *Journal of Teaching in Social Work*, Harworth Press, 20(5), pp. 577-592.

Moorthy, M.V. and Narayana Rao (1970), *Field Work in Social Work*, Waltair Press, Andra Pradesh, India

Pathan, K.G., and Lawani, B.T., (1990), *Field work training in social work education*, Bharathi Vidyapeeth Publication, Maharashtra, India

Phippen, M. The 1993-4 survey of counseling services in further and higher education. Newsletter, Association for Student Counseling. 1995; 26-36.

Rao, S. Narayan (2005), *Counselling and Guidance*; published by Tata McGraw-Hill Publishing Company Limited, New Delhi, Page 8-10

Ramana, K.V., Presentation of Key Issues, Challenges, and Strategies Emerging from the Zonal Meetings by Convenors National Consultation on National Network of Schools of Social Work for Quality Enhancement of Social Work Education in India May 2-3, 2012.

Ross S., Cleland J., Macleod M.J. Stress, debt and undergraduate medical student performance. *Med Educ* 2006; 40(6): 584-9.

Rowntree, D. (1987) Assessing students: how shall we know them? (London, Kogan Page) In: Social Work Education: A Review of Literature.

Schultz, S.E. and Schultz, D.P. (2001), *Theories of Personality*. Published by Woodsworth Thomson learning, Australia, 7th edition, page 219-220, 232.

Shankar Pathak, (1978), *Social Welfare, Health and Family Planning in India*, Marwah Publications, New Delhi, India.

Shylaja Nagendra, (2005), *Social Work and Social Welfare*, ABD Publishers, Jaipur, India.

Sheafor, B.W., Horejsi, C.R. and Horejsi, G.A. (2000). 5th ed. Allyn and Bacon, Boston.

Social Work Foot Prints, (2010-12), Volume I (Issues 1 to 12), *Monthly Journal of Kannada & English*, Nirutha Publication, (Bangalore) Karnataka, India.

Subhedar, I.S., (2001), *Field Work Training in Social Work*, Rawat Publications, Jaipur, India.

Surendra Singh and Srivastava, S.P, (2003), *Social Work Education in Indian: Challenges and Opportunities*, New Royal Book co, Luknow, India.

Tajularipin Sulaiman *et al*. The Level of Stress Among Students in Urban and Rural secondary Schools in Malaysia. *European Journal of Social Sciences,* 2009; 10(2): 179-184.

The Global Agenda for Social Work and Social Development Commitment to Action. (2012).

The Indian Journal of Social Work, (2011), Volume 72 (Issue 1 and 2), Quarterly Journal of English, TISS Publication, Mumbai, India

Turkish Board of Higher Education (YOK), Current Situation of Higher Education in Turkey. November, 2004. Website (Dec 06, 2004).

Vasuki, K. and Charumathy, P.J., (2004) in Sibling Rivalry and its relation to Achievement Motivation Frustration Mental Health and Self Conflict of Adolescents; *Indian Psychological Review*, Vol. 62, No. 2, pp. 72-78.

Visvesvaran, P.K. 9200) Admission criteria and internal assessment in a school of social work: an analysis, *The Indian Journal of Social Work,* 61, pp. 255-268. in: Crisp, B.R., Lister, P.G. (2002) Assessment methods in social work education: a review of literature, *Social Work Education*, 21 (2), pp. 259-267.

Chapter 12

B., Ruiz P., Galanter M., eds. *Handbook of Clinical Alcoholism Treatment*. Philadelphia, PA: Lippincott Williams and Wilkins; 2003: 208-216.

DHSS, Causes of Addiction and Modalities for Treatment (1994) *Treatment for Alcohol and Other Drug Abuse: Opportunities for Coordination*. Technical Assistance Publication Series 11.Chapter 3. DHHS Publication (SMA) 94-2075.

Dowd, E.T. (1989). Stasis and change in cognitive psychotherapy: Client resistance and reactance as mediating variables. In W. Dryden & P. Trower (Eds.). Cognitive therapy: Stasis and change (pp. 139-158). New York: Springer.

Murthy Pratima. *Psychosocial Interventions for Persons with Substance Abuse*

National Institute of Social Defence *Newsletter*, volume7 No. 3, March 2005

Nystul, M.S. (2001). Overcoming resistance through individual psychology and problem solving. *Journal of Individual Psychology*, 58, 182-189.

Pope, B. (1979). The mental health interview. New York: Pergamon.

Smith M.O., Culliton P, Voyles C. Auricular acupuncture in alcohol treatment. In: Johnson

Smith M.O. Ear acupuncture in addiction treatment. In: Brizer D, Castaneda R, eds. *Clinical Addiction Psychiatry*. New York, NY: Cambridge University Press; 2010: 230-249.

www.acudetox.com and www.acudetoxindia.com

www.huffingtonpost.com/dr-michael-o-smith/addiction-acupuncture_b_1665796.html

www.richardelovich.com/articles/article_acupuncture_and_treatment_readiness.html

Chapter 13

Anthony, W.A. (1993). Recovery from mental illness: The guiding vision of the mental health service system in the 1990's. *Psychosocial Rehabilitation Journal, 16*(4), 11-23.

Becker, D.R., and Drake, R.E. (2003). *A working life for people with severe mental illness.*New York: Oxford University Press.

Bond, G.R. (2004). "Supported employment: Evidence for an evidence-based practice". *Psychiatric Rehabilitation Journal,* 27(4): 345–359.

Bond, G.R., Drake, R.E., and Becker, D.R. (2008).An update on Randomized Controlled Trials of Evidence – Based Supported Employment.*Psychiatric Rehabilitation Journal,* 31(4): 280-290.

Bond, G.R., Salyers, M.P., *et al*. (2007). A Randomized Controlled Trial Comparing Two Vocational Models for Persons With Severe Mental Illness. *Journal of Consulting and Clinical Psychology*, 75(6): 968-982.

Chandrashekar, H., Prashanth, N.R., Kasthuri, P., Madhusudhan S. (2010). Psychiatric Rehabilitation.*Indian Journal of Psychiatry*, 52: S278-80

Corrigan, P.W., Larson, J.E., and Kawabara, S.A. (2007). Mental illness stigma and the fundamental components of supported employment.*Rehabilitation Psychology,* 52: 451-457.

Crowther, R., Marshall, M., Bond, G., *et al.* (2001). Vocational rehabilitation for people with severe mental illness. *Cochrane Database of Systematic Reviews*, issue 3.

Grove, B. (1994). Reform of mental health care in Europe. Progress and change in the last decade. *British Journal of Psychiatry*, 165: 431-433.

Hardiman, E.R., and Hodges, J.Q. (2008). Professional Differences in Attitudes Toward and Utilization of Psychiatric Recovery. *The Journal of Contemporary Social Services,* 89 (2): 220-227.

Jacobson, N., and Curtis, L. (2000).Recovery as Policy in Mental Health Services: Strategies Emerging from the State. *Psychosocial Rehabilitation Journal.*

Kumar, S.P.N. (2008). Impact of vocational rehabilitation on social functioning, cognitive functioning and psychopathology in patients with chronic schizophrenia. *Indian Journal of Psychiatry*, 50: 257-261.

Lefley, H. (1999). Mental health systems in cross-cultural context. In A.V. Horwitz & T.L. Scheid (Eds). *A handbook for the study of mental health: Social contexts, theories and systems.* pp 566-584. New York: Cambridge University Press.

Liberman, P.R. (2012). Recovery from Schizophrenia: form follows functioning. *World Psychiatry.* 11 (3): 161-162

Onken, S.J., Dumont, J.M., Ridgway, P., Dornan, D.H., and Ralph, R.O. (2002). *"Mental Health Recovery: What Helps and What Hinders? A National Research Project for the Development of Recovery Facilitating System Performance Indicators; Phase One Research Report: A National Study of Consumer Perspectives on What Helps and Hinders Recovery."* Alexandria, VA: National Technical Assistance Centre for State Mental Health Planning.

Ralph, R.O. (2000). Recovery. *Psychiatric Rehabilitation Skills*, 4(3), 480-517.

Rinaldi, M., and Perkins, R. (2007). Comparing employment outcomes for two vocational services: Individual placement and support and non-integrated pre-vocational services in the UK. *Journal of Vocational Rehabilitation,* 27: 21-27.

Rinaldi, M., Perkins, R., *et al.* (2008) Individual Placement and Support: from research to practice. *Advances in Psychiatric Treatment,* 13, 50–60 doi: 10.1192/apt.bp.107.003509.

Rossler, W. (2006). Psychiatric Rehabilitation Today: An Overview. *World Psychiatry.* 5(3): 151-157.

Stanhope, V. (2002). Culture, Control and Family Involvement: A Comparison of Psychosocial Rehabilitation in India and the United States. *Psychiatric Rehabilitation Journal*, 25(3): 273-280.

Tsang, H.W.H. (2011). Supported employment versus traditional vocational rehabilitation for individuals with severe mental illness: a three-year study. *Hong Kong Medical Journal*, 17(1), Supplement 2: 13-1.

Tsang, H.W.H., Fung, K.M.T., *et al.* (2010). Three year follow-up study of an integrated supported employment for individuals with severe mental illness. *Australian and New Zealand Journal of Psychiatry,* 44: 49-58.

Vaughn, C.E., and Leff, J.P. (1976). The influence of family and social factors on the course of psychiatric illness: A comparison of schizophrenic and depressed neurotic patients. *British Journal of Psychiatry,* 129: 125-137.

Wig, N. (2000). World Health Organization and Mental Health: A view from developing countries. *Bulletin of WHO*, 78 (4): 502-506.

Chapter 14

Barnett T., and Whiteside, A. (2000), *AIDS in the Twenty-First Century: Disease and Globalization*, Palgrave-Macmillan: Basingstoke.

Barnett, T. (2002), "HIV/AIDS and Globalization: What is the epidemic telling us about economics, morality and pragmatism?" *AIDS Economics*, July 2002, IAEN.

Brown L.D. *et al.* (2000), 'Globalization, NGOs and Multi-Sectoral Relations'. In J.S. Nye and J.D. Donahue (eds.) *Governance in a Globalizing World*, Brookings Institution Press: Washington D.C.

D'Adesky, AC (2004), *Moving Mountains: The Race to Treat Global AIDS*, Verso: London.

Dommen, C. (2001), Background Note of the Workshop on "The impact of globalisation on the full enjoyment of economic, social and cultural rights and the right to development", held at Kuala Lumpur, Malaysia, 8-10 May 2001.

Fowler, A. (1997), *Striking a Balance: A Guide to Enhancing the Effectiveness of Non-Governmental Organisations in International Development*, Earthscan: London, pp. 43-68.

GFATM (2002), Report of Global Fund to Fight AIDS, T.B. and Malaria, 2002.
www.globalfundatm.org

GFATM (2007), Global Fund to Fight AIDS, T.B. and Malaria, Press Release, 27th September 2007. www.theglobalfund.org

Gordenker, L. and Weiss, T.G. (1996), 'Pluralizing Global Governance: Analytical Approaches and Dimensions'. In Gordenker and Weiss (eds.), *The UN and Global Governance*, Lynne Rienner: Boulder, p. 17.

Haslegrave, M. (1988), 'Resource guide to NGOs concerned with AIDS in Africa based in UK'. In *AIDS in Africa: The Social and Policy Impact*, Meller Press: Lewiston, New York.

Irwin A, J. Millen and D. Fallows (2003), *Global AIDS: Myths and Facts—Tools for Fighting the AIDS Pandemic*, South End Press: Cambridge, MA.

Mercer, M.A., L.Liskin and S.J. Scott (1991), "The role of NGO in the global response to AIDS", *AIDS Care*, 3(3): 265-270.

Merson, M. (2005), "HIV/AIDS: A Truly Global Response Needed For a Global Scourge", *Yale Global*, 20 November 2005, New Haven.

Morna, C.L. and PANOS (1991), "South African NGOs Seize the Initiative", *World AIDS*, 12: 5-9.

Narain, J.P. (2004), *AIDS in Asia – The Challenge Ahead*, Sage: New Delhi.

Osmani, S.R. (2005), 'An Essay on the Human Rights Approach to Development'. In A. Sengupta (ed.) *Reflections on the Right to Development*, Sage Publications: New Delhi.

Salamon, L.M. (1994), "The Rise of the Non profit Sector", *Foreign Affairs*, 73, 109-116.

Schoepf, Schoepf, and Millen (1992), 'Theoritical Therapies, Remote Remedies'. In Steven Feierman and John M. Janzen (eds.) *The Social Basis of Health and Healing in Africa*, University of California Press: California.

Seckinelgin, H. (2005), "A Global Disease and Its Governance: HIV/AIDS in Sub-Saharan Africa and the Agency of NGOs.", *Global Governance*, Boulder: Jul-Sep 2005, Vol. 11, Issue 3.

Stover J., *et al.* (2006), "The Global Impact of Scaling Up HIV/AIDS Prevention Programs in Low- and Middle-Income Countries", *Science*, 10 March 2006: Vol. 311. no. 5766, pp. 1474 – 1476.

Sukai, T.B. (2010), *AIDS, NGOs and Globalization,* Akansha: New Delhi.

UNAIDS (2002), Report on the Global HIV/AIDS epidemic. http: //www.unaids.org

UNAIDS (2007), Financial Resources Required to Achieve Universal Access to HIV Prevention, Treatment, Care and Support, UNAIDS.http: //data.unaids.org/pub/Report/2008/20080801_jc1509_universal_access_en.pdf

WHO (2000), WHO Policy perspectives on medicines, globalisation, trips and access to pharmaceuticals, 2000, WHO: Geneva.

WHO (2001), Report of the Commission in Macroeconomics and Health. Jeffry Sachs (ed.), WHO: Geneva.

WTO (2001), WTO/WHO Secretariats Workshop on Affordable Drugs, 2001. www.wto.org/english/tratop_e/trips_e/tn_hosbjor_e.htm

Chapter 15

Bauer, P.T. (1981) The Third World and Economic Dellusion. *Weinfield and Nicholson*, London.

Bendell, J. (2006) Debating NGO Accountability; *United Nations; UN Non-Governmental Liaison (NGLS);* Switzerland.

D.N. (2003) Aid: Old Morality and New Realities; *Economic and Political Weekly*, Vol. 38. No. 24, pp. 2353.

Fuherer, H. (1994). The Story of Official Development Assistance; *Organisation for Economic Co-Operation and Development*

Hansen, H., and Tarp, F. (2000). "Aid Effectiveness Disputed." *Journal of International Development* 12(3): 375-98.

Mosley, P., J. Hudson, and A. Verschoor, 2004."Aid, Poverty Reduction and the 'New conditionality."*Economic Journal* 114: F217-43.

Planning Commission. Eleventh Five Year Plan Documents. Available at www.planningcommission.nic.in.Retreived on 28th January 2013.

Pratt, B. and Myhrman, T. (2009) Improving Aid Effectiveness: A review of recent initiatives for civil society organizations: *International NGOs training and research centre.*

Quibria, M.G. (2004) Development Effectiveness: What Does Recent Research Tell Us: *ADB Working Paper Series/Evaluation:* ADB.

Roy, B. (1988) "Voluntary Agencies Twenty years from now", *Mainstream,* Vol (26), pp. 17-19.

Society for Participatory Research in Asia (1991) *Voluntary Development Organizations in India: A study of History, Roles and Future Challenges;* New Delhi: PRIA.

Society for Participatory Research in Asia (1993) *Voluntary Organizations: Yesterday and Today*; New Delhi; PRIA.

Srivastava, S.S.; Tandon, R.; (2000). *Defining the Sector in India: Voluntary; Civil or Non-Profit*; Report for PRIA in Collaboration with the Centre for Civil Society Studies, Johns Hopkins University, USA.

United Nations (2003) Financing for Development: Monterrey Consensus; *United Nations Department of Economic and Social Affairs*, Switzerland.

United Nations Development Programme (UNDP). (2010). Human Development Report 2010. New York, USA: UNDP.

World Bank (1995) *Strengthening the Effectiveness of Aid: Lessons for Donors.* The World Bank, Washington D.C.

Chapter 16

Archna Shukla, July 07, 2010) Read the complete story at: http: //bit.ly/c1nVvv

Bart Muusse (2010) Accountability Practice in Northern Development NGOS, Master Thesis Policy, Communication & Organization, Free University of Amsterdam

Chandrasekhar, S.F. and P. Anjaiah. (2002), Organizational Commitment: A study of employees responses from select NGOs, Management and Labour Studies, 27, 3, 205-209.

Desai V (1999) Anatomy of the Bombay NGO sector, Environment and Urbanization, Vol. 11, No. 1, April, 247-266.

Ibrahim AKSEL and Muhtesem BARAN (2010) Organizational Problems of Non-Governmental Organizations (NGOs).

Kudva, N. (2005) Uneasy relations: NGOs and the state in Karnataka, India, Cornell University, paper presented at Karnataka conference, ISEC/Cornell University/ The World Bank, Banglore, June 10-12.

S.F. Chandrasekhar (2009) Employee Engagement as a Function of HRD in NGOs: A Study of

NGOs Employees in South Indian, *Sugyan, Management Journal*, Shiva Sivani Institute of Management, July 2009.

Smillie Ian and Hailey John (2000) *Introduction, Managing Change-Leadership, Strategy and Management*, Oxford University Press, Karachi, *op. cit.*, P1.

Chapter 17

Appiah, Kwame, Anthony. (2005). *The Ethics of Identity*. Princeton, NJ: Princeton

Asia Watch. (1991). *Kashmir under siege*. New York: Human Rights Watch.

Behera, N C. (1996). *Making and Unmaking of Identities*. Delhi: Himal South Asia.

Behera, Navnita. Chadha. (2006). *Demystifying Kashmir*. Washington, D.C: Brookings Institution Press.

Census of India. (1941). Jammu and Kashmir, Parts I & II. Vol. XXII.

Chaturvedi Sanjay. (2005). The ethno and geo: A new look into the Kashmiri's autonomy, in Rannbir sammadara. (Ed), *Politics of Autonomy: Indian Experiences*. New Delhi: Sage Publications.

Chowdhary, Z. (2011). Beyond reservations, Gujjars have nothing or little against paharis. *Epilogue*, 5(1): 23-27.

Copp, David. (2002). Social unity and the identity of persons. *The Journal of Political Philosophy,* 10(4): 365-91.

Eisenberg, A. (2009). *Reasons of Identity A Normative Guide to the Political and Legal Assessment of Identity Claims*. New York: Oxford University Press Inc.

Hall, Stuart. (1996). Introduction: Who needs, 'identity'?, in Stuart Hall and Paul Du Gay (Eds.) *Questions of Cultural Identity* (pp. 1 17). London, UK: Sage.

K. Warikoo. (2000). Tribal Gujjars of Jammu and Kashmir. *Himalayan and Central Asian Studies*, 4(1): 3-15.

Khatana, R.P. (1991). *Dilemma of the Gujars in Jammu and Kashmir*. Paper Presented at the Symposium on the Himalaya. Delhi: Jawaharlal Nehru University Delhi.

MC Donell, J.C. (1899). *Annual Report of the Forest Department Jammu and Kashmir State* for the Year Samwat 1955 (AD 1898 –1899), Lahore: Government Publication.

Negi, R.S. and M.K. Raha. (1982). The Gujjar of North-western Himalayas: From Pastoralism to Settlement. In K.S. Singh (Ed) *Economies of the Tribes and their Transformation* (pp200-207). New Delhi: Concept Publishing House.

Rao, Aparna. (1995). From Bondsmen to Middlemen, Hired Shepherds and Pastoral Politics. *Anthropos*, 6(2): 149-167.

Rao, Aparna. (1999). The many sources of identity: an example of changing affiliations in rural Jammu and Kashmir. *Ethnic and Racial Studies*, 22(1): 56-91.

Sen, Amartya. (1999). *Development as Freedom*. New York: Anchor Books.

Sen, Amartya. (2006). *Identity and Violence: The Illusion of Destiny*. New York: WW Norton and Co.

Taylor, Charles. (1994). *Multiculturalism and the 'The Politics of Recognition'*. Princeton, NJ: Princeton University Press.

Chapter 18

Bulloug, V.L. (1979). Homosexuality, A History. *Press New York and London: Garland STMP.*

Colfax, G.N. *et al.* (2001). Drug Use and Sexual Risk Behavior Among Gay and Bisexual Men Who Attend Circuit Parties: A Venue-Based Comparison. *JAIDS Journal of Acquired Immune Deficiency Syndromes*; 28 (4).

Gelder, M. Mayou, R. Cowen, P. (1996). *Oxford Textbook of Psychiatry.* Oxford University Publications.

Herek, G.M. Cogan, C.J. Gillis, J.R. (2009). Internalized Stigma Among Sexual Minority Adults:

Insights From a Social Psychological Perspective; *Journal of Counseling Psychology*, 1, 32-43.

Pando, M.A. *et al.* (2003). High human immunodeficiency virus type 1 seroprevalence in men who have sex with men in Buenos Aires, Argentina: risk factors for infection; *International Journal of Epidemiology*, 32, 735-740.

Trioden, R.R. (1979). Becoming Homosexual: A Model of Gay Identity Acquisition. *Psychiatry,* 42, 288-299.

Chapter 19

Benería, L., and Floro, M. (2005). Distribution, gender, and labour market informalization: A conceptual framework with a focus on homeworkers. In N. Kudva and L. Benería (Eds.), *Rethinking Informalization: Poverty, precarious jobs, and social protection*. Cornell University Open Access Repository. Retrieved November 30th, 2006, from dspace.library.cornell.edu/bitstream/1813/3716/1/Rethinking+Informalization.pdf

Bhatty, Z. (1987). Economic contribution of women to the household budget: A case study of the beedi industry. In A.M. Singh and A. Kelles Viitanen (Eds.), *Invisible*

Egger, P. (2002). Towards a policy framework for decent work. *International Labour Review, 141* (1 and 2), 161-174.

Fields, G.S. (2003). Decent work and development policies. *International Labour Review, 142* (2), 239-262.

Gallin, D. (2007). *The ILO Home Work Convention - Ten Years Later*. Paper presented at Women Work and Poverty: SEWA/UNIFEM Policy Conference on Home Based Workers of South Asia (January18-20, 2007): New Delhi. Retrieved March 9th, 2011, from http: //www.wiego.org/program_areas/org_rep/Gallin_homework_speech.pdf

Ghai, D. (2005). *Decent work: Universality and Diversity*. Geneva: International Institute of Labour Studies; (DP/159/2005). Also retrieved May 7th, 2005, from http: //www.ilo.org/public/english/bureau/inst/download/dp15905.pdf

Heyzer, N. (2005). *Preface. Progress of the world's women 2005: Women, work and poverty*. New York: UNIFEM. Retrieved November 30th, 2006, from www.un-ngls.org/women-2005.pdf

ILO (2005*a*). *Decent work: The heart of social progress*. Retrieved April 5th, 2005, from http: //www.ilo.org/public/english/region/asro/newdelhi/download/koldecnt.pdf

Jhabvala, R. (2002). Bringing informal workers centrestage. In R. Jhabvala, R.M. Sudarshan and J. Unni (Eds.), *Informal economy centre stage: New structures of employment* (pp. 258-275). New Delhi: Sage Publications.

Jhabvala, R., and Tate, J. (1996). *Out of shadows: Homebased workers organize for international recognition*. Retrieved June 4th, 2007, from http: //www.popcouncil.org/pdfs/seeds/seeds18.pdf

Kuruvilla, S. (2006). *Social dialogue for decent work*. Geneva: International Institute of Labour Studies. Retrieved October 17th, 2007, from http: //www.ilo.org/public/english/bureau/inst/download/pedmat.pdf

Mishra, L.D. (2002). Problems of home-based workers. In Self Employed Women's Association (Ed.), *Report on workshop on national policy for the home-based workers*. Ahmedabad: SEWA.

Mohan, B. (2003). *The practice of hope-diversity, discontent and discourse*. XLIBRIS: Xlibris corporation.

Pathak, S. (1989). Social development and Social Work Education: Some unresolved issues in R.K. Nayak and H.Y. Siddiqui (Ed.), *Social Work and Social Development*. New Delhi: Gitanjali Publishing House

Rao and Hussain (1987). Invisible hands: Women in home based production in the garment export industry in Delhi. In A. Menefee Singh and A. Kelles-Viitanen (Eds.), *Invisible hands: Women in home-based production* (pp. 51-68). New Delhi: Sage Publications.

Rodgers, G. (2001). Decent work as a development objective. *The Indian Journal of Labour Economics*. *44*(1), 14-26.

Sinha, S. (2006). *Rights of home-based workers*. New Delhi: National Human Rights Commission.

Sudarshan, R.M. (2007). *Social security for women homebased workers in South Asia*. Published in Women, work and poverty (Policy conference on homebased workers of South Asia (January 18th-20th, 2007). New Delhi: SEWA & UNIFEM.

Wright, D. (2004). Sub-contracting, small-batch production and home-based workers. In A. Kaur (Ed.), *Women workers in industrialising Asia: Costed, not valued* (pp. 129-148). Hampshire: Palgrave Macmillan.

Contributors

Dr Ajay Vats, Chairman, Indian Association of Acupuncture Detoxification Specialist (IAADS), New Delhi-110074.

Dr Abraham Francis, Senior Lecturer, Social Work and Human Services, College of Arts, Society and Education, Division of Tropical Environments and Societies, James Cook University, Douglas, Townsville LD 4811 Australia.

Dr Atul Pratap Singh, Assistant Professor, Department of Social Work & Programme Officer, NSS, B.R. Ambedkar College, (University of Delhi), Delhi-110094.

Dr B.P. Nirmala, Associate Professor, Department of Psychiatric Social Work, PSW Consultant, Department of Psychiatric and Neurological Rehabilitation, NIMHANS, Bangalore- 560029.

Ms Faseela Jaleel, Research Scholar, Department of Psychiatric Social Work, Department of Psychiatric and Neurological Rehabilitation, NIMHANS, Bangalore-560029.

Prof Gracious Thomas, Director, School of Social Work, Indira Gandhi National Open University (IGNOU), New Delhi-110068.

Prof H.Y. Siddiqui, Department of Social Work, Maulana Azad National Urdu University, Hyderabad-500032.

Mr Iqball Majeed Bhat, Department of Social Work, University of Delhi, Delhi-110007.

Dr J. Harini Christopher, Assistant Professor, Department of Psychiatry, St. Johns Medical College Hospital, Sarjapur Road, Bangalore-560034.

Dr Jagadisha Thirthalli, Department of Psychiatry, National Institute of Mental Health and Neurosciences, Bangalore-560029.

Dr Jaimon Verghese, Assistant Professor, BPHES' CSRD Institute of Social Work and Research, Ahmednagar, Maharashtra-414001.

Dr Jitendra Kumar Misra, Assistant Director (TI), Delhi AIDS Control Society, Dr Baba Sahib Ambedkar Hospital, Rohini, Delhi-110085.

Dr Kaivalya T. Desai, Assistant Professor, Department of Social Work, Assam University Silchar-788011, Assam.

Prof Kalpana Sarathy, School of Social Work, Tata Institute of Social Sciences, Uzanbazar, Guwahati-781001, Assam.

Ms Namita Jainer, Junior Research Fellow, Department of Social Work, University of Delhi. Delhi-11007.

Ms Subhashree Sanyal, Assistant Professor of Social Work, Palli Samgathan Vibhaga (Institute of Rural Reconstruction), Visva-Bharati, Santiniketan, Bolpur, West Bengal-731235.

Dr Shivani Chauhan Barooh, Assistant Professor, Tata Institute of Social Sciences, Uzanbazar, Guwahati, Assam-781001.

Mr Suneel Vatsayan, Chairman, Nada India Foundation, New Delhi-110074.

Prof Suresh Pathare, Director, Center for Studies in Rural Development, Institute of Social Work and Research, Ahmednagar, Maharashtra-414001.

Dr Tarun Bikash Sukai, Assistant Professor, Department of Social Work, Assam university Silchar, Assam-788011.

Dr Teddy Andrews J., Lecturer (Senior Grade), MSW, Department of Public Health, Manipal University, Manipal, Karnataka-576104.

Ms V. Vindhya, Trainee, Nada India Foundation, New Delhi-110074.

Prof Vidya Rao, Professor and Head, Department of Social Work, Jain Vishva Bharati Institute, Ladnun, Rajasthan-341306.

Ms Zothankimiralte, Guest Faculty, Department of Social Work, Mizoram University, Tanhril, Aizawl, Mizoram-796009.

The Editors

Sanjai Bhatt is a Professor of Social Work at the Delhi School of Social Work, University of Delhi. He is proactive social work educator, researcher and activist. Prof. Bhatt has also served faculty of social work at University of Lucknow; Kashi Vidyapeeth, Varanasi, Kurukshetra University, and Chitrakoot Gramodaya Vishwavidyalaya. His areas of interest are social work education, social development, social security, occupational social work, climate change and corporate social responsibility. He has authored/edited five books, contributed a dozen book chapters and around 80 research papers on various themes. He is presently President of National Association of Professional Social Workers in India. He was Organizing Secretary of the first Indian Social Work Congress 2013.

Suresh Pathare has obtained Master of Social Work from University of Pune and Ph.D. in Social Work from University of Delhi. He is Director of Institute of Social Work and Research, CSRD, Ahmednagar. He has served as Faculty of Social Work at Delhi University, School of Rural Development at Tata Institute of Social Sciences, Mumbai and School of Social Work, IGNOU, New Delhi and Vidyajyoti College of Theology as Programme Coordinator. His areas of interest are Urban and Rural Community Development, Sustainable Development, Human Rights, Religion, Spirituality and Social Work. He has conducted a dozen research projects, published research papers and attended number of national and international seminars and conferences. He has recently completed Post doctoral from University of North Carolina, Chapel Hill, USA. He is Secretary of National Association of Professional Social Workers in India.

Index